Praise for *Solidarity Is the*

T0268115

"It is very rare to have access to the internal dynamics of any political movement, more so when it is rife with internal fissures and external pressures that threaten to unravel it daily. *Solidarity Is the Political Version of Love* provides that for us with biting nuance and tender self-reflection in regards to the transformation of Jewish Voice for Peace from a local anti-occupation Jewish organization into an international anti-Zionist Jewish organization leading a revival of Jewish leftist traditions. Situating themselves both within and adjacent to the organization, Rebecca Vilkomerson and Rabbi Alissa Wise have offered an enduring historical document for generations of anti-Zionist Jewish organizers to come." —**Noura Erakat**, human rights attorney, professor, and author of *Justice for Some: Law and the Question of Palestine*

"*Solidarity Is the Political Version of Love* is timely, not only because Jewish Voice for Peace is the leading force resisting Israel's current genocidal war on Palestinians but also because it is a success story. And today, as we confront the threat of fascism and political despair, movements need success stories. Veteran organizers Rebecca Vilkomerson and Rabbi Alissa Wise guide us through two decades of JVP's history, revisiting mistakes, drawing lessons, and revealing the secrets to the movement's sustained growth, coherence, longevity, and radical vision. Beautiful, inspiring, insightful . . . this book is for every organizer and anyone willing to fight for a world grounded in the principles of peace, justice, decolonization, and love." —**Robin D. G. Kelley**, historian, professor, and author of *Freedom Dreams: The Black Radical Imagination*

"Two of the most effective solidarity workers in American politics offer a tough-love, how-to-get-it-done gift to those ready to confront oppressive power while building deep relationships with our political partners. Focused, realistic, and above all impactful. A book of practical and emotional insights that are so, so helpful." —**Sarah Schulman**, novelist, playwright, screenwriter, and author of *Let the Record Show: A Political History of ACT UP, New York, 1987–1993*

"Jewish Voice for Peace has done some of the most difficult and morally courageous organizing I have seen, standing in unwavering solidarity with the Palestinian liberation struggle at one of the most difficult times in its history, while simultaneously deepening the tradition of Jewish left internationalism. Two amazing women have been key to JVP's evolution as a galvanizing political force for justice, Rabbi Alissa Wise and Rebecca Vilkomerson. Fierce, formidable, and deeply compassionate, their insights offer inspiration and clarity in a moment where grief and uncertainty abound. This book is so necessary, and these authors are the only ones who could have written it. I am in awe of them both as movement visionaries and unrelenting organizers."
—**Barbara Ransby**, historian, activist, and author of *Making All Black Lives Matter: Reimagining Freedom in the Twenty-First Century*

"*Solidarity Is the Political Version of Love* is a unique and beautiful book. Masterfully mixing memoir, organizational history, and political criticism, Vilkomerson and Wise have crafted a text that affirms their lifelong commitment to revolutionary love, radical action, earnest self-critique, and unrelenting hope. Although rooted in their own personal and professional experiences as leaders within Jewish Voice for Peace, this project provides powerful and necessary insights for anyone invested in the struggle for justice." —**Marc Lamont Hill**, journalist, professor, and coauthor of *Except for Palestine: The Limits of Progressive Politics*

"The movement for Palestinian freedom that is upending American politics did not arise from nowhere. It stems from many years of difficult work, including by American Jews like Rebecca Vilkomerson and Rabbi Alissa Wise. You don't need to agree with them on everything to be inspired by their commitment to Palestinian and Jewish liberation. And whatever your views, this book will help you understand the political earthquake that is shaking the ground beneath our feet."
—**Peter Beinart**, journalist and author of *The Crisis of Zionism*

Solidarity Is the Political Version of Love

Lessons from Jewish Anti-Zionist Organizing

Rebecca Vilkomerson
and Rabbi Alissa Wise

Foreword by Omar Barghouti
Afterword by Stefanie Fox

Haymarket Books
Chicago, Illinois

Published in 2024 by
Haymarket Books
P.O. Box 180165
Chicago, IL 60618
www.haymarketbooks.org

ISBN: 979-8-88890-095-6

Distributed to the trade in the US through Consortium Book
Sales and Distribution (www.cbsd.com) and internation-
ally through Ingram Publisher Services International (www.
ingramcontent.com).

This book was published with the generous support of Lannan
Foundation, Wallace Action Fund, and Marguerite Casey
Foundation.

Special discounts are available for bulk purchases by organizations and institutions. Please email info@haymarketbooks.org
for more information.

Cover artwork, "Solidarity with Palestine" © 2023 by Wendy
Elisheva Somerson, www.wendysomerson.net.

Printed in Canada by union labor.

Library of Congress Cataloging-in-Publication data is available.

10 9 8 7 6 5 4 3 2 1

For our children: Tali, Amalia, Sammy, Lev, and Samara

"What do I mean by home? Not the nation state; not religious worship; not the deepest grief of a people marked by hatred. I mean a commitment to what is and is not mine; to the strangeness of others, to my strangeness to others; to common threads twisted with surprise. . . . Solidarity is the political version of love."

—Melanie Kaye/Kantrowitz z"l, *The Colors of Jews*

Contents

Foreword

On July 9, 2015, the Palestinian-led Boycott, Divestment and Sanctions (BDS) movement celebrated its tenth anniversary. Over the preceeding decade, BDS established itself as a critical part of Palestinian popular resistance to Israel's system of oppression and as *the* most effective form of solidarity with the Palestinian liberation struggle. Speakers from across the world participated virtually in this event. One of the most memorable moments of that celebration was the short video speech by Rebecca Vilkomerson, then director of Jewish Voice for Peace (JVP). It not only conveyed a strong message of Jewish American support for the BDS movement and solidarity with the Palestinian liberation struggle, it also inadvertently reminded many of a different era, when Jews in Palestine were considered as Palestinian as anyone else, an inseparable part of the Palestinian people resisting the onslaught of Zionist settler colonialism enabled by British imperialism.

As early as 1919, the General Syrian Congress, consisting of elected representatives of the people of Palestine, Syria, and Lebanon, adopted a historic resolution regarding the encroaching settler colonialism in Palestine that said:

> We oppose the pretensions of the Zionists to create a Jewish Commonwealth in the southern part of Syria,

known as Palestine, and oppose Zionist migration to any part of our country; for we do not acknowledge their title but consider them a grave peril to our people from the national, economical, and political points of view. *Our Jewish compatriots shall enjoy our common rights and assume the common responsibilities.*[1] (emphasis added)

Decades later, the Palestine Liberation Organization, representing the Palestinian people in historic Palestine and in exile, envisioned a secular democratic state with equal rights for all, including Jewish Palestinians. This history, buried under the weight of decades of Zionist domination of Jewish communities worldwide, is as relevant today as ever.

In her speech, Rebecca said:

I am here to tell you that in the Jewish American community, as well as the United States at large, there is a fundamental shift in the understanding of Israeli systems of oppression and control over Palestinian lives. Jewish support for BDS shatters the claim that Israel represents all Jews, or that all Jews support Israel. My organization, Jewish Voice for Peace, has by just about every measure tripled in size in the last year, and polls of the Jewish American community show a growing generational divide. . . . How can it be antisemitic to hold a state—any state, including Israel—accountable for its human rights violations, for enforcing inequality and for its systems of oppression?[2]

To many in the Palestinian BDS National Committee (BNC), the largest coalition in Palestinian society, leading the global BDS movement, this principled position came as no surprise. But the sentiment behind it and JVP's strategic work in solidarity with the struggle for Palestinian liberation rekindled among

Palestinians a warm feeling of Jewish solidarity and Jewish anti-Zionism that had become all but a faint memory.

Palestinians, and with us other Arabs, have for decades experienced the consequences of overwhelming Jewish support for Israel's regime of oppression and for Zionism, a racist and colonial ideological pillar of this regime. The social justice tradition in Judaism, Jewish opposition to Zionism (until World War II) and to racist and oppressive systems worldwide, and Jewish support for Palestinian rights have not been present in Arab thinking and Arab reality, especially in Palestine, for a very long time. JVP has demonstrated resolute condemnation of Zionism and principled solidarity with the Palestinian struggle for liberation, including through its especially effective role in the BDS movement in the United States. It has, more than any other Jewish group in contemporary history, shone a bright light on and effectively revived these emancipatory aspects of Jewish tradition—in the ten-year period that this precious book by Rebecca Vilkomerson and Alissa Wise covers and ever since. Instead of the typical Jewish American PEP (progressive except on Palestine) culture, JVP has evolved among many Jewish Americans, especially younger ones, a PIP culture: progressive *including* on Palestine.

§

This gem of a book was written months before the October 2023 escalation of Israel's ongoing genocide against 2.3 million Palestinians in the occupied and besieged Gaza Strip. Yet it is even more needed, more valuable, and more useful today, amid our relentless struggle to stop the genocide and, ultimately, to dismantle the underlying 76-year-old regime of settler-colonial apartheid that has spawned it.

In the weeks and months after Israel's latest attack on Gaza commenced, powerful footage captured hundreds of Jewish activists peacefully occupying a congressional building, the Statue of Liberty grounds, and Grand Central Station in New York while chanting "Never again for anyone!," "Not in our name!," and "End the genocide!" These demonstrations enacted and projected that hardly ever discussed nexus between Palestinian liberation from Zionist settler colonialism and Jewish liberation from Zionism that Rebecca and Alissa so eloquently explore in this book.

With Israel's latest massacre in Rafah on Sunday, May 26, when its US-supplied fighter jets—with parts coming from across Europe—bombed forcibly displaced Palestinians huddled in their tents with US-supplied missiles, burning many children, women, and men alive, it is easy to be filled with a debilitating and all-consuming level of grief, anger, or both. The fact that this massacre is only the latest in the world's first televised genocide, now in its eighth month, only inflames our passions and our utter disgust with the horrific complicity of states, corporations, and institutions in enabling this genocide to continue unabated. There are no more words, really, to describe the horrors that the international legal system, dominated by the colonial West, has allowed to continue against the Palestinian people for decades.

International law and ethical principles are necessary but woefully insufficient conditions for justice and emancipation from colonial subjugation, as Palestinians have known for decades. Only more people power, grassroots power, can lead to wider boycotts, divestment, and lawful sanctions to force the genocidal US-Israeli axis to stop. Winning these measures requires many factors, primary among them strong organizations and movements that can connect justice struggles in an ethically consistent manner, create spaces for shared learning and shared acting toward emancipation, and strategically transform the creative agency and energies of the many into a power that challenges the powers that be. To get there, we need to reach a golden balance between ethical principles and strategic effectiveness. In this cathartic and uniquely illuminating guide, the authors shine an especially valuable light on the path to achieving such a balance.

JVP's theory of change, as the book explains, focuses on base-building, bringing together "a critical mass of American Jews to collectively serve as a counterweight to the various legacy Jewish institutions." The authors offer an insightful take on power dynamics and what they mean in struggles for justice. They further explain JVP's sophisticated and very effective perspective, writing:

> Put simply, power is the ability to make things happen. In organizing, oppressive power is challenged and shared power is cultivated. As organizers we seek to build grassroots power by bringing together enough people to make those in charge change. Power in grassroots movements is measured in our ability to develop leaders and the communities around them to have the resolve, knowledge, and skills to seize organizing opportunities, develop strategic campaigns, and win specific outcomes, as well as create further organizing opportunities, leaders, and a wider base out of successful campaign wins.

And, indeed, JVP has succeeded in many such campaigns, against all odds. This is no small feat, given the immense power stacked against JVP and the relentless vilification, marginalization, and more recently outright war waged on the organization and movement by the anti-Palestinian Jewish Zionist establishment in the United States. "Through tethering the present and future to the past," the authors write, JVP's leadership team managed to "develop organizing that heals and motivates" and to create a "political home" for tens of thousands of Jewish Americans, mobilizing them to play an indispensable role in growing the US solidarity movement with the Palestinian liberation struggle.

In the current student-led uprising on campuses, for example, JVP campus chapters have been important partners to Students for Justice in Palestine (SJP) groups in calling for a boycott of Israel and its complicit universities and for divestment from companies that support Israel's regime of oppression. With its membership and number of supporters rising exponentially in the last months in response to its strategic and principled contribution to the struggle to stop the genocide and end US complicity in it, JVP is welcoming to this political home many new, young (and some older) members with all the opportunities and challenges they bring with them to the movement.

Now more than ever, our much more powerful enemies aim to wear down our movement by relentlessly attacking, smearing, bullying, intimidating, demonizing, and sometimes criminalizing our work. Most significantly, they seek to colonize our minds with despair, as Israel's settler-colonial regime has always desperately tried to do to Indigenous Palestinians resisting its system of oppression. By ruthlessly trying to crush us under the weight of their propaganda and lawfare, they try to sear into our collective consciousness that, no matter what we do, we can never *accumulate* enough power to reach victory, to prevail over oppression and enjoy freedom, justice, equality, and dignity.[3] Some organizations, while understanding these insidious machinations, insist on marching ahead with unstrategic work that indeed has no possibility of building people power to eventually change policies. Rebecca and Alissa, on the other hand, remind us that the protracted war on us should never make us complacent about the need to be not just principled but also strategic, effective, goal-oriented, and cumulative in our work. We must never lose sight of the fact that it is not our bubble that we seek to alter, but society at large to achieve the golden balance mentioned above.

JVP has done impressively well in never letting its detractors obscure that need for developing great strategies, reflecting on them and attenuating them, evolving them, correcting them to always get the movement closer to its goals. "A for effort" and "D for results" can only go so far before we burn out and resign ourselves to the conclusion propagated by our detractors, that indeed it's not worth it, as we can never succeed. Too many potentially good initiatives have folded not just because of the vicious wars waged against them by repressive forces but also because those wars succeeded in diverting the attention of those struggling for justice away from the absolute need for effective strategizing and consistent execution of those strategies to build people power as the only guaranteed, ethical, and sustainable way to overcome an unjust reality and build a really better world.

§

In this cathartic and uniquely illuminating guide, the authors share the most important lessons of their ten years of organizing in and re-inventing JVP. A small organization with a mixed membership of anti-Zionists and "soft" Zionists transformed into an anti-Zionist force that had ambitions and potential to change the Jewish landscape in the US and possibly beyond in support of Palestinian freedom.

It took JVP years of internal, at times emotional, debates to finally issue a statement of principle opposing Zionism as "a settler-colonial movement, establishing an apartheid state where Jews have more rights than others." It recognized that by design, "Zionism has meant profound trauma for generations, systematically separating Palestinians from their homes, land, and each other. Zionism, in practice, has resulted in massacres of Palestinian people, ancient villages and olive groves destroyed, families who live just a mile away from each other separated by checkpoints and walls, and children holding onto the keys of the homes from which their grandparents were forcibly exiled."[4] This declaration of opposition to Zionism and the Jewish-led struggle to "liberate Judaism from Zionism" was seen by the BNC, and Palestinian society at large, as nothing less than a tipping point in Jewish solidarity with Palestinian liberation.[5] While many observers thought at the time that JVP would disintegrate, given the dominance of support for Zionism in the Jewish American community, its membership actually increased dramatically. Crucially, the average age of JVP members decreased drastically over the years, as many young Jews who were reluctant to join any Jewish group that had no clear position against Zionism finally found their political home in JVP.

Steering the organization and movement through this process of coming out against Zionism and welcoming a remarkable influx of young members may now look simple in retrospect. The details and intricacies of the discussions and debates shared in this book about these processes show that they were more like navigating a large ship, ultimately successfully, in a tumultuous sea during a punishing storm. Israel and the international Zionist movement have been busy pushing their revisionist, racist, pernicious, and deeply flawed International Holocaust Remembrance Alliance (IHRA) definition of antisemitism to shield Israel's regime of oppression from accountability, to silence Palestinians, and to police and suppress any expression of solidarity with Palestinian liberation.[6] Meanwhile Jewish American supporters of BDS, many represented in JVP, along with Jewish Israeli supporters of BDS in Boycott from Within, have been showing what true co-resistance to oppression looks like. Cognizant of its particularly influential role, JVP has strived, as Rebecca's 2015 speech revealed, to shatter the Zionist establishment's claim of representing all Jews, to undermine its putative moral authority used to bully and smear Israel's critics, and to relatively and gradually diminish its political power. JVP's contribution to the movement for Palestinian freedom, justice, and equality is therefore vital and indispensable.

Throughout this book, the authors emphasize the unparalleled importance of building "communal spaces" that "allow people to express their whole selves, in all their complexity, often for the first time." Other than offering a Jewish space for Jews to be their whole selves, I think JVP offers something else that is truly unique: it is the only organizational collective space in the US where progressive or liberal Jewish Americans can disabuse themselves of the heavy burden of moral inconsistency—of living the PEP contradiction—as a price they must pay to stay in relative harmony with their families and traditional Jewish communal spaces. I can imagine how oppressive and unsettling it must be for an otherwise progressive person to have to consistently, dogmatically, unethically defend oppression against some "lesser" people while still claiming to be progressive. Shedding that massive inner contradiction must be emancipatory.

The authors elucidate how this "sense of belonging—a core human need that many people fulfill at synagogue, church, mosque, ethnic heritage associations, block associations, labor unions, and more—is part of what makes JVP an enduring political home for so many, and is the 'secret sauce' that keeps movements vibrant even when the political work is daunting."

Rebecca and Alissa show how JVP has become a beacon of hope in the fight against anti-Jewish racism and bigotry while dedicating most of its energies to fighting US complicity in Israel's regime of settler-colonial oppression against Palestinians. A key feature of antisemitism is essentializing all Jews, considering them as a monolithic group or even a separate "race." Zionism and Israel, regardless of intent, are guilty of fanning the flames of antisemitism by insisting on speaking for all Jews, treating them as if they were all part of the same "tribe," all "belonging" to Israel, calling on them to "go home" to Israel in the face of rising antisemitic attacks in their home countries, whether in France, the United States, or elsewhere. Equating Israel with Jewry, holding all Jews responsible for Israel's crimes and apartheid policies, is a feature of today's rising antisemitism. Decoupling Jews from Israel, Jewishness from Zionism, or "liberating Judaism from Zionism," as the authors write, therefore becomes an essential ingredient in the struggle against anti-Jewish racism and for Jewish safety, well-being, and freedom. And, of course, this is all inseparable from the struggle for Palestinian liberation. History will one day mark that now, as the Zionist establishment works overtime to enable Israel's ongoing genocide against 2.3 million Palestinians in Gaza, JVP, with its almost one million supporters, and smaller anti-Zionist Jewish groups similar to it across the globe, have made clear that Jews and Judaism are not equatable with Israel and Zionism.

In 1967, soon after Israel's occupation of the Gaza Strip and the West Bank, including East Jerusalem, the prominent Jewish American writer I. F. Stone wrote:

> Israel is creating a kind of moral schizophrenia in world Jewry. In the outside world the welfare of Jewry depends on the maintenance of secular, non-racial, pluralistic societies. In Israel, Jewry finds itself defending a society in which mixed marriages cannot be legalized, in which non-Jews have a lesser status than Jews, and in which the ideal is racial and exclusionist. Jews must fight elsewhere for their very security and existence—against principles and practices they find themselves defending in Israel.[7]

This "moral schizophrenia" has reached an abyss of moral collapse in those supporting the current Israeli genocide. In contrast, the most lush, fertile, fast-growing oasis in this Zionist desert in the US is JVP. In this precious book, Rebecca Vilkomerson and Alissa Wise share part of the untold story of how JVP has countered this contradictory stance to emerge as the most effective Jewish anti-Zionist organization in solidarity with the struggle for Palestinian liberation worldwide.

This book paints a complex, beautiful, challenging picture of a decade in building a quintessentially *Jewish* movement, which through thought, principles, and consistent strategic practice engages in effective, meaningful solidarity with Palestinians in our liberation struggle, while evoking the most progressive Jewish values and traditions. In parallel, it demolishes antisemitic tropes and their most stubborn common denominator: erasing Jewish diversity, debate, difference, and reducing Jews to a monolith. By reviving the rich and prevalent pre-WWII Jewish anti-Zionist tradition, especially as expressed in Bund trade unionism, JVP has been, in effect, building the foundation for a new international Jewish anti-Zionist movement that can finally challenge Israel and Zionism—not just for their unspeakable crimes and regime of settler-colonial oppression against Indigenous Palestinians but also, crucially, as menaces to Jewish safety, community, and well-being. It reminds us that ethical coexistence demands ethical co-resistance, against oppression, against injustice, and against racism in all its forms.

—Omar Barghouti
Palestinian human rights defender, cofounder of
the BDS movement for Palestinian rights and
corecipient of the 2017 Gandhi Peace Award
May 28, 2024

Introduction

In 2002, Jewish Voice for Peace (JVP), then a Bay Area organization, made headlines on *PBS NewsHour* for blocking traffic in front of the Israeli consulate in San Francisco during the height of the Second Intifada, the Palestinian uprising that had begun in the fall of 2000. Members who were demonstrating wore T-shirts that read, on the front, "Jews Say: End the Occupation," and, on the back, "Peace for Israel Requires Justice for Palestinians." The media attention garnered at that action catapulted JVP into the national spotlight and inspired the organization to continue to invest and grow to become a force to reckon with.

In 2014, JVP organizers gathered in a multifaith vigil in a cavernous conference center in Detroit to pray, as the Presbyterian USA General Assembly was preparing to vote on a resolution to divest from the Israeli occupation of the West Bank, Gaza, and East Jerusalem. In bold letters, our T-shirts read, "Another Jew Supporting Divestment." A few hours later a historic vote was made in favor of divestment, the first major decision of its kind in the US.

In preparation for the 2016 Democratic convention in Philadelphia, JVP printed hundreds of T-shirts that read, "Palestinians Must be Free" on the front. On the back was a checklist of issues that summarized progressive priorities that year: Medicare for All, Black Lives Matter, Fight for $15,

1

Fighting Anti-Muslim Hate. Right in the middle of that list was checked: Palestinian Human Rights. The T-shirts flew out of our hands and onto the backs of delegates to the convention. Palestinian freedom was in the process of shifting squarely into the heart of progressive organizing.

JVP has consistently offered a home for Jewish Americans searching for a new paradigm of Jewish support for the Palestinian movement, but our politics have evolved over time. JVP went from seeing Palestinians as an instrument of peace for Israel to centering Palestinian liberation, eventually leading to the organization adopting a clear anti-Zionist stance. JVP nested itself inside and was welcomed by the Palestinian rights movement and the broader left, assuming a key role in the shifting of Jewish communal politics about Israel and support for Palestinian freedom. In each iteration, JVP was pushing the envelope inside American Jewish communities about as far as it could go, offering both a challenge and a vision of a more just future.

§

Weeks before this book went to press in fall 2023, our worlds, on every level, were forever altered on October 7th. Without knowing what will come next, we can say that the ensuing assault is undoubtedly the most consequential violence and ethnic cleansing since Israel's founding in 1948. It will likely be decades until we can fully understand the impact of this horrific time. Right now, grief, rage, and fear are overwhelming everyone.

What have been long festering fractures in the Jewish world have become complete ruptures. Led by JVP, Jewish anti-Zionist organizing against genocide has erupted on an unprecedented scale. As part of JVP's national organizing effort the two of us jumped in to help organize the first mass Jewish civil disobedience in the Rotunda of the US Congress. We were able to mobilize 350 Jews to take arrest in seventy-two hours, which helped to set the tone for large-scale protests at a level none of us can remember. This book can now also be read as a backstory to the flourishing of Jewish solidarity with Palestinians worldwide unlike the world has ever seen.

§

This book focuses on the ten-year period from 2010 to 2020, when we were both in positions of staff leadership of JVP. As two of its core leaders, among many, during a time of rapid movement building and political dynamism, we are proud that we helped steer our organization and the movement we are a part of in unique ways: JVP grew larger as it shifted to the left and altered the public narrative about Palestinian liberation while creating a space for Judaism beyond Zionism. Between 2009, when Rebecca became executive director (ED), and 2021, when Alissa left, the organization grew from six staff to more than thirty; from six chapters to more than sixty; its hundreds of members increased to tens of thousands; and its budget expanded from about $400,000 to nearly $4 million. These numbers are just a snapshot of the massive transformation of the American Jewish perspective on Palestinian rights over that period.

In addition to the steep growth in members, chapters, staff, and budget during our time on staff, JVP made some crucial political decisions, including to move further left by endorsing the Boycott, Divestment, and Sanctions (BDS) movement and becoming officially anti-Zionist, even as JVP grew larger and more powerful. JVP became known, and in some corners feared, for our insistent voice, our well-designed and well-executed campaigns, and our ability to activate thousands of people across the country. Although these effects are ephemeral and thus difficult to quantify, JVP's existence and growth agitated and challenged existing legacy Jewish institutions while becoming an exciting alternative for Jewish Americans who had previously felt exiled from Jewish communal life. In other words, JVP became both a beacon and a litmus test of Jewish politics, central to the Jewish communal conversation.

The question of Palestinian rights is often a third rail in Jewish settings. Many American Jewish organizations take great pains to avoid touching the issue at all costs, especially when it can cost them donors, while others make support for Israel a baseline criterion for inclusion. JVP's success in pushing the needle forward on this issue in the face of such a well-funded and powerful opposition was thanks to tried-and-true organizing practices, strong organizational structures, and visionary messaging that were baked into every facet of the organization, from our approach to communications and fundraising to how we cultivated leaders and structured staff and participated in intersectional movement building. JVP's success reflects the collective work of thousands of member leaders who poured their hearts and souls and time and energy into meetings, writing, conversations, actions, relationships, and campaigns locally, regionally and nationally.

Organizing was the key to how, during our ten-year tenure, JVP was able to build support for pushing the boundaries of the conversation on Palestinian rights in Jewish communities and, by extension, of the mainstream conversation in the US. We developed strategies as an organization to stake out our position and move people toward it in the public square. We created space for Jews to normalize the challenging of Zionism in their families, communities, and places of work. We figured out how to inculcate a spirit of dynamism and political courage into a growing organization while balancing being right and being relevant effectively. And of course, the two of us as leaders made mistakes, faced both internal and external challenges, and went through some heartrendingly difficult times.

It's a painful reality that many JVPers and others supporting Palestinian freedom pay a price for our organizing—through lost family relationships, friendships, jobs, and communal comfort. And we are very aware that, while we are telling our own story of these experiences, they were not nearly as severe as the consequences felt by Palestinian Americans, Muslim Americans, and people of color more generally who organize for Palestinian liberation, who can face FBI investigation, imprisonment, character assassination, career loss, and inability to access their homeland. A lot of the organizing and organizational strategies JVP developed, borrowed, and/or made our own are applicable to many movements that seek—however imperfectly—to weave together community, culture, tradition, politics, action, and power building. The intention of this book is to pull back the curtain on all of it. At a time when strong and sustainable organizing is essential, our greatest hope is that this book will be of use to a broad array of progressive activists and organizers regardless of their specific focus.

We want to give an extra shoutout to those of you reading this who are trying, despite enormous odds, to shift the status quo of your own communities when they are complicit in the oppression and dispossession of other people. We hope our reflections on the pain, frustrations, victories, and revelations we outline here will support you in your journey.

Political Context

To place ourselves in the world in which JVP waged its organizing struggles, we want to first offer a bit of historic context about JVP's evolving relationship to the Palestinian freedom and justice movement, as well as a very brief introduction to Jewish American communal life and JVP's emergence in that context. Especially for readers who are not fluent in these details, we want to emphasize that our circumstances are specific to our time, place, and history, but the questions we grapple with will ring true across movements.

We did not weep
when we were leaving—
for we had neither
time nor tears,
and there was no farewell.
We did not know
at the moment of parting
that it was a parting,
so where would our weeping
have come from?
We did not stay
awake all night
(and did not doze)
the night of our leaving.
That night we had
neither night nor light,
and no moon rose.
That night we lost our star,
our lamp misled us;
we didn't receive our share
of sleeplessness—
so where
would wakefulness have come from?
—Taha Muhammad Ali

Palestinians refer to Israel's establishment in 1948 as the *Nakba* (catastrophe), when more than 750,000 Palestinians fled or were forced to leave their homes, denied return to this day, even as many elders still hold the keys to their childhood homes. Israel's premeditated plans of dispossession and violation of Palestinian land, rights, and freedom, as wielded during its founding, have only intensified since. Palestinians, whether in the West Bank (including East Jerusalem), Gaza, in present-day Israel, or in forced diaspora, are enduring an ongoing Nakba to this day.

Over the twenty plus years of JVP's existence, conditions on the ground have deteriorated steadily, clarifying the urgency of our work. In 2002, Israel began constructing the apartheid wall, snaking through the West Bank, de facto annexing large swaths of fertile Palestinian land and water resources, and further restricting freedom of movement. Israel's ongoing apartheid policies of administrative detention—holding Palestinians without charge or trial—left Palestinians stranded in prison indefinitely. At the same time, home demolitions are a daily occurrence, with more than nine thousand structures destroyed since 2009.[1] In addition to the daily indignities faced by Palestinians at checkpoints, Jewish-only settlements proliferated in the West Bank, siphoning water, developing a network of Jewish-only roads connecting the settlements to Israel, and bringing into Palestinian communities thousands of armed settler vigilantes, who regularly harassed and violently attacked Palestinians, vandalizing their property with the blessing of the Israeli army, felling ancient olive trees, and shooting at Palestinians that need to cross Jewish-only roads to reach their farms or graze their flocks. In Gaza, the situation became even more dire for Palestinians after Jewish settlers were removed in 2005, when Israel turned Gaza into an open-air prison, maintaining an illegal siege by controlling what goes in and out by air, land, and sea. Between 2008 and 2022, there have been four major military assaults of Gaza by Israel, leaving more than four thousand Palestinians dead with tens of thousands more critically wounded and traumatized. Palestinians living inside Israel face increasing systemic racial discrimination, amounting to at least sixty-five laws that discriminate against Palestinians by "limit[ing] the rights of Palestinians in all areas of life, from citizenship rights to the right to political participation, land and housing rights, education rights, cultural and language rights, religious rights, and due process rights during detention."[2] Palestinian refugees, now numbering in the millions, still cannot exercise their UN-stipulated right to return home, and are often barred entry even to visit.

Against this gruesome backdrop, global solidarity with Palestinians blossomed. The BDS movement was launched in 2005 by Palestinian civil society, which called on the international community to boycott, divest from, and sanction Israel until freedom, equality, and justice were achieved. It was brought to worldwide prominence with Israel's devastating assault on Gaza in 2008–2009. In June 2014, after at least five years of working in solidarity with the Israel-Palestine Mission Network (IPMN) of the Presbyterian Church, their General Assembly voted in favor of divestment from companies profiting from the Israeli occupation, making the front page of the *New York Times* as the first mainline church to do so.[3] Just days later, Israel began to bomb Gaza without mercy, resulting in over 2,200 deaths in Gaza, at least 17,000 injuries, and untold destruction of homes, schools, mosques, health and higher education infrastructure, and ongoing trauma to the Palestinians of Gaza living through periodic bombardment and permanent siege. The word "apartheid" as it applies to Israel was extremely controversial in 2010, particularly in Jewish circles. By 2021, every major human rights organization had named Israel as an apartheid regime, a mark of the impact of the global movement.[4]

At the same time, the US was experiencing a resurgence of Black resistance. When Michael Brown was murdered by police in Ferguson, Missouri, the nascent Black Lives Matter movement, which had begun as a hashtag after the acquittal of George Zimmerman in the shooting of Trayvon Martin, expanded to ongoing protests in Ferguson. Ferguson residents were tear-gassed by police during protests, and messages of solidarity and practical tips on how to handle the tear gas flowed in publicly from Gaza and Ramallah to Ferguson, the product of several years of building relationships between Palestinian and Black American activists, based on their shared conditions.[5] Outrage continued to build when Eric Garner was killed by police in August 2014, and twelve-year-old Tamir Rice was killed by police in Cleveland later that fall. It was the genesis of the Movement for Black Lives, and a moment of public reckoning about the roots of racism and white supremacy in this country.

During this period, the US went from the administration of president Barack Obama into the presidency of Donald Trump and the growth of an emerging and increasingly self-confident white fundamentalist Christian, and even fascist, right. At the same time, the left in the US grew stronger than it had ever been in our lifetimes, beginning with the Occupy movement in 2011 and led by the emergence of the Movement for Black Lives, Indigenous Land Back movements, increasingly loud and proud anticapitalism, and increasing awareness of the interdependence of movements.

Relationship to the Palestine Movement

Against enormous odds and in the face of fierce pushback, the Palestinian rights movement in the US has succeeded in shifting the discourse and politics of Palestinian liberation from being an untouchable topic in even liberal political circles to becoming a central rallying cry in grassroots progressive discourse and demands. As we unpack in detail throughout the book, JVP prized its relationship with Palestinian organizations, maintaining strong working relationships and actively consulting with partners when we undertook big strategic or political shifts in the organization.[6] Our most successful partnerships with Palestinian organizations were with those with whom we shared values. How we articulated those values shifted over time, but they always included a commitment to transnational solidarity; an anti-oppression and anti-apartheid framework; and dedication to full equality and grassroots leadership of Palestinians, as well as liberating Judaism from Zionism. As BDS became a central demand and rallying cry of the Palestinian rights movement, it correspondingly gained increasing importance to JVP. Of course, just as in the Jewish community, the Palestinian community is not a monolith, and throughout our time we strove to adjust to the shifting currents of internal Palestinian politics. Ensuring an effective solidarity stance requires understanding your unique role and responsibility as part of the broader movement with whom you are in solidarity. As part of a movement ecosystem, different people join through different entry points, each element of the movement taking part where they can be most impactful.

Solidarity is typically understood as when people outside a specific community dedicate themselves to supporting the rights and aspirations of that community, taking direction on what actions to take from the community itself. A classic internationalist example is the global solidarity movement with Black South Africans against apartheid. As a Jewish organization fighting against Israeli apartheid, which hijacked Jewish symbols and traditions in the service of the repression of Palestinians, JVP's solidarity model was slightly different. We included independent actions affirming our cultural traditions and detethering and reinventing them so they could be part of our struggle for justice rather than symbols of repression against Palestinians. Our hope and belief is that by doing so we made our movement richer and more effective. For JVP, that has entailed organizing Jews by building a political home where people could find a warm embrace and avenues of expression of their Jewishness

that are both familiar and liberatory, while also understanding the dangers of regarding Israel and Zionism as a source of
Jewish safety and community. This has meant doubling down
on political education to deepen our members' understanding
of the root causes of Palestinian oppression and to strengthen
their brass-tacks organizing skills. The spirit of patience we
strove to cultivate (and in which we did not always succeed) in
organizing Jewish communities—meeting people where they
are and understanding how they got that way through their
Jewish education, family history, and dominant myths—was not
a role for our Palestinian comrades to play. The conversations,
let alone the compromises that we might be ready to make (such
as engaging in good faith with those who are not yet willing to
acknowledge the Nakba or current manifestations of Palestinian
suffering) would rightfully feel unbearable to those whose very
identity is regularly denied and rejected. At the same time, we
prioritized the creation of welcoming spaces for people to "come
home to" when they are ready, without tying ourselves in knots
or sacrificing our principles for people who aren't yet ready.

Relationship to Jewish World

JVP is a Jewish organization that is part and parcel of the spectrum and history of Jewish communal organizations in the United
States. Since early in the twentieth century, Jewish organizations
have sprouted to address the needs of Jewish communities as they
arose, whether to provide services to new immigrants; address
structural antisemitism; advocate for a more pluralistic, multifaith society; offer solidarity with Jews trying to survive under
Nazism; or, eventually, to advocate for (and in our case organize
against) the interests of the State of Israel.

The first Jews to come to this continent were Sephardi Jews[7]
(Jews from the Iberian Peninsula), who made up the majority

of the Jewish population here until the mid-1800s. In the late nineteenth and early twentieth centuries, in response to swelling violence pre– and post–World War I, the Jewish population of the US ballooned, with more than two and a half million Jews, mainly Ashkenzi, immigrating from Eastern Europe to the US. From 1840 to 1920, the Jewish population went from 15,000 to over 3 million. These Jews were by and large poor and working-class racialized minorities, making them among the natural standard-bearers for the Communist Party and unions, prominent in the left of their day. In the wake of World War II, Jews from Europe were racialized in the US as white, the majority enthusiastically moving into the middle class thanks to the opportunities provided by the GI Bill, the easing of antisemitic restrictions on opportunities like college entrance and purchasing homes, and the other more intangible benefits and privileges of whiteness.[8]

The scars of the Holocaust dominated the Jewish communal psyche over the coming decades. While well into the 1930s the majority of American Jews were anti-Zionist, the post-Holocaust milieu inspired fierce organizing on behalf of Israel, with the impact of the Nakba for Palestinians deliberately denied by the most established and well-resourced organizations that found their initial missions evolving as Jews found affluence and comfort in American life. Especially after the 1967 war, when Israel conquered the occupied West Bank (including East Jerusalem and its Old City) and Gaza, support for Israel became a litmus test for almost the entire Jewish community and its institutions.

The Jewish non-Orthodox community in the US, overall, has remained relatively liberal, voting for Democrats at higher rates than all other demographic groups apart from Black people (of course, there are Black Jews who bridge these two categories). Since the 1980s, Jewish Zionist groups like the powerful

American Israel Public Affairs Committee (AIPAC), alongside enormous evangelical Christian influence, rising state-sponsored Islamophobia, and military corporations with an economic interest in weapons provision, created a status quo that required whoever was elected to higher office, or aspired to be, to act as if the US alliance with Israel was unbreakable. In practice, that meant support for virtually unconditional economic and military aid beyond what any other country receives. Legacy Jewish organizations continue to wield enormous influence as they demand toeing the line on Israel as a prerequisite for access to resources and communal inclusion, brandishing accusations of antisemitism as a cudgel to silence critique of Israel.

That does not mean there was not dissent. The remnants of the early left never disappeared entirely. The Jewish Peace Fellowship was founded in 1941 to be "a Jewish voice in the peace community and a peace voice in the Jewish community." Other organizations, such as Breira, founded in 1983, and New Jewish Agenda (NJA), in 1980, emerged with a similar ethos to bridge the progressive and Jewish worlds. Breira lasted just four tumultuous years, NJA's Middle East Task Force lasted about eight years, both facing ruthless attacks from legacy Jewish organizations that would stop at nothing to shutter a Jewish voice in support of Palestinians.

It was into this world that JVP matured, as a local Bay Area organization, in the early 2000s, with these histories well known to its founding generation. Other similar local groups were scattered around the country, but post 9/11 was nevertheless a low point for the US left overall, as well as the Jewish left. Ever since, JVP has sat at the farthest left point of the Jewish communal spectrum when it comes to Israel and Palestinian freedom. That spectrum ranges from right-wing Zionist organizations like the Zionist Organization of America (ZOA) to legacy Jewish organizations like the American Jewish Committee (AJC) and the

Anti-Defamation League (ADL) to liberal Zionist organizations like J Street and T'ruah.[9] JVP, which began with members who spanned from anti-Zionist to left Zionist, was never a Zionist organization and became formally anti-Zionist in 2019. Thus, JVP's work was cut out for it in fighting for recognition and legitimacy in the Jewish world, which only became more intense as we grew and the mainstream Jewish world began to fear JVP's influence and what it indicated about changing Jewish perspectives on Palestinian liberation.

Shifts were just beginning to be noted in the Jewish American world early in our tenure. Peter Beinart's 2010 essay "The Failure of the American Jewish Establishment" made waves when it was published by naming the widening divide between Jews in the US and Israel.[10] That piece proved prescient as Israel's governing coalitions moved further and further to the right—as they have continued to do ever since, espousing fascist and even genocidal views—even as not just young Jews but all younger Americans have grown more and more supportive of Palestinian rights, according to polling.[11]

Despite the manipulative insistence on communal homogeneity regarding Israel, the reality is that as long as there was Zionism there's been anti-Zionism. JVP and the two of us personally are part of a lineage of Jews who reject the idea that Jewish safety and prosperity rely on the establishment of a Jewish supremacist nation-state in historic Palestine. From the outset, opposition to Zionism in Jewish communities ranged from theological to political. Ultra-Orthodox Jews reject the idea that humans can return Jewish sovereignty to the Land of Israel by force, believing that only God can do that in messianic times; Bundists preferred to link arms with the working class in their home countries to together struggle for democracy and social justice. The Reform movement of Judaism, today the largest denomination of Judaism in the US, was adamantly anti-Zionist initially, stating in 1885: "We consider ourselves no longer a nation, but a religious community, and therefore expect neither a return to Palestine . . . nor the restoration of any of the laws concerning the Jewish state."

JVP did not declare itself anti-Zionist until early in 2019, late in the period considered in this book. While JVP had anti-Zionist members since its inception, the proportion of individual members and staff who identified as anti-Zionist grew and grew as the years passed. Anti-Zionist thought and legacy were a constant source of inspiration long before JVP's formal adoption of an anti-Zionist position, and, particularly after we adopted the full BDS call in 2015, an inherent anti-Zionist critique flavored our public positions. Throughout the time period covered in the book, therefore, you'll see us referring to anti-Zionism as a guiding concept. That being said, there was never a litmus test, before or after JVP took a formal position, for how members identified.

The particular flavor of Jewish anti-Zionism JVP embodies today is unique to our historical moment. Our rejection of Zionism is rooted in a sense of solidarity with Palestinians living under the boot of Jewish supremacy, a broader critique of settler colonialism, and an interdependent understanding of realizing freedom and liberation for all people. Over the years, as JVP evolved into an explicitly anti-Zionist organization, we were moved and inspired by Jewish anti-Zionist lineages across the political and religious spectrum as we devise new/old ways to be Jewish for our time.

The Emergence of JVP

JVP is a grassroots membership organization that was founded in the Bay Area in 1996 by three University of California, Berkeley, students named Julie Iny, Julia Caplan, and Rachel Eisner. From the beginning, JVP's culture was feminist, largely queer, unapologetically left and included both Mizrahi (Jews of Middle East and North African Heritage) and Ashkenazi (Jews of Eastern European heritage) leadership.[12] JVP's first few years focused largely on social and cultural events and exchanges. When the Second Intifada began, in 2000, an influx of new members, who brought decades of experience in movements ranging from reproductive justice to antiwar to Central American solidarity, as well as earlier Jewish/Palestinian solidarity formations, turned JVP's focus to opposing Israeli government actions. With a "big tent" ideology that ranged from liberal Zionist to anti-Zionist, JVP built common ground around a strong anti-occupation stance, becoming known for creative actions and effective messaging. But even then, JVP went far beyond just about any other Jewish peace group by talking about the Nakba and acknowledging that Israel's very founding was implicated in Palestinians' ongoing dispossession and oppression. Unusually for the time, we didn't take a position on one state or two states for final parameters. The two-state solution had long been the consensus position for the peace camp, and eventually the US establishment, but JVP was cognizant both that many Palestinians analyzed Israel first and foremost as a European settler-colony in the heart of the Arab world and wanted to maintain the integrity of historic Palestine, and second, perhaps more important, that as a group of people in the US it was not JVP's place to determine the number of states at all, but instead to do what we could to support a liberatory future.

In 2002, at the height of the Second Intifada, members began to take seriously the idea that JVP had a responsibility to build power in order to change the status quo of unconditional US support for Israel. With that analysis, a decision was made that money and staff were needed to implement JVP's ambitious agenda. Around 2005, JVP began to be in touch with other similar organizations around the country about merging to create a single national organization. JVP was at this point the largest of similar local groups with more of a national reach, due to investments in tech infrastructure and strong communications. When JVP "went national" in 2006, there were tensions almost immediately among the disparate small groups that had come together under one banner. There was some nuance in political positioning, but the challenges largely centered around competing cultures and leaders among different groups that were used to operating independently, struggles over power and tone, and differences around the degree and structure of democratic decision-making and the importance of raising money. For two years the new national formation struggled to find its footing and then began to split apart in 2007.

Rather than giving up, the remaining members decided to embark on a "moving forward" process, which took on interviewing as many current and recently resigned members as possible to ascertain what had gone wrong. This was possible because the total membership was around a hundred people.[13] Using the results of the interviews and the trust that had been reestablished through the process, the committee overseeing it built a new blueprint for organizing and organizational structure going forward. An emphasis was placed on cultivating new members and chapters from the ground up along guidelines set by the national organization. Rebecca inherited this blueprint when she became executive director in 2009, after it was ratified by the members.[14] This history, although not addressed explicitly in the pages to come, is noteworthy for how JVP's early days influenced its later structure, approaches, and politics.

JVP's organizational structure was born at this time, with a strong national staff and a network of members and chapters. Since then, JVP has been a structural hybrid between a movement and a traditional nonprofit organization—with a board, staff, and the governance and decision-making hierarchies that entails, entwined with a robust membership, chapter network, and constituency groups (such as rabbis, artists, and students)—that has driven its political trajectory. Within this model, members were involved in setting national strategy, and also autonomously developed campaigns, coalitions, and unique cultures locally. We discuss the advantages and tensions of this structure in detail in chapter two.

Theory of Change

JVP's theory of change has always centered on building a large and powerful enough grassroots movement to shift US policy on Israel and Palestinian rights. JVP understood our responsibility as Jewish Americans to target our own government, which, by giving essentially unconditional economic and military aid and diplomatic cover to Israel, enables Israel to continue its apartheid toward Palestinians. JVP saw the Jewish community specifically as a key pillar that would need to shift its position in relation to Israel and the Palestinians in order for US policy to move. Inspired by the civil rights movements in the US and the anti-apartheid movement in South Africa specifically, we took as our models successful grassroots interventions that were up against superior resources but built power through sheer numbers. That meant always centering organizing and visionary messaging, regardless of whichever campaigns, programs, or projects we were pursuing. Especially because Jewish communal support for Israel was overwhelming, JVP recognized our role as just one prong in a multifaceted movement, led by Palestinians in the US and Palestine, with organizations proliferating to take aim at the other pillars holding up the unconditional US support for Israel: Christian Zionism, Islamophobia, and the military-industrial complex, to name just a few.

The core of JVP's theory of change was base-building, to bring a critical mass of American Jews to collectively serve as a counterweight to the various legacy Jewish institutions. That's why JVP invested in building an institution that had within it a structure to contain our ambitions and the daily work of movement building. As we will dissect further in chapter 2 (on building a movement inside a nonprofit), we relied on a fairly traditional hierarchical staff and board leadership structure, nested in a membership organization, nested in the Jewish community, nested in the broader movement for Palestinian rights. JVP's organizing influences were multiple, as our active members, staff, and board brought with them pieces of their previous organizing formations and schools of thought, pulling from Paulo Freire, Ella Baker, Saul Alinsky, Dolores Huerta, and more. The result is an organizing theory of our own that was a hybrid of community, faith-based, political, and movement-building organizing practices.

This organizing mélange is a comfort zone for JVP, as we thrived in the space of "both/and." JVP always self-identified as an organization of the left and was also simultaneously struggling to be accepted as part of the Jewish communal world. In the Jewish world, JVP began as small and relatively marginal, but, in the broader Palestinian solidarity movement in the US, JVP was often the largest organization in the room. Even as JVP identified as a movement, we also operated within the constraints of a nonprofit 501(c)(3) organization. We explore each of these contradictions and how they impacted our thinking and action throughout the book.

About the Book

We offer this book even as JVP's urgent work continues. Someday, we hope, the definitive history of JVP and its role in moving American Jewish communities to support justice for Palestinians will be written. But that is not this book. Instead, it focuses on a very specific and decisive time within JVP's broader history: the ten-year period from 2010 to 2020, when we were both on the staff of JVP. The two of us took on this project because we think the lessons of building a sustainable, functioning, effective left movement in the face of difficult conditions can help address the urgent need for interlocking left movements to be able to thrive over the long haul under challenging political contexts, even the existential threat of fascism.

We are in a very serious moment in American political life, as the left struggles to contend with an ever-evolving set of conditions including intense threats to democracy, climate disaster looming, the repercussions of a pandemic, and now the aftermath of October 7th. Historically, too many left movements have experienced damaging and sometimes lethal splits. It is sometimes difficult to recognize the enormous value of simply keeping a unified movement together, as JVP has done. We are very aware that, all too often, as mainstream opinion shifts—which is our goal—that the more left or radical groups that have labored to make those positions viable are erased. We offer these lessons as part of the first draft of that history. And, of course, JVP has continued to grow and evolve beyond us! We want to underline that we are not speaking for the JVP of today, nor on behalf of the JVP that predated us. By focusing on this specific time period, we hope to illuminate a time of crucial growth and evolution that informs JVP's present but is not confined to it.

Our focus is not at all comprehensive. We examine some of the most illustrative political and organizational moments and challenges in the ten years of our leadership in order to map out relevant lessons for organizers in our movement and beyond. We look at not just outcomes but also the intricate processes that made them possible, drawing back the curtain on what it takes organizationally to build people power and shift politics, with the aim of being useful across movements. Happily, tens of thousands of people, maybe hundreds of thousands, identify themselves as affiliated with JVP. They include kick-ass member leaders, past or current staff or board leaders, online followers, petition signers or phone bankers, dues-paying members, members of the rabbinical, artist, academic, or other councils, or any combination therein. We cannot tell their stories, only our own. We cannot possibly do justice here to the enormous amounts of dedication and work that JVP members bring to its success every day, in some cases for decades.

We are very conscious of writing from our own, very specific perspective as two of many staff leaders. We want, in particular, to acknowledge with love and appreciation our friends/comrades/coconspirators Stefanie Fox (JVP's current ED), Cecilie Surasky, and Ari Wohlfeiler, who were each deputy directors during much of the time under discussion. In various configurations, we made up the Leadership Team (LT), which we discuss further in chapter 2. It was the full LT that together made most of the plans and decisions we examine in this book. We want to lift up their often unspoken role in the pages to come, because they were intimately involved even when they are not explicitly named. Of course, as we are the authors of this book, the lessons and conclusions offered represent only the two of us. Even those who shared daily leadership with us, we have no doubt, would have somewhat different recollections and analysis than we do. While we did our best to fact-check documents within the existing JVP archive, and perspective-check through interviews with others who were there at the time, we are very aware that this is just one angle on a multifaceted view of the inner workings of JVP.[15]

As white and Ashkenazi leaders in JVP, we had and continue to have blind spots that can make it easy for us to ignore or downplay the ways our actions impacted other people or groups of people. And we know that in the very act of writing we are smoothing down the messy edges of real life. At the same time, as white organizers as part of multiracial movements, we want to hold and show the complexity of making mistakes and remaining valuable and impactful as part of a larger ecosystem.

As we map the political evolution of the organization, we also need to map the evolution of the language we used. Over the ten years we were at JVP, the language we used changed dramatically as external political conditions shifted in response to JVP's organizing, guided by our Palestinian comrades. For example, when we began, JVP was focused on challenging the Israeli occupation of the West Bank (including East Jerusalem) and Gaza, and our campaigns concentrated on forcing corporations and institutions to divest their resources from companies that profited from the occupation. But when JVP endorsed the Palestinian call for BDS in 2015, we moved closer to the global solidarity movement, and our understanding of the root causes of Palestinian oppression continued to deepen. It was clear that the word "occupation" was insufficient to capture the realities on the ground, which impacted Palestinians who lived within Israel and in exile across the planet. So, JVP sunsetted talking just about "occupation" and began to describe the current reality as "apartheid."

Throughout the book, when we reference campaigns that predate JVP's endorsement of the Palestinian call for BDS, we may use the terms that we used at that time, even if they read as outdated today. During our tenure the organization was on a journey to identifying as anti-Zionist, even before it was officially established as such in early 2019. Many, if not most, of our members and staff identified as anti-Zionist before then. The evolution of our vocabulary is a way to track the maturation of the organization's analysis and a way to experience the impact of political dynamism in an organization's life cycle. In that same vein, we struggled with what tenses to use. It had happened in the past for us, but some of what we describe are ongoing dynamics and realities for JVP. At the same time, we are also making present-day reflections and observations with the advantage of hindsight. So, you might find our verb use uneven, and we invite you to roll with it!

§

Even as we ask for readers' flexibility, we do want to ensure the book is accessible if you are new to Jewish communal dynamics, organizing, the movement for Palestinian rights, or all of the above. Here are some definitions of the concepts we refer to repeatedly:

Antisemitism: We understand antisemitism as discrimination, prejudice, hostility, or violence against Jews as Jews.[16] It can take many forms, including violence, threats of violence, repeating or circulating antisemitic tropes or conspiracy theories, and other aggressions.

Anti-Zionism: Political opposition to Zionism, based on an understanding of Zionism as a racist, settler-colonialist movement.

Base-building: Building a social base of support that helps an organization accomplish its goals. A classic base-building model involves identifying a key constituency (for us that is American Jews and friends), bringing people from the constituency into a base that identifies with the organization's goals, then facilitating the base's participation as members, supporting those members to step into leadership roles that help the organization grow and accomplish its goals. Key activities of a base-building organization include door knocking, flyering, phone banking, one-to-one meetings, collective meetings, educational workshops, social media, petition drives, community events, and more.

BDS: Inspired by the South African anti-apartheid movement, BDS stands for boycott, divestment, and sanctions. BDS is a Palestinian-led movement launched in 2005 to pressure Israel to comply with international law and to end its discriminatory apartheid policies through mounting boycott, divestment, and sanction campaigns targeting corporations, governments, and other institutions that are invested in or otherwise enabling Israel's practices that violate Palestinians' human rights. Its three baseline demands are 1) end the occupation and colonization of Palestinian lands; 2) full and equal rights for Palestinians inside Israel; and 3) the right of refugees to return home.

Grassroots Organizing: Winning justice by identifying, recruiting, and developing leaders, cultivating community around and among those leaders, building and strategically deploying the power of that community to win concrete changes that allow all people to flourish.

Legacy Jewish Institutions: We use this phrase to refer to the collection of American Jewish organizations established between 1850 and 1950.[17] These organizations began with missions related to Jewish civic and social standing as minorities and new immigrants, but, as Jews assimilated into whiteness and climbed the class ladder post–WWII, these institutions' missions shifted. They have amassed millions of dollars, pivoted to pro-Israel advocacy, and are focused on maintaining the status quo even as Jewish communities are evolving rapidly around race, sexuality, gender, and other social issues. These organizations now work in tandem with Israel as the main organized opposition to the Palestinian rights movement.

Left: The left seeks a radical transformation of our social systems toward democracy and justice. The left rejects capitalism, colonialism, and imperialism and opposes forces of domination including prisons, police, militaries, and corporations.

Movement: When we say "movement" in an organizing context, we mean the ecosystem of organizations, individuals, ideologies, and practices that combine to push for social change, whether to expand rights (such as the civil rights or women's rights movements), change government policy (such as the antiwar movement), or shift culture and demand accountability (such as the MeToo movement), or, in the case of the movement for Palestinian rights—all of the above! Movements are always multifaceted and are not held by one organization, even as organizations play a key role in forwarding the demands of the movement at large, as is the case of JVP.

Power: Put simply, power is the ability to make things happen. In organizing, oppressive power is challenged and shared power is cultivated. As organizers we seek to build grassroots power by bringing together enough people to make those in charge change. Power in grassroots movements is measured in our ability to develop leaders and the communities around them to have the resolve, knowledge, and skills to seize organizing opportunities, develop strategic campaigns, and win specific outcomes, as well as create further organizing opportunities, leaders, and a wider base out of successful campaign wins.

Zionism: A settler-colonial movement that successfully advocated for the establishment of a Jewish state in historic Palestine. While Zionism was hotly contested within Jewish communities when it first emerged in the late 1890s, since the mid-twentieth century, most Jewish institutions and a majority of Jews have seen Zionism as a movement of self-determination for the Jewish people. Zionism today is focused on maintaining a Jewish state through a violent, militarized apartheid system in which Jews have more rights than the Indigenous Palestinian population.

Reviewing the Agenda

We are facilitators by nature, so of course we want to orient you to making your way through this book by reviewing the agenda!

- The book begins at the core of JVP: a political home where members celebrate holidays and reimagine Jewish rituals, build relationships, and get refilled from the relentless work of organizing.
- From there, in chapter 2 we look at the actual container we built to hold the work. This includes the limits, contradictions, and successes of JVP's movement/nonprofit hybrid organizational model that emerged over time, affecting everything we did, from fundraising to staffing structures, hierarchy to leadership development.
- In chapter 3 we unpack the challenges and possibilities of organizing against the grain as part of and counter to our family and communities of origin. This is important political and emotional context for JVP's work and will likely resonate with all those doing similar intimate community organizing.
- Jewish community organizing cannot be understood without exploring antisemitism. Chapter 4 is focused on the cynical manipulation of accusations of antisemitism from pro-Israel forces as a key strategy to undermine the movement for Palestinian rights, even in the face of rising anti-Jewish hatred in the US.
- In chapter 5 we look at the work of tending to the wider circle of partnerships and coalitions that deepen and strengthen the web of relationships that undergird thriving movements.
- Chapter 6 brings together all the preceding elements to show the power of how JVP pushed our positions farther to the left even as we grew, including the yearslong processes that resulted in endorsing the Palestinian call for BDS and officially becoming anti-Zionist, as well as how JVP slowly and

carefully built out our engagement with Congress based on our relative people power.

- In the final sections of the book, we turn to some key challenges we faced. Chapter 7 outlines the reckonings we faced toward the end of our tenure as we grappled with white supremacy and Ashkenazi hegemony within JVP.

- That leads into our final chapter, which details the tactics of a "continuum of repression" that our movement and so many others face, especially as our organizing proves effective, ending with reflections about ways in which we made victories out of attacks and remained resilient.

Throughout the book we posit a theory of JVP's unique solidarity stance, which informed each of our reactions to the rejections we faced from our community for our countercurrent political positions and reinforced our own sense of stakes in Palestinian freedom. We also explore the complications of the power JVP amassed, disproportionate to other organizations in the Palestine solidarity movement. At the end of each chapter, we have included organizing strategy reflection questions that highlight important aspects of organizing strategy that we've explored in the chapter. These are questions that have no easy or essential answers but are important to grapple with proactively. We imagine that teams can discuss these questions together as part of a reading group or use the questions as a guide during strategic sessions or work planning. In the appendices, we have included a glossary of the various organizations we mention throughout the book and primary texts of various statements we reference throughout the book. We encourage you to make use of those appendices, as they will put more meat on the bones of the stories we share.

There is so much that happened in the ten-year period we are covering that we do not address here. But we hope that by the end of the book you'll have a rich sense of the ways our organizing and organizational structures added up to a powerful whole.

Solidarity Is the Political Version of Love

Our title and epigraph use the words of our beloved Jewish writer and activist ancestor Melanie Kaye/Kantrowitz, z"l, which echo how we used the same phrase in the 2019 statement with which JVP officially became anti-Zionist.[18] In many ways, our years on staff at JVP were one long love letter to our ancestors, comrades, and descendants, the manifestation of our deepest, greatest hope for their ongoing protection, happiness, and flourishing.

Our subtitle is just as important: we offer this book for organizers of all stripes who are striving for answers to pretty universal movement questions. Left movements are engaged in some of the hardest work there is—politically, emotionally, and spiritually—because it involves changing people's perceptions of the world, fighting against a status quo that is accepted as a given. That is true of abolitionists, of queer people fighting for trans rights, Indigenous people in the US organizing for sovereignty over the land, and when groups of non-Black people in solidarity with Black people or rich people seeking to equitably redistribute wealth are seen as race or class traitors. This kind of struggle often requires challenging the people who raised you, engaging with and moving through painful feelings, and building a vision of a new world that can be very lonely for a long time. That has been the reality of our work, too, and we would like to share it in all its complexity, pain, beauty, and strategic utility as an offering to our sibling movements.

Our hope is that our reflections on what worked and where we missed the mark will be of interest not only to those involved in the Jewish communal world or the movement for Palestinian freedom (or both) but also to people in other movements who face similar challenges in building healthy, sustainable, effective organizations capable of moving communities toward justice. We hope that these reflections on JVP's organizing successes—and failures—can offer to every social justice movement opportunities to draw crucial lessons and strategies for the ongoing collective work of building hope, justice, and power always rooted in love.

Chapter 1

Building a Political Home

The first big national JVP campaign of our era was to pressure TIAA-CREF, the retirement pension fund giant, to divest from companies profiting from the Israeli occupation. When, in 2010, our team began to plan an action at the first TIAA-CREF annual meeting since our campaign began, we realized it would coincide with Tisha B'Av, a solemn Jewish fast day that commemorates the many disasters that have befallen the Jewish people over our history. While there are no restrictions on working that day, the rabbis among us urged us to incorporate the significance of the day into our plans.

The planning group decided on a brief communal ritual that would begin a half hour before the official start of the action. We sent out a carefully worded email that invited folks who wanted to be part of the observance to arrive earlier, and suggested that folks who weren't interested in participating should arrive when it would already be over. One of our newest and most enthusiastic members, Jethro, reacted angrily. He had been very active in his synagogue until he left in rage and despair over the censure he had faced over his insistence on talking about the Israeli occupation and was in a stage when he found Jewish communal life, apart from political action, absolutely unbearable. He questioned why we needed to

integrate observance of Tisha B'Av into our work at the wholly secular TIAA-CREF annual meeting at all, and said that he would
feel alienated by it. We agreed to disagree on the approach, and he
grudgingly accepted the compromise of the early call time for those
that wanted to be part of it.

The day arrived. We had been busy with all the standard logistics of action planning, elevated by its being our first public action
of the campaign. We had recruited TIAA-CREF shareholders
who were going inside to attend the meeting as well as supporters
who took up posts outside the building. It involved complicated
timing and careful calibration of tone since we weren't yet ready to
escalate, and everyone was nervous. Layered on top of this was the
additional complication of marking Tisha B'Av.

TIAA-CREF's headquarters on Third Avenue in Manhattan
were one convenient block away from a small corner park covered
by a blue awning, offering relief from the summer sun. We had
put together a short service that linked the traditional lamenta-
tions with our purpose for the day. Before lighting a candle, we
read:

> There is a tradition that the Messiah will be born on
> Tisha B'Av and thus that out of destruction, redemption
> is born.
>
> Today as we gather together, Jews and friends who
> are working, struggling and seeking justice for all peo-
> ple, we are supported by the wisdom of Jewish tradition
> that inspires us to trust that out of Occupation, libera-
> tion can be born.[1]

Rebecca was not surprised to find herself moved to tears by
our gathering—but was shocked to look across our small circle
and see Jethro, who had arrived right on time, also wiping his
eyes. It is a moment we both have always remembered—how
deeply the pull of our rituals can link our histories and our

reasons for showing up to this work. In this case, it was Jewish ritual that resonated, but just about every powerful movement has its own history, rituals, songs, and poetry that has an emotional impact, nourishing us to maintain the light inside.

This was a time we did it just right. Our team had created a sense of deep calm, community, and spiritual purpose on the corner of Third Avenue, without making any assumptions about who "we" were. And the action was a huge success.

What We Mean by Political Home

We don't know exactly what was going through Jethro's mind that led him to decide to come early to the TIAA-CREF action or what moved him to tears once he was there. But, over time, the two of us have reflected upon the importance of building a political and communal home as part of our, or any, movement work. It makes our feelings bearable when we are heartbroken, it enables us to be joyful even when the work is hard. It tethers us together as a community that exists alongside and beyond the work itself. Yes, it is critical for our longevity and sustainability, but it also exists for its own sake.

Existing as a political home beyond JVP's organizational structures—but hopefully facilitated by them—bound us together as a community. Whether in local chapter meetings in members' living rooms, virtual gatherings on Zoom, our biannual national member meetings, or staff retreats, our staff and leaders were intentional about creating spaces where we could express our Jewishness—whatever that means to us—while also expressing our full political, cultural, and social selves. It felt urgent to create such a community because, except in a few isolated places, it was something that had not existed before.

Too many JVP members had experienced a sense of alienation or rejection in other Jewish spaces. It's hard to remember now, but for the vast majority of Jewish people who had deep criticisms of the Israeli state project before JVP became established nation-wide, the choices were either to stay away from Jewish communal life entirely or to continue to participate but not share aloud political concerns or critiques, forcing a kind of split reality. This forced choice is one that queer Jews have long had to make, so it has an uncomfortable echo among our queer-dominant organization. Foundational to movements for justice is ensuring everyone can be exactly who they are, everywhere. No one is going back in the closet!

Some of us show up to build a political home as Jews because we care about the future of Judaism and Jewishness. Some Jews are observant, expressing our Jewish identity through prayer, ritual, adherence to Jewish laws, and so on. Some Jews are secular, expressing our Jewish selves through language, art, food, philosophy, and other cultural dimensions of Jewishness. For some, our Jewish identity exists along the spectrum of religious to secular, eschewing divine and rabbinic authority but valuing the holiday cycle and the sense of belonging as part of a synagogue, while identifying strongly as Jewish.

Some show up to organize with JVP simply because they're looking for the most effective and transformative place to fight for Palestinian liberation. Some, of course, hope to do both simultaneously. While previous organizations such as Breira and New Jewish Agenda had offered a Jewish home for those skeptical of Israel, by the mid-1990s both had shut down and only scattered local groups carried on independently.

We believe what has made JVP's communal spaces—whether in person or online—powerful and meaningful beyond the constant stream of campaigns and projects is that they allow people to express their whole selves, in all their complexity, often for the first time. This sense of belonging—a core human need that many people fulfill at synagogue, church, mosque, ethnic heritage associations, block associations, labor unions, and more—is part of what makes JVP an enduring political home for so many, and is the "secret sauce" that keeps movements vibrant even when the political work is daunting.

This lesson was brought home to us both in 2017 at our national member meeting's Shabbat morning services. JVP held national gatherings for members biannually, which offered opportunities for far-flung members to meet, strategize, and learn together. It also always included, for those who wanted them, various Shabbat observances led by JVP rabbis and student rabbis. A longtime leader in our Tucson chapter rose to recite *birkat hagomel*, a blessing for making it through a life-threatening event. A few months earlier, doctors gave her a clean bill of health after a battle with cancer, but she waited months to offer the blessing in front of the open Torah because there was no Jewish community in her hometown that felt safe and welcoming for her, as an anti-Zionist Jew, to recite this very personal prayer.

The hard-fought circumstances that bring people into JVP also means that the stakes of what happens inside feel incredibly high. For many members, JVP became a proxy for Jewish family. This created a warmth and intimacy and commitment that served us well, but it also meant that the intensity of internal battles was sometimes very high, as people refought the battles of their childhood or young adulthood through the JVP lens. Building a political home is not without its risks. A political home is not immune from—perhaps, in fact, it is more vulnerable to—the tussles and insensitivities that arise around any family's table. The sense of belonging offered by a political home makes any incongruency in values or sense of rejection that much more painful. Disagreements reverberate with the rejections and alienation that led people to this political home in the first place. This lesson became most evident to us when, in 2015, Jews of color and Mizrahi and Sephardi Jews began to raise the ways they were excluded from that sense of home within JVP.

The specific cultural and sometimes religious milieu is specific to JVP, but these dynamics are probably familiar to anyone who is part of a movement that has taken on the transformation of its own community from the inside—from white people organizing against racism to men organizing against patriarchy to cis people organizing in solidarity with their trans siblings. Whatever movement you may be part of, it is worth it to build a political home as part of a hard-hitting political movement because the rewards are so profound. Rewards for each person who is a part of the political home and who reap the emotional benefits. Rewards to the organization and broader movement as deeply invested and connected circles of members assure the sustainability of the organization for the long haul. Rewards for future generations, as through the work of building a political home we ensure the evolution of our cultural and religious traditions as an enduring force for justice.

The "J" in JVP

Part of building a political home requires wading into the fraught waters of personal identity. When people talk about their identities, you never quite know what you will find. After all, identity taps into questions of lineage and upbringing that might raise legacies of trauma and violence, feelings of rejection, nostalgia, longing, separation. Over the course of JVP's history, there has been a constant, productive struggle over which holidays to observe, and how. JVP is not a religious organization and includes Jewish people of every stripe of observance and nonobservance, as well as non-Jewish sympathizers who find meaning in doing their political work with JVP. Complicating matters further, JVP has Jewish members who have been marginalized in their own home communities, whether because of their queerness or their interfaith relationships or being a Jew of color, or simply for their outspoken politics around Israel. For these members, associations with Jewish practice can be painful and alienating. That being said, JVP also has many members (often the same people!) whose political commitment to Palestinian freedom is deeply rooted in their understanding of Jewishness. The expression of the "J"—that is, Jewish—in JVP can be fraught and painful but is also deeply meaningful and necessary for building our own sense of identity and community as Jews going against the grain of the mainstream. All those who organize against the grain know the challenges and rewards this entails.

JVP clearly defines itself as a Jewish organization. This is politically significant because the "Jewish state" claims to speak on behalf of all Jews on the world stage. Our collective understanding of what that means has shifted and evolved—and remains one of the most powerful elements of our communal identity while also being sometimes confusing and awkward. For one thing, "Jewish" is an exceptionally broad term. People who identify as Jewish range from simply having Jewish parentage or cultural identification to every level of observance and lived experience. JVP has folks who went to Jewish summer camp, attended Jewish high school, and took a free trip to Israel in college, and we have folks whose relationships to their Jewishness—and especially Jewish communal institutions—are full of pain. There are also people who are culturally Jewish but unconnected to Jewish community or practice. This web of messy relationships to JVP's organizing targets, issues, and our selves is part of what organizers across movements seek to uncover and heal through organizing.

There has always been an inherent tension in JVP's Jewishness. As a political organization committed to ending apartheid based on ethnic and religious identity, it is nevertheless an organization based on ethnic and religious identity. JVP has striven to be very conscious of the imperative not to reproduce in our own space the same framework that Israel is based on, while recognizing (and often being reminded of it by Palestinian friends and comrades) the importance of a specifically Jewish organization doing our work. This tension has manifested in everything from qualification for membership to content at our annual National Membership Meeting (NMM) to the voice we use in our op-eds and social media feed and which holidays we closed the offices for.

The underlying assumptions and prejudices held by the vast majority of JVP's members and leaders about what Jewishness is in the US have also tripped us up over the years. While our political positioning was certainly far outside the Jewish mainstream, our cultural makeup largely reflects the white, Ashkenazi (Jews of Eastern European heritage) power structures of almost every other Jewish organization. It is important for organizers not to lose sight of these identity-related tensions over time, as they reveal areas where politics need sharpening or where there are gaps between values and actions. Because Israel and pro-Israel advocacy organizations gatekeep Jewish identity ruthlessly as part of enforcing Jewish supremacy over Palestinians, JVP's expansive and inclusive vision of what Jewishness is, and therefore what JVP membership is, can be understood as an anti-Zionist practice. While the details of our approach shifted back and forth over the years, our fundamental principles remained largely the same: Jewishness is self-identified; membership is open to everyone, with an understanding that self-selecting into work with JVP will mean opting into a Jewish framework for the work; and part of the power of JVP is creating a political and, for some, spiritual home for Jewish expression.

From 2010 to 2015, JVP's organizing model was predicated upon embracing all those who came toward us. This approach led to a cultural homogeneity and predominance of white, Ashkenazi Jews. There was such steady and ongoing growth that organizers were playing catch-up and not adequately engaging and integrating the new members who found us on their own, let alone being systematic about reaching out to specific subcommunities or geographies. Along with our own ongoing blind spots as leaders, we hadn't done the work of embedding guardrails into our organizational structures and accountability standards to interrupt or even slow down the practices that were so comfortable to us and that perpetuated a hegemonic culture that prioritized white, Ashkenazi Jewishness. Many staff and members who were Jews of color or Mizrahi/Sephardi did not find JVP an automatically comfortable, healthy, accessible home. Our white and Ashkenazi leadership set the culture, the values, and the narrative of the organization, and that meant it was one that revolved around whiteness.

Because most members struggled in some way, whether spiritually, politically, or communally to arrive at JVP, most also brought some Jewish communal baggage with them. Many of us had stories of disappointment and disillusionment from our brushes with or upbringing within Jewish institutions. In fact, when the JVP Rabbinical Council was formed, a surprising number of members pushed back vociferously. This was a bit mysterious at first, since it seemed like a no-brainer both strategically and for our community to organize sympathetic rabbis. They would have a stronger public voice collectively, would be able to support one another in their often lonely positions, and would be able to support the membership with relevant Jewish practice. Yet, when the formation of the council was announced, one member, speaking for many, said angrily, "I am not going to submit to rabbinic authority." This rather innocuous sentence reveals an entire lineage. To be concerned with rabbinic authority indicates a personal history with Jewish practice that is far from neutral. For generations, rabbis exerted almost absolute authority over Jewish life. Political movements like the Bund, which, in its commitment to the struggle of working-class Jews in their own countries included a fierce anti-Zionism, were part of the direct family history of some of our members, passed on from generation to generation.[2] For better or worse, our membership, us included, brought all of our old stories, histories, traumas, and joys with us into this new arena.

The JVP rabbinical council is overwhelmingly Reconstructionist, a movement of Judaism that understands Judaism as an evolving religious civilization.[3] This evolution means it is incumbent upon Jews to engage actively with Jewish tradition and history, and weaved contemporary political, spiritual, ethical, and psychosocial understandings and commitments into how to live a Jewish life in our time. When Alissa applied for admission to the Reconstructionist Rabbinical College (RRC) in 2003, despite the movement's commitment to Zionism, she was drawn there because Reconstructionists have been on the forefront of challenging American Jewish orthodoxies, integrating feminism and queerness into study and practice, taking a critical view of "chosen people" language in Jewish liturgy, and infusing ethics into every facet of Jewish life, making it a natural home for challenging the Jewish community politically as well—including when it comes to support for Palestinian rights. As it turned out, Alissa's experience of being an anti-Zionist rabbinical student was quite difficult, as it was for her predecessors who challenged the status quo in their time around queerness.

Of course, JVP did have members who had no prior connections to Jewish practice or community—by choice or by family upbringing or by being pushed away. In fact, as an organizing strategy, JVP's leadership at the time was pretty clear that we could grow faster and more easily by going after the low-hanging fruit of Jewish communities—those who, for whatever reason, were not yet part of any organized Jewish community. And the numbers backed us up: Pew Research consistently shows that about 25 percent of the Jewish community overall identifies as Jewish without being an active part of any Jewish organization or congregation.[4]

In an organizing sense, we have found that it is always easier to invite someone to join a vibrant community when they don't have one than to ask them to leave a community where they already have comfort, familiarity, networks, and family. At the same time, we found that some of our most vibrant member leaders were themselves displaced from Jewish communities of origin, finding themselves in the role of building and creating new ones, rooted in their investment in being and living Jewish. As in all organizing, the magic is made when you have members ready to join, ready to lead, and everything in between. In retrospect, our members' forthrightness about their hesitations related to their individual Jewish histories was a gift that pushed JVP as an organization, and us as leaders, to struggle productively to encompass it all.

From Generation to Generation

Jewish cultural traditions are not the only ones woven into the culture of the JVP political home. JVP's founding generation (early 2000s) was largely made up of committed leftist activists who had been in movements as varied as the anti-apartheid movement in South Africa, the Central American solidarity movement, reproductive rights, antiwar, ACT UP, and earlier iterations of Palestine solidarity organizations like New Jewish Agenda.

JVP's founders and early members were led to take action on Palestine by connecting the dots between Zionism, militarism, homophobia, sexism, and settler colonialism, and they brought with them the insights, practices, knowledge, and experience from those movements to the Palestine solidarity movement.

Although not universally the case, many early members in the Bay Area brought their experience from being active in multiple movements. For them, it was relatively easy to fit their work in support of Palestinians in the context of their already established political principles. One way to think of it is that they were Jewish activists as opposed to activist Jews, meaning that up to this point their activist work had not been organized around their Jewishness but around their broad political commitments.

The next generation of members that came in—roughly, from 2009 to 2014—were mostly younger and politicized through their engagement with what was happening at the time in Israel/Palestine, many having begun to grapple with it during Israel's assault on Gaza known as Cast Lead in 2009/2010. JVP, which at that point had existed for over a decade, was well equipped (thanks to smart forethought on digital infrastructure, still in its infancy, thanks to Cecilie Surasky) to absorb the surge of new members that came as a result of outrage over the level of destruction and death in Gaza, evidence of the brutal power imbalance between Israel and Palestinians in the besieged Gaza Strip. These newer members tended to have less of a sense of political context for where the struggle for Palestinian freedom fit into other struggles historically, and JVP was a vehicle not only for becoming seasoned Palestine solidarity activists but also for beginning to identify as part of a wider left.

During these years, when JVP still was not formally grappling with Zionism, a perhaps surprising detail was that the most religiously observant were often also the most dedicated anti-Zionists. For those with a strong Jewish practice, there was less of a need for Israel to play an anchoring role in their identity, making this subgroup within JVP the leading edge in creating a culture of Jewish anti-Zionism. This is not unlike, for example, the key role progressive Christians can play in the fight against Christian nationalism. For more secular members, who had largely been brought up on an exclusive diet of the Holocaust and Israel as their Jewish education, it was harder to come to grips with under-standing their Jewishness without Zionism. Jewish members who had been alienated from Jewish life through a superficial and jingoistic upbringing came to find nourishment in Jewish culture thanks to their commitment to Palestinian liberation.

Of course, within Jewish communities are many other inter-secting identities as well. What all the generations of JVP have in common, like many organizations on the left, is that JVP has always been disproportionately queer. This queerness is about whom we love but also how we think about politics, how we relate to the Jewish community and the mainstream world at large, and how essential it is to our safety and health to create a vibrant community around us. Queer people have a superpower, which is the will and experience to reimagine and re-create structures within our communities that exclude us. Having developed that muscle, we knew what we had to do when it came to questions of justice and rights of Palestinians. Our cultural queerness influ-enced our HR policies, the aesthetics of our street protests, and everything in between. As the organization grew and more for-mal policies were put into place, we created those policies to have an expansive conception of family when it came to health insur-ance, family medical leave, or bereavement policies, before it was commonplace to do so. And, of course, the queer community is practiced at fighting for inclusion and weathering rejection—emotional skills we needed to cultivate in spades while counter-ing the Jewish community's aggressive repression of our activism, as we will discuss in more detail in chapter 8, on repression.

In tandem with JVP's queerness, one of the joys of JVP orga-nizing is that in many places, and as an organizational ethos, it is truly intergenerational. That means there is a willingness to learn from one another's different experiences—from growing up as red-diaper babies or children of the Holocaust, or bringing lessons from deep immersion in 1960s civil rights struggles or the anti-apartheid movement in South Africa, to embracing evolving definitions of queer and trans identities, understandings of sexual harassment, and the urgency of climate crisis. It also means, at its best, creating a social world where people of all ages feel at home. And, as in so many ways at JVP, these relationships are often not only a lot of fun but also offer healing tonics for those who have lost relationships with grandparents, children, or parents due to diverging politics or identities.

JVP members were mostly middle-aged and older when it was founded, and it took a concerted effort to change the culture of the organization to bring in younger people, including, for a while, separate youth chapters. Eventually, there were enough younger members to balance out the founding generation, and the culture of individual chapters as well as the national staff began to shift accordingly. Younger members brought new practices to meetings—such as doing a go-around at the start of meetings, where everyone responds to a prompt from a facilitator to share something about themselves, as a way of building relationships and connection. It took time to integrate these cultural practices, with some older members complaining that they just came "to do political work, not go to therapy," just as some also resented the rituals that were regularly integrated in our direct actions, seeing them as navel-gazing, especially if their Jewish identity was more cultural than religious. Some older members who came to do political work resented a sense that younger generations were primarily there to build relationships with each other. The divides were, notably, not about political analysis—there was broad consensus on approaching the work with an intersectional analysis and a shared sense of Jews' place in the movement. The rub came more around how to relate to each other. Older members, the majority of whom had been involved in movement work for decades, did not feel respected for their wisdom and expertise, while younger members resented that older members were negligent toward community-building aspects that they valued as integral to successful political work. While in some cases this meant losing a subset of members from the chapter, most of the time these challenges led to opportunities to make explicit values and practices, challenging the various generations to meet each other in the middle. And, since JVP did create its own unique culture, it also meant that not everyone felt comfortable inside of it. For folks who had already experienced alienation in Jewish communal spaces— whether for their politics or their identity or some combination, it was even harder to take. It wasn't until the Jews of Color and Sephardi/Mizrahi (JOCSM) Caucus organized themselves to challenge this hegemony, slowly and painfully, that we grappled with how the new Jewish world JVP had created had left some members feeling even more alienated and alone.[5]

Jews of color, Sephardi Jews, and Mizrahi Jews were among JVP's cofounders, yet JVP has always been predominantly white, and Ashkenazi. JVP was not immune to the dynamics of white supremacy, which is a factor for any majority-white organization. In the years since the emergence of the Movement for Black Lives in 2014, in particular, just about every white-led movement or organization has had to grapple with the internal dynamics of white supremacist culture that have been increasingly and rightly challenged. In our case, even as the two of us thought of ourselves as antiracists, we were unsuccessful at navigating how to represent Jews of color in non-tokenizing ways in our communications and fundraising; we carelessly used Yiddish as a universal Jewish language; we focused staff hiring outreach on our own networks, which were likewise predominantly white and Ashkenazi, leading to homogeneity among our staff; and our senior leadership remained entirely white. Despite our best intentions, we were unable to prevent the culture from feeling exclusionary and unwelcoming to Jews of color or to allow Jews of color and Sephardi and Mizrahi Jews to influence our culture as deeply as queerness had. As we explore further later in this book, JVP did take on a thorough racial justice transformation process to redirect ourselves to where we aspire to be. The work of culture change is long and slow, and repairing the harms caused likewise takes time. JVP was never a one-size-fits-all organization, so there need to be spaces where our members, with their various and often contradictory needs, can flourish. We were not always successful at making this a reality, but the work continues.

Building a Culture of Belonging

In JVP's early years, we actively tried to be accepted as part of broader Jewish communities, going as far as to apply for membership in the local Jewish Community Relations Council (JCRC) in San Francisco, when JVP started as a local organization.[6] Over the years, all around the country, JVP members were excluded from consideration for jobs or fired from positions, joint events with JVP were canceled, and JVP chapters were blocked from joining local coalitions, even on issues that weren't related to Israel/Palestine. Once Hillel (the national Jewish college campus organization) created guidelines that explicitly excluded those with JVP positions from participating in Jewish communal life on campus, to name just one example, it became clear that we were banging our heads against a brick wall.

Even as JVP was being denounced from all sides in the Jewish community, the ironic truth has always been that JVP has brought people back into Jewish community or helped them find Jewish community for the first time. We knew that many of our members not only wanted to speak out against Israeli apartheid but also wanted to do it in a Jewish context, rather than abandoning their identity in despair. As one participant in our 2015 NMM wrote, as quoted in the *Forward*, "For three days, I was immersed in a Jewish community unlike I have ever been a part of, one rooted in justice that welcomed all of me."[7]

It's relatively unusual for people to be willing or able to give up familial and communal comforts in order to live in alignment with their values. It is especially important, no matter the cultural entry point for your organizing, to create opportunities to engage in and continue that culture and participation in communal life for those that do make that choice. These opportunities are the threads that tie us to each other and offer a glimpse into the future we are building. For those of us that refuse to check our politics at the door when we try to be a part of legacy Jewish institutions, it is emotionally impossible to sit through a Rosh Hashanah service, one of the holiest days of the Jewish year, when an Israeli flag is positioned on the *bimah* (stage), right next to the rabbi. A former JVP board president left his synagogue when, in the throes of the 2006 Israeli attack on Lebanon, his liberal synagogue had a video on their website's home page of Israeli soldiers petting kittens. An invitation to a Yom Ha'atzmaut (Israeli "independence" day) event from the local JCC stings, as it shows a callous disregard for the pain of that day for Palestinians who commemorate it as the Nakba. So, re-creating acts of care and ritual signals welcome and home-coming for those who love being Jewish, seek to mark time in sync with Jewish tradition, and continue the sacred obligation to evolve and nurture Jewish culture without sacrificing our deeply held and Jewishly rooted commitment to Palestinian freedom. That's one reason we've always maintained that the mainstream Jewish community, perpetually concerned with Jewish intergenerational continuity, should be thankful for JVP![8] Apart from our politics, JVP is doing everything that is the elusive holy grail of the Jewish world: fostering genuine engagement, connection, and attachment to Jewish community. That is certainly not the primary motivation of JVP's work, but for those of us who care about a meaningful Jewish future in this country, it is a moving by-product. And as JVP moved toward and ultimately adopted an anti-Zionist framework (as we discuss in more detail in chapter 6), it created even more opportunities to imagine and embody Judaism liberated from Zionism.

The ongoing and formalized rejection from mainstream Jewish communities both took a toll and illuminated a way forward that, ultimately, was freeing. Rather than continuing to beg to be included within inadequate existing institutions, JVP made a conscious decision to forge its own path, to create our own institutions, culture, and definition of Jewish life, one where we could be our full political and spiritual selves. That led JVP to create programs such as the Rabbinical Council and Havurah Network, whose members are now leading some of the most vibrant—and successful—communal projects in progressive Jewish life in the US.[9]

Inevitably, our organizational and institutional experiences in the mainstream Jewish world had an impact on our approach. JVP was undeniably a relatively small, though always growing, thorn in the side of legacy Jewish communal life. JVP's spokespeople and messaging brought that underdog attitude with us everywhere, insisting on recognition and loudly proclaiming our every victory. As underdogs seek to build political power, we have to make ourselves bigger, both to our adversaries as well as to ourselves. That sense of rejection led us to build something new organizationally in response, fostering a kind of "us against the world" vibe. This is a familiar theme in leftist organizing. It was fine, even justified, in the context of the Jewish organizational ecosystem. We had a bit of a chip on our shoulder from experiencing ongoing rejection and critique. Given our small size relative to the rest of the Jewish world, it made sense that we were screaming to make sure we were heard. But how that screaming landed in the Palestine solidarity movement was a very different story. Very early on, JVP had become the largest and most organized group in the loose network of Palestine solidarity organizations in the US. JVP members and leaders built deep and overlapping partnerships based on shared work and values with the dozen or so organizations with whom we worked most closely.[10] They let those of us in leadership know—gently and kindly—that what we had perceived as making sure people knew we existed and insisting on raising our voices was being read as grabbing credit and erasing our allies. This was, of course, particularly fraught, given our Jewish identity in a political space that was fighting for Palestinian voices to be heard at all. Given the ways that American culture normalizes and centers whiteness, together with the ways Ashkenazi Jews colluded with and assimilated into whiteness, Jewish voices (whether Ashkenazi or not) were routinely privileged above Palestinian voices. Countering this anti-Palestinian racism was a value JVP held in tandem with our commitment to winning our rhetorical battles. We think we sometimes held this contradiction more successfully than others, as later examples throughout the book will show.

Honoring Our Lineages with Visionary Political Action

One of the gifts that organizing offers is the chance not just to change oppressive conditions and policies today, to dream up and organize toward a different future, but also to be in relationship with our ancestors. In any movement work, creating space for members or participants in your organizing community to connect to the histories and traditions of their people can provide inspiration and deeper meaning for how you frame your demands and design your actions, pulling from the cadence in liturgical traditions, the rituals of the holidays, the reinterpretation of sacred texts, or calling back to communal memories, commemorations, or victories. Tethering the present and future to the past can develop organizing that heals and motivates. The traditions passed down to us—whoever the "us" may be—are the building blocks of rooted and visionary political action. In Jewish tradition, the act of repentance on Yom Kippur is done in the first-person plural, *ashamnu, bagadnu, gazalnu,* WE are guilty, WE have betrayed, WE have robbed. We take collective responsibility for our actions. With this liturgical inspiration, we gather for collective action to end Israeli apartheid with the knowledge that Israel claims to speak in our names. While we refuse that claim, we also recognize that, at any time, we can exercise "privileges" that are, in fact, tactics to further entrench settler colonialism—such as getting citizenship from Israel, which is specifically offered to Jews in order for Israel to retain its Jewish demographic majority.[11] Further, US foreign policy offering virtually unconditional military and economic aid to Israel is often couched in terms of protecting Jewish lives, despite the outsized role of the Christian Zionist lobby. We thus feel even more urgently the need to disrupt and contest the idea that there is a consensus within Jewish communities. Undermining perceived notions of consensus is a critical part of discourse shift in all countercurrent-culture movement building efforts, from undoing white supremacy to climate crisis to police and prison abolition. So, the simple slogan JVPers printed on placards early on in JVPs life, "Another Jew Against the Occupation," was empowering and represented a radical cultural reclamation of voice and place. An affirmation of Jewishly standing up against occupation and apartheid is itself a Jewish cultural practice—with no religion involved. JVP's Artists Council created powerful art and cultural objects that contributed to a sense of building a public powerful movement. As the years went on, members of JVP's Artists Council would go on to create moving, powerful art of all kinds that could transmit messages more powerfully than prose, from giant colorful menorahs that were used in "Jews Against Islamophobia" actions across the country to "Refugees are Welcome Here" posters that popped up in bodegas from city to city; from poetry and song to fiber arts, puppetry, and every medium imaginable. Each contributed to the public sense that there did exist a Jewish voice in support of Palestinian freedom.[12]

The day after the horrific shooting that killed eleven worshippers during Shabbat morning services at a Pittsburgh synagogue in 2018, JVP members gathered on Zoom to connect, grieve, and reflect together. We were trying organizationally to hold, on one hand, a full-throated condemnation of the antisemitism on display and, on the other, a rejection of the attempts by some supporters of Israel to change the definition of antisemitism to include criticism of Israel. We needed to carve out a space, to refuse all attempts to cynically muddy the waters between real antisemitism and those who are engaging in legitimate criticism of Israel's human rights abuses. For those wanting a safe space to mourn and grieve, these spaces are essential. We recited the mourners' *kaddish* together, broke into small groups to share more intimately how we were feeling, and heard words of solidarity and comfort from Christian and Muslim comrades.[13] In the wake of the Pittsburgh massacre, our longtime partners MPower Change quickly organized $50,000 for the victims of the shooting. Also, in Washington, DC, JVP–Metro, Justice for Muslims Collective, New Synagogue Project, March for Racial Justice, and Showing Up for Racial Justice (SURJ) collaborated on a vigil of resistance and resilience that drew thousands. It was a healing balm to find comfort in the solidarity offered by our allies and the reaffirmation of our vision that safety comes through solidarity.

Because JVP organizes as Jews, we relied primarily—but not solely—on Jewish traditions to deepen our experience of organizing for justice, and we integrate Jewish values of justice, stories, knowledge, and rituals into our organizing. We are deeply influenced by leftist movements, contemporary and historical. We learned from the Bund to embrace diaspora with a commitment to *doikeit* ("hereness" in Yiddish). We're inspired by their sophisticated mutual aid strike funds, daily newspaper circulations, and self-defense groups. We also find inspiration from following the rhythms of the Jewish holiday cycle, each holiday with its own moral focus and invitation to reflection, offering a scaffold for integrating contemporary political commitments through the symbols and rituals of our ancient practices. We embrace the multivocality of Jewish traditions, allowing the myriad strategies our ancestors figured out to influence and guide us.

JVP chapters often first encounter their future members and leaders at their annual holiday celebrations, particularly during Rosh Hashanah and Passover. Often these celebrations are open to all, embraced as a time to bring new people into the work and build community apart from the work. The JVP chapter in Seattle, one of the first chapters outside of the Bay Area, has held a Passover celebration annually since 2006. In the tradition of feminist, liberation seders dating back to the 1970s, these Passover gatherings take familiar rituals and stories and tie them to the current political crises of our time, a reminder that these ancient traditions still live and breathe as long as we do. The Seattle seder has an enduring tradition to invite local community partners who do racial justice organizing to speak at the seder, drawing connections to the themes of the holiday and the interlocking struggles for Palestinian rights and racial justice. During Rosh Hashanah, chapters gather for a Tashlich (casting away) ritual. Dating back to the medieval period, during Tashlich, bread is tossed into a moving body of water to symbolize release and regret of mistakes we've made in the past year. This tradition is ripe for reinterpretation, political education, and agitation.

For example, the JVP Tashlich ritual guide for 2011 offered participants this framing: "While it is false to claim that all Jews are guilty of the sins committed by the Israeli government, as Jews we acknowledge that these acts are being done in our name and we must take ownership of these sins." As each participant tossed bread into the water, a litany of wrongdoings was read. After each line of the litany, the group recited together, "We take responsibility and will work to make it stop." The 2011 litany included these transgressions, among others:

1. Attacking, starving, and strangling Gaza while claiming it is no longer occupied.

2. Allowing violence against Palestinians to be committed in our name.

3. Stealing Palestinian land and destroying Palestinian homes.

4. Not fighting for the rights of Israeli Palestinians who are treated as second-class citizens.

5. Allowing fear, instead of compassion, to dictate our actions.

6. Not speaking out against anti-Arab racism and Islamophobia.

7. Elevating antisemitism above other oppressions and refusing to see its interconnectedness with other oppressions.

8. Forgetting that being a Diasporic people means that we come from multiple cultural traditions.

9. Assuming all Jews are Ashkenazi and assuming every person of color is not a Jew.

No Hebrew words were recited in this ritual. There was no mention of God. The attendees need not have had any previous knowledge about Israel/Palestine or Jewish communities, but they would most certainly leave much more informed. This ritual could be done any day of the year, but doing it during the traditional time all Jews are doing this ritual allows those Jews that feel a need to integrate their political, spiritual, and cultural lives a chance to do that. It works well to take advantage of the holiday cycle or national days of remembrance and integrate the themes of your work into it when people are looking for ways to mark the day themselves (or just have the day off).

Too often, in non-JVP settings, Jewish rituals can ring hollow when we don't hold the complexity and acknowledge the pain of the gap between our values and the reality in Israel/ Palestine. For example, Passover is a holiday driven by the commemoration of Jewish struggles for freedom and liberation, even as today Palestinians in the occupied West Bank are put under curfew for the eight days of the holiday, and Palestinians in Gaza are put under ongoing yearslong siege. Rather than abandoning Jewish practice altogether in disgust or despair when we experience this disparity, we are able to draw inspiration from our revised texts and rituals to continue to work toward freedom and liberation. This work of reclamation and reinterpretation of inherited texts and practices breathes new life into our movements and our selves while honoring those who came before us.

Jewish practices around life cycles provide a similar scaffolding for rooted and visionary political action. It is common at JVP actions, during the horrifically frequent Israeli assaults on the Palestinians of Gaza, that the assembled will close their action by reciting the Jewish prayer of mourning. *Yitgadal v'yitkadash shimei rabah.* The words are in Aramaic, the syllables are familiar, rolling off many of our tongues or echoing in our ears, the mystery of the meaning of the words a comfort. The power of the recitation lies, then, in the mantric cadence and ubiquity of the words that, for many Jews, our ancestors have recited in grief. Because of this deep-seated familiarity with those words, our recitation of them in memory of Palestinian lives lost is profound. Not as a political stunt or theater, but as catharsis.

On the date of Trump's inauguration, we gathered again in grief. We had sent an invitation to our members to gather on Zoom (a tool we were using well before the pandemic!) at the time of his inauguration. Even more than two months after the election, most of us were still in shock that this was really happening. A couple hundred people gathered online at noon. There were music, poetry, readings, prayer, calls for action, and lots of tears. The feelings of relief in being together, shared fear and resolve, were palpable. Compared to the 2011 Tashlich ritual, the venue was different, the vibe was different, but in the end the purpose was the same: being together in community, whether in grief or resolve or celebration, drawing upon our Jewish traditions to make meaning, while not excluding our members who, for whatever reason, did not get meaning or comfort from Jewish ritual, but did get comfort from JVP ritual. When it comes to rooted and visionary political action, this felt like we were hitting our stride.

Home Building Is Movement Building

Building a political home is a crucial, and often unacknowledged and unplanned, aspect of creating a vibrant movement. When a movement is also a place where people live, learn, love, celebrate, and grieve together, it offers comfort to its members and sustainability through hard times. This is all the more true when, as in the case of JVP, people are being asked to leave behind institutions we grew up in, as well as beloved mentors, friends, teachers, and community because they no longer reflect or welcome our political values. A political home is where people choose to return again and again to organize, protest, and strategize with the cultural and spiritual guides that they've inherited or invented. Political homes are where movements dedicate the time to develop a shared culture that tends to the emotional and spiritual well-being of everyone inside; innovate inherited cultural traditions to deepen commitment to the larger goals and values of its members; and challenge dominant perceptions and demonstrate possible futures, tethered to practices of those who came before. Of course, there are risks to building political homes. You can reinforce or mirror harmful power dynamics you are actively working against. You can create a new out-group if the political home focuses more on litmus tests and exclusions than a strong culture of belonging. In building the unique culture of your political home, you can obfuscate the cherished diversity of the paths and stories and traumas and victories that led each member to the home you're building.

When an organization commits to building a political home, it is also affirming an embrace of the whole person because, ideally, home is where you let it all hang out, where you find comfort and peace, where you dream and imagine and find the nourishment to keep on going. Ideally, political homes are places of profound cultural mixing, the hybridity birthing new and retrieving more ancient or forgotten practices, across generations, identities, and struggles. Building a political home requires confidence and chutzpah. You need to know who you are, where you are from, and where you want to go. And those are the exact same ingredients needed to cook up impactful campaigns, recruit a wider base of support, and win concrete changes toward your organizing goals. The comfort that the two of us take in adapting and evolving our inherited traditions to match our contemporary values is one we have learned from the feminist and queer Jews who came before us: women who fought for the rabbinate, queers who fought for the chuppah. Their courage is an inspiration and reminder that we too can fight for—and realize—Judaism beyond Zionism.

Organizing Strategy Reflection Questions
Building a Political Home

1. What are you doing in your organizing to create a sense of belonging and home while pursuing strategic campaigns? How do your organizing structures/practices tether you together as a community?

2. Are your members able to express their whole selves in your organization/movement? How? In what ways? How are you creating opportunities for your members to bring rituals, texts, and practices of their spiritual or communal traditions in your political actions?

3. When creating your organizational/movement culture, how do you grapple with and ideally avoid re-creating harmful dynamics that may already exist in your larger community?

4. What role does identity, in all its facets, play in your formation, and how does it a) feed your sense of home and b) help determine power, access, culture, and ritual?

Chapter 2

Forging a Movement
Inside a Nonprofit

Like many aspects of JVP's work, the internal structures and organizing model had an aspect of "both/and." Both/and is a concept we used frequently in our organizing, analysis, and whenever we had to make hard decisions. It was meant to help us hold somewhat contradicting ideas at once, to be expansive rather than binary about our thinking, and work to reconcile seemingly disparate threads.

JVP has, almost since its founding, been both a movement organization and a nonprofit. As a movement-building organization, JVP focused on growing a massive base of members, donors, and supporters to build and deploy power as part of the broader Palestine solidarity movement within the legal confines of a nonprofit. As a nonprofit, issues of staffing, governance, fundraising, and the other core functions of a workplace ensured the movement-building work could thrive. JVP's structure, with a strong national staff and a network of members and chapters, is a somewhat common arrangement for social justice organizations (a few similar examples include SURJ, Working Families Party, and 350.org). JVP has always been a structural hybrid between a traditional nonprofit organization, with a board, staff, and the governance and decision-making hierarchies that entails, and a robust membership organization and chapter network that informed its political trajectory. Within this model, members were involved in setting national strategy and also autonomously developed campaigns, coalitions, and unique cultures locally, some of which were then adapted nationally.

At the core of JVP during our tenure was a network of chapters and constituency groups that took action together as well as separately. This at times included a rabbinical council, a health advisory council, a Jews of Color, Sephardi and Mizrahi (JOCSM) Caucus, an academic advisory council, a *Havurah* (DIY Jewish community) network, an artist's council, a student network, and as many as sixty-five chapters in communities and on college campuses nationwide. These member collectives were tethered to the national organization in practical ways—like through bank accounts and databases—and through a commitment to organizing in line with the guiding principles and political positioning of the national organization. This is why the processes to endorse BDS and become anti-Zionist, which we discuss later in this book, were so necessary.

The nonprofit-industrial complex comes in for rightful criticism on the left, and JVP was not immune from all the pitfalls it entails, which have been exhaustively described, most thoroughly in the seminal anthology *The Revolution Will Not Be Funded.*[1] The initial critique, as described by INCITE! Women of Color Against Violence, actually came out of their experience of losing funding from the Ford Foundation when they took a strong position on Palestine, demonstrating the long tradition of funders' trying to control the political positioning of organizations to whom they offer funding. JVP's funding model, discussed in depth in this chapter, ensured that we had guardrails to help avoid the pitfall of funders dictating political positions. Even within the nonprofit framework, we strove to maintain an emphasis on membership, leadership development, organizing, collective action, and fiscal independence. Navigating being staff-led and member-driven is tricky, and on occasion we did have to wrestle with the ways that the hybrid model could impede grassroots energy.

JVP's Structural and Cultural Roots

In JVP's earliest configuration (in the late 90s/early 2000s), when its membership was several dozen people in the San Francisco Bay Area, those members made decisions based on consensus, bringing people representing a fairly wide range of ideologies (that is, Zionist and anti-Zionist, one-state and two-state) together by identifying common political ground: being against the Israeli occupation. At the same time, there was a group of men who, in an informal and unacknowledged way, were leading JVP's positions and development. At some point, women in JVP, many of whom had histories in radical feminist movements, started circulating the essay "The Tyranny of Structurelessness" by Jo Freeman.[2] The essay, written in the early 1970s, reflects upon Freeman's experience in radical feminist spaces that were trying to establish organizations without hierarchies. Freeman outlines how, in the absence of transparent formal structures, organizations become sites of informal and unaccountable leadership. She suggests formalizing structures and placing them under democratic control. Early leaders of JVP remember this as an influential moment in the evolution of JVP's approach to leadership. While maintaining a process-intensive collaborative model of political decision-making, JVP moved—with resistance from some members—toward more formal leadership. At the same time, JVP actively made that decision that staff and fundraising were needed to effectively pursue its ambitious goals. This decision was political—it reflected the seriousness with which JVP took the responsibility to change the status quo, and recognized that serious resources would need to be organized to have any hope to accomplish that vision. Because of the legal constraints under which we function in the US, a nonprofit structure went along with that. Nonprofit status allows for direct fundraising and hiring staff, which were seen as crucial to JVP's ambition by the folks who made that decision before the two of us came on staff. That early decision, and our ongoing, if unconscious, affirmation of it on the organizational level, impacted everything from how we raised money to HR policies and how membership was engaged.

There are still echoes of the way these decisions were embedded into JVP's DNA, especially since so many of the early leaders of JVP are still active members today (Rebecca also became a member during the early years, around 2002). The striving for political agreement across some degree of ideological differences is reflected in our BDS and anti-Zionism processes fifteen or more years later! The constant balancing—between member input and discussion with staff leadership, along with the simultaneous sense of being a movement as well as an organization—has been in delicate balance ever since.

In doing research for this book, we noticed that the JVP culture our team inherited and largely replicated during our tenure was set very early. This included a highly collaborative and process-oriented work style, an eagerness to embrace technology, a strong sense of urgency and ambition, as well as the overwhelming queerness and white, Ashkenazi dominance of the membership. When we did manage to change these patterns successfully, such as when we became more multigenerational, it was through very concerted effort. It's not impossible to change founding characteristics that get baked in, but it is certainly harder and requires deliberate attention. At the very least, it is important to be aware of the traits that have perhaps inadvertently become part of your model without your even realizing it—some may be highly prized, some may have upsides and downsides, and some may need to be jettisoned completely, but the important thing is to pay attention. No organization's culture is static, of course, but cultural markers set early do tend to have more staying power than later generations of an organization may realize.

Because being a nonprofit is a legal framework and not an organizing model, it required us to go through some legal hoops that distracted from JVP's organic organizing energy. JVP aspired to a movement culture, where collectives build trust and relationships, feel ownership, set strategy, and take action together. As we on staff often reminded ourselves, members could always vote with their feet: if they didn't like what we were doing, they wouldn't stick around, giving them ultimate veto power over our work. Some members at times appreciated the structure the national organization offered, while others struggled against it (sometimes both at the same time!).

Organizing Lineages

JVP's approach to organizing has always been an amalgamation of different organizing traditions. Our approach had at its core traditional community organizing (including base-building, leadership development, and staff support), layered with a commitment to direct action focused on shifting public discourse as well as solidarity practices that tethered us to Palestinians in Palestine and throughout the Diaspora. JVP's approach was heterodox but leaned on a more structured organizational model than, for example, Momentum, which emerged around 2014 as an incubator for more decentralized movement building focused on civil disobedience and mass training.[3] We also engaged in more cultural and discourse-shifting work than a traditional Alinsky model, which dates back to the 1940s and focuses on one-to-ones and relationship building to build a base that pushes for concrete changes on issues identified by the base.[4] While we did have multiple committees or working groups active providing guidance and leadership to our campaigns and projects and regularly brought chapter leaders together for strategy sessions, we did not embody the participatory democracy model of the Occupy Movement, which used consensus-based decision-making and general assemblies to allow all participants to shape the demands, tactics, and evolution of the various Occupy encampments. JVP's members came out of and were part of all these organizing traditions, and the language and practices in JVP chapters borrowed from all of these approaches.

Alissa and Stefanie Fox, as co–organizing directors from 2011 to 2016, were the architects of our organizing philosophy and what it looked like in practice. Before Alissa joined staff, Stefanie had begun throwing the door open to base-building, moving the organization from one of hundreds of members to one of thousands. As part of this, she focused on strengthening the small set of chapters that had developed nationally as JVP began to spread its wings from being a solely Bay Area organization, growing quickly in the first couple of years from seven chapters to twenty-seven. When Alissa came on staff, they took on developing JVP's leadership development program, chapter infrastructure, launched a new nationwide campaign targeting retirement fund giant TIAA-CREF, and coordinated our National Member Meetings. With a steadily expanding staff team, Alissa and Stefanie developed all the crucial elements of the organizing program referred to here.

As organizers, we believed that to be successful in recruiting and retaining an active, vibrant base of member leaders we must allow them to bring their specific passions, experiences, and talents to the movement. We know that some people love to hold a placard and chant on a picket line, while others feel more comfortable in business attire at the office of a local member of

Congress. We know that academics had a specific vantage point and role to play, not just developing analysis and thinking to undergird our political work but also being a vital bulwark against our opposition that was seeking to turn college campuses into the main stage where the multimillion-dollar effort to restrain the movement for justice for Palestinians would be played out. We wanted our rabbis to be rabbis in the movement, and artists to be artists. And each of these organizing constituencies had a role to play in our work to topple the multiple pillars holding up US support for Israeli apartheid.

This organizing strategy was helpful as our base ballooned. It's a delightful problem to have in organizing—when you have more people ready to be organized than the organizing structure to plug them into! Identifying a multipronged strategy that likewise mirrored our theory of change fed two birds with one seed. We focused on creating organizing structures that encouraged everyone to play the role that fits who they are and that allowed each member to grow the organization through their strengths. JVP's organizing grew around the strengths, relationships, and access that members collectively brought to the movement for Palestinian rights. Our rabbis played an essential role supporting Presbyterian, Methodist, UCC, and other church partners as they organized for divestment in their denominations. Students and academics together fought off attempts to enshrine activism for Palestinian rights as antisemitism on college campuses. Street activist members brought their skills to the doors of weapon manufacturers profiting off the immense loss of life in Gaza in 2014.

The flip side of this bountiful menu was the danger of losing focus and trying to do too much. We were terrific at experimenting with new campaigns and strategies but less good at sunsetting them when they no longer had much utility, so they would linger as underresourced ghost programs. Overall, it also contributed to a sense of being overwhelmed with work, not allowing the time to

really pay attention to the perennial questions that need maintenance, such as our accountability to Palestinians or our staff culture.
That longer-term work would rarely get the time or attention it was
due, as we were drawn to keeping the programmatic balls in the air.

Membership

JVP, from its earliest days as a Bay Area organization, had a
dues-paying membership structure. It was an integral part of our
identity and self-conception as a movement. Membership at JVP
meant paying your annual dues, electing the board of directors,
being brought into organization-wide processes (such as the BDS
and Zionism processes we detailed in the previous chapter), and
the opportunity to take part in leadership development programs
and semiannual National Member Meetings. The question of
membership was not without its political complications, largely
because of questions of identity: What did it mean to be a member if you weren't Jewish? That was an especially fraught question since we didn't want to re-create the very same patterns of
privilege that we were fighting. Israel, you could say, is the ultimate example of membership based on identity. So, we relied on
people self-identifying as members and didn't spend time gate-
keeping peoples' Jewishness. That felt like an accurate reflection
of Jewish communities in the US, which vary widely in terms
of what Jewishness looks like and integrate the reality of most
non-Orthodox Jewish families in the US, which often include
non-Jewish members. We imagine that other organizations might
have similarly fraught political issues related to identity that can
only be answered by your context, values, and strategy.

A devastating reality of JVP's growth and trajectory is that
it can be mapped onto moments of Israeli aggression. Just as in
other high-stakes moments, such as when *Roe v. Wade* was overturned or George Floyd was murdered, it can be overwhelming for

organizations to adapt to the cascade of attention, money, and new members or volunteers that those moments can bring. After Israeli assaults on Gaza, new cohorts of members would join our movement—whether from organizations slightly to our right or those who were suddenly galvanized to take action. This is certainly not the worst problem an organizer can have! But the truth is that it took several years to fully absorb the new members who flocked to us during moments of crisis. We needed both to keep people engaged in noncrisis moments and to spend the time, money, and energy to invest in the infrastructure needed to be ready to absorb people when they are ready. JVP's first burst of growth, during the 2008–2009 Gaza assault, was largely possible because JVP's leadership at the time had invested in online organizing tools before that moment came. If they hadn't been infrastructurally ready for that moment, we would have lost the momentum as well as thousands of people who were ready to be organized, if they had no place to go. That decision to invest in infrastructure became a template and a reminder to us to think of the more plodding years, when most of the world didn't see the ongoing crisis, as a key building period for the times when it would.

A central challenge of JVP's rapid growth in the wake of intensified Israeli aggression was that we had to integrate new members when they came in full of energy and keep them engaged after those moments of crisis ebbed.[5] A big part of retaining these new members, of course, was the sense of political home and community that we discussed in the first chapter. But it also consisted of concrete operational tasks, such as supporting local chapters to create membership committees tasked with conducting one-to-one welcome meetings with new members and offering regular new-member orientations as well as roles for new members in long-term campaigns. It may seem obvious, but it is important to carve out roles for new members to play in the local work as well as the national work, whether leading a section of an upcoming meeting or making art for an upcoming action. Creating clear ways for new people to plug in was the most essential thing to ensuring that new members became longtime members. We held in-person, cross-regional gatherings focused on political education to help new members move past their initial rage and betrayal into a deeper understanding of our political analysis and JVP's place in the movement ecosystem. These bursts of rapid growth followed by long tails of integration and education challenged all of us at JVP to be willing to adjust our structure as conditions changed. Picture us as a tennis player, crouched, bouncing, expectant— ready to pivot as needed to meet the ball.

When it came to growing our membership, we had a pretty lax approach and relationship to accountability for our organizers. Where unions, electoral, and mass base-building organizations are extremely demanding of the number of members their organizers get to sign on and take action, we were much looser with what we demanded from organizers, as far as implementing targets for membership recruitment and retention went. Our occasional attempts to be more strict or formulaic with organizers never really took root. This could be attributed to our hybrid organizing model that sought to go deep and broad; it might be because members flocked to us in moments of crisis, because organizing Jews against the grain of support for Zionism requires patience and finesse, or perhaps because it was against our nature as feminist leftists to be as ball-busting as some organizing shops are.

As an essential building block in JVP's budget, membership dues lent weight not only to our political independence but also to our theory of change and our ability to speak as representatives of our tens of thousands of members—even if, cumulatively, they contributed a relatively small portion of the budget overall. Membership dues play an important role in cultivating a sense of commitment to the organization. As we know from the labor movement and some community organization models, dues, no matter the amount, create a sense of identification and ownership in organizations. Perhaps even more important, as an organization that was seeking to shift the reality and perception of Jewish American support for Israel, declaring membership in JVP made explicit a critique of Jewish American communal positions, and membership numbers overall were a way to contest legacy Jewish organizations' claims of Jewish hegemony. Yet, JVP never aspired to be structured as a pure membership organization, choosing the ability to make decisions rapidly over the more deliberative and time-consuming process of direct democracy, especially with members spread all over the country. The structure JVP chose offered greater flexibility, the ability to pivot as needed to be responsive to our partners, and day-to-day functionality, but at the cost of transparency of decision-making for members. There was always a segment of JVP's membership who did not endorse this lack of direct democracy. Of course, what we ended up with is not the only valid way to structure an organization, but it is the one we chose, for reasons internal to our organizational history, the context of when we emerged and the models that were available to us, and our ongoing belief—at least at the leadership level during our tenure—that this model fit best within our theory of change of growth and power building. Many movement organizations have eschewed formal membership, especially in recent years. But we found that the sense of ownership it offered members, and the political power and independence that membership numbers offered JVP, made membership an essential part of our structure and culture throughout our history.

Staff-Led, Member-Driven

For us, being staff-led meant that staff held responsibility for the day-to-day operations of the organization; designed political education opportunities; facilitated organization-wide decision-making processes; coordinated long-term and rapid response campaigns; maintained relationships with journalists, donors, and movement partners; and ensured we had the resources to continue organizing for the long haul. Being member-driven meant that members were the lifeblood of the organization, by executing national strategy on a local level throughout the country and influencing national strategy through the relationships, campaigns, educational workshops, community events, and actions they organized. Members were crucial to fundraising efforts and communications work by authoring op-eds in their local papers, drafting letters to the editor, and bringing our messages into progressive movement coalitions in their towns. Members created the drumbeat of movement energy indicating that JVP was effective and engaged everywhere, because it was. Members pushed the national organization to live up to our own commitments, including member agitation and leadership that led to BDS and Zionism policy changes. Members also filled more formal roles by joining national committees or serving on our national board.

Serving on the board is a key way members help drive the organization. The board, as a whole, fulfilled the legal fiduciary duties as required by nonprofit law and also provided leadership on key strategic questions and expertise in specific issue areas. The board brought in the perspective of various constituencies within JVP, including chapter leaders, rabbis, and students, though this was not a prescribed part of their board duties. One animating dynamic of JVP's board members, which holds true at many mission-driven nonprofits, is that the core reason people stepped up to be on our board is because they are intensely passionate about ending Israeli apartheid, each in their own ways and for their own reasons. Board members were eager to have big political strategy discussions on our campaigns and messaging as well as to play roles moving forward the programmatic work fueled by their perspective as members before stepping into board leadership. Like many other boards, JVP's skewed older than the membership as a whole. In later years, the multigenerational-ness of the board allowed it to be a microcosm of the generational differences that played out on the membership level. As staff members working closely with the board on issues that would later come to be organization-wide conversations, we found it a really helpful space for talking through the various assumptions and experiences at play, and for practicing how to balance advocating for where we wanted things to go with listening and engaging substantively to help us get there. In our experience, board members and the board as a whole were crucial resources for the overall functioning of the organization and a way we embodied being member-driven and staff-led.

Individual members and the membership as a whole had a somewhat ambivalent relationship to staff-led organizing and program development. Members and chapters developed their own practices, rituals, expertise, and campaigns, some of which were eventually "nationalized" by virtue of their popularity and effectiveness, a reflection of the vibrancy and sense of autonomy that members felt. Especially as we grew, members and chapters often wanted more from the staff—more help with specific needs, more campaign support, or even their own staff person to bolster their local organizing. They might chafe at their perception of being treated as cogs in a machine that the national organization created, such as with National Days of Action, but they also asked for more guidance and tools to enable them to pull off successful local actions.

Because we were explicitly a staff-led organization, the staff did get out ahead of members and chapters at times. Time is never on your side, with rapid response in particular. What might take staff a few hours to throw together would take much longer if it was first necessary to integrate local members—who are otherwise occupied during the day—into a rapidly flowing stream. In our frenzied media culture, a moment of hesitation can make the difference between being part of the media moment or missing it completely. This is where being staff-led can aid and accelerate your growth and power building.

Honest Hierarchy

As JVP grew, the leadership bodies we created affirmed over and over again, both consciously and unconsciously, an embrace of hierarchy. Of course, we are writing about hierarchy from the perspective of having had power within it, so we can only speak to how we felt the organization functioned overall, not how it felt for those that had less power in the hierarchy. Even in the relatively short time since we were in leadership, the political context has shifted in workplaces, where hierarchical structures have become increasingly fraught, especially for those in movement-nonprofit hybrids. In the early years of our tenure, everything was quite informal, as JVP was small enough for everyone to do a little bit of everything. But, as we grew, it became evident that we needed a clearer leadership structure. Rebecca, who supervised most of the staff at that time, noticed that she had become the hub of a wheel: if each staff member was a spoke, it meant that she held information that could be much more efficiently shared within a structure that enabled people to share information directly with each other. An early version of the staff team structure was born, with autonomous, project-based teams that could be led by the person accountable to the work of that project, rather than defaulting to the person highest in the hierarchy.

In 2014, when the staff grew to ten people, Rebecca got some excellent advice from board member James Schamus: to be attentive to the structures that we built as the staff entered the ten-to-fifteen-person range. With under ten people, almost any structure will do. But at ten to fifteen, patterns are put into place that get baked in as you continue to grow. This is the size at which care and forethought are needed to ensure that, as you grow, information sharing and collaboration are relatively easy. As JVP grew, Rebecca found that she wanted to formalize the informal team she relied upon for strong leadership and strategic direction. This was another example of preferring to name power structures that already existed rather than allowing them to remain invisible, but it was also an example of the lack of forethought given to the impact of hiring and promotions before we implemented our racial justice transformation (RJT) process. The leadership team (LT) was initially five: Rebecca, Alissa, Cecilie Surasky, Stefanie Fox, and Ari Wohlfeiler, all of us white and Ashkenazi. At the beginning of 2016, Cecilie left JVP after thirteen years on staff, so it was the four of us. Our posture as leaders regarding hierarchy flowed from the assumption from JVP's early years that power exists within all organizations or formations of any kind. Pretending otherwise would obscure the power dynamics that exist in ostensibly horizontal groups. As Maurice Mitchell of the Working Families Party articulated it in 2022, "Pretending formal leadership doesn't exist can obscure hierarchies and create centers of informal power. Formal leadership, when healthy, provides clarity and transparency, which leads to greater accountability. This in turn fosters more avenues for support to develop new leadership."[6]

Inherent in hierarchy are questions of power. In movement organizations that prioritize being attuned to questions of power in the world, it is both especially difficult and critical to be attentive to how power operates internally. As the staff grew from less than a dozen to almost three dozen between 2014 and 2016, the LT led a process of creating a more explicit and complex organizational hierarchy. In addition to the board of directors and the LT, the hierarchy included a layer of supervisory and management staff and another layer of organizers and coordinators. This structure was an attempt to be transparent about where decision-making power was centered. Within this hierarchy there was permeability and a commitment to participation of all the layers in decision-making and implementation of the work in ad hoc teams—ranging from hiring, fundraising, strategy setting, and beyond. That permeability allowed staff at various levels to weigh in beyond their silos but also created confusion at times about where decision-making really was located. We found that a strong yet flexible structure was liberating and actually facilitated more creativity and experimentation. When it worked best, this flexibility was essential to allowing the hierarchy to work for us, not against us. Even as we sought to create participatory spaces for feedback and deliberation, ultimately it was up to a few of us to make the final call. As leaders, we exercised our power by determining how time and resources were utilized and by getting to choose the format for the decision-making process. No matter what micro- or medium-sized decisions we had allocated to teams, there was no denying the buck stopped with the LT.

In the years we were in leadership, we never seriously considered becoming a truly horizontal organization. Despite, at times, variations on horizontal formations being favored in left organizations, it always felt incompatible (to us) with moving the work forward at the scale and speed we aspired to. We were not aware of any models of national nonprofit organizations with an organizing program that combined base-building, political education, leadership development, and both rapid and long-term campaigns that were truly nonhierarchical. For better or worse, we never considered pioneering such a model, given the needs of a fast-paced organizing program and the reality that we were both a 501(c)(3) and a movement organization, not to mention the already grueling nature of our work.

Leadership Team

The two of us, in writing this book, are conscious of the ways that the individual contributions of each member of the LT are hard to convey in writing about our collective decisions and practices. As a body that worked out decisions among ourselves before sharing them more widely, our public unity could hide the individual skills, strengths, and weaknesses we were each bringing to the mix—and the ways in which we had areas of specialization. We also each contributed well beyond those areas, as we learned from each other and stretched past our comfort zone as we developed as a team. As an LT, we all became generalists in the sense that we held holistic responsibility for the direction and functioning of JVP across communications, operations, fundraising, and organizing. But, of course, we each brought our own special concerns, strengths, and natural areas of focus to the table. In the interest of illustrating the point, we'll be a bit reductive here in terms of specifics: Alissa, as a rabbi, was attuned to Jewish communal relationships and dynamics; Stefanie, as an organizer, brought a focus on systems, structures, and supervision; Ari, who had been development director, thought about growth and impact; and Rebecca (who, as longtime ED, had always been a generalist), brought a particular eye toward our external relationships and the perception of JVP in the world.

As the two of us see it, we complemented one another with our unique perspectives, emphases, and skills and combined them to beautiful effect through our shared belief in building power through organizing. We worked our way through ideas together until we came up with something that worked. We worked at an exhausting pace and yet thrived on it (at least in the short term). We were ambitious and confident in our skills, and we thought holistically about the ways the different constituencies and programs fit together. We were fiercely committed to seeing this work as movement work, and we were getting our social, political, and emotional needs met with each other. We had epic team retreats where we got enormous amounts of work done and set strategies that we were all prepared to implement in our own areas of work. And, not surprisingly, we increasingly became extraordinarily close friends with large reservoirs of trust in each other and in our collective group wisdom. Our bonds extended outside of the organization—Rebecca was a doula for Alissa during the birth of her second child, and Alissa officiated at Stefanie's wedding. These life cycle intimacies only deepened our sense of accountability and commitment to each other.

The two of us credit the LT for much of JVP's success during our years on staff. But it also had several downsides. All of our synchronicities were also shared blind spots. We were seen by the rest of the staff as somewhat of a locked black box. Staff knowing we were such dear friends reinforced the feeling of inaccessibility. And the fact of our whiteness as a team compromised staff trust that we wouldn't miss important considerations. The LT worked by consensus. Looking back on it, we can see, given our close relationships, how we often prioritized getting to that consensus without undue conflict. That was especially true during the times, especially in the later years of the team, when we faced hard challenges internally and externally, making the mutually supportive space of the LT even more important to us. Each of us can remember times when, in retrospect, we may have compromised beyond where we felt comfortable for the sake of that perceived unity. This would then lead us to contain or close off discussing issues with the rest of staff when we were not confident or clear ourselves.

Democratic-ish Decision-Making

JVP's big-picture decision-making functioned best when there were comprehensive research, reflection, and feedback-gathering processes that included the varied constituencies within JVP, which were then relayed to the board for a final decision. Some of JVP's most successful projects began as chapter initiatives, but in practice the staff set the overall political agenda. Chapters varied widely in their focus, functioning, structures, and level of connection to national, though all chapters had some degree of staff support. Individual JVP members were integral to the teams charged with stewarding big political shifts for the organization, strategic planning, which campaigns to pursue, and so on. Of course, in an entity the size of JVP, decisions are made every day. They're made by staff teams that own projects, by staff/member committees that govern campaigns or congressional work, or by members in chapters as they decide how much to engage in national work and what their own priorities are.

In 2015, as part of a refreshed strategic plan, board and senior leadership developed both public guiding principles and internal filters to help us make decisions about which programs, projects, and campaigns to pursue. The strategic answers to all these questions could shift, but the basic understanding of the underlying need for a mass grassroots movement was so deeply entrenched that we consciously chose not to revisit this core understanding as part of the process, rather to focus on updating the tactics that flow from it. The strategic planning team developed categories of "must have," "it's best if it does," and a set of guiding questions to ask ourselves as we sought to operationalize how we chose our priorities. It was a somewhat clunky system at first, but with practice all of us on staff internalized scanning our proposals on the basis of that framework. It didn't eliminate our penchant to try everything but helped to contain it so we could harness our creativity and experimental energy within some limits.[7]

Of course, phrases like "strategic planning" and "organizational development strategies" and even "theory of change" are examples of pretty standard nonprofit lingo. It is notable that each was driven by staff and board, specifically those of us in leadership. This is yet another example of the sometimes uneasy balance of movement work in a nonprofit structure. JVP was not immune to the problems that many organizations have faced around the ways in which organizational culture can be too hierarchical and opaque. We recall hearing concerns that there was a lack of transparency around decision-making processes on a national level, which would lead to frustrations and mistrust between members and staff. That was especially true with decisions that impacted chapters and members directly, such as organizing priorities and the resultant staffing decisions, campaign selection, and other budgetary questions. Often the issue members had was not that it was illegitimate for staff to make these decisions, but that they would often hear about a decision after the fact, without even knowing that a change or reevaluation was in the works. We learned that taking the time to give members a heads-up about what is under discussion, the options on the table, and an invitation to give input can often be enough to reassure. We were careful and deliberate with the processes around our big political decisions, but for smaller ones we often took shortcuts—and members noticed. To further complicate things, internal decision-making was always being balanced by the needs and requests of JVP's coalition partners and allies, at both the national and local levels. Inevitably, at times, the local and national priorities and alliances did not match. At those times, staff would talk through the incongruencies with chapter leaders to figure out the best way forward. The length and depth of the relationship between staff and members would make or break the ability for us to stay together in those times of nonalignment. In chapter 6 we will further discuss this dynamic, where national policies stymied local alliances and actions but were essential to successfully completing our BDS process and changing our BDS policy.

Urgency

There's no way around it: organizing is not a forty-hour-a-week day job. Movement building requires unpredictable and often long, irregular hours. The nonprofit model exacerbates the contradictions, with salaried staff organizers available all day, but for member leaders, only after their day jobs or school days are done. Rapid response requires dropping everything to push hard at key moments and is crucial to base-building and narrative shifting, but it reinforced the primacy of staff leadership in uncomfortable ways. We are certain these tensions will be familiar to every organizer reading this!

Discourse in movement organizations around white supremacist cultural norms often associates a sense of urgency with the exacerbation of power imbalances and exploitation of workers.[8] The two of us, upon reflecting on this tension, don't see the perceived problem of urgency as simply a manifestation of our whiteness. We saw the need for urgency as being, on some level, objective—life under apartheid for Palestinians was unacceptable, as was our level of complicity, as US taxpayers, in enabling this system of injustice. As every gruesome image, story, or new Israeli policy emerged, our sense of urgency grew. Palestinian liberation cannot wait. As organizers and organizational leaders, we think urgency matters for base-building, is essential for media work, and is inspirational and motivating if implemented in a way that allows for opportunities for rest and rejuvenation. Urgency is also a critical ingredient for organizing—to get people's attention, you need a deadline and a sense that what you are fighting for cannot wait.

Because our organizing model was working toward a tipping point of American Jewish solidarity with Palestinians, we were constantly striving for massive growth: of members, of resources, and of internal and external attention to sustain the organization and to realize Palestinian freedom. Combined with the devastating conditions on the ground, which intensified during our tenure, all of it led to a perpetual sense of urgency for us as leaders. The idea of urgency within a culture of basically working around the clock was a constant source of tension as we professionalized. The trappings of the nonprofit structure often conflict with the rightful demands of workers for fair working conditions, and concerns arose among staff that the pace we set did not allow for enough time for the deep reflection we needed to evaluate and shift our organizing priorities to address the overall whiteness of our membership, for example.

The question of urgency came to the fore during the RJT process we discuss in chapter 7. Likewise, one of the core critiques of the JOCSM Caucus was that we move too fast and need to slow down to be able to address core questions. The consultants we brought in to lead the process shared the analysis that urgency was a manifestation of white supremacist cultural norms. Some staff saw our sense of urgency as a misguided political analysis, in which we were positioning ourselves as white saviors. Some saw it as a flawed understanding of solidarity. Some saw it as egotistical and self-aggrandizing. Some shared our embrace of urgency. Over the years, we have mulled over our approach and believe that our sense of urgency was a genuine and appropriate reflection of our commitment to Palestinian liberation and the dehumanizing and untenable reality of Palestinian life under apartheid. We also understand that urgency can obscure a focus on underlying issues such as staff culture, sustainability, or our approach to accountability to Palestinians. Our intensive years-long processes to endorse BDS or become anti-Zionist were evidence that we did have within us reservoirs of patience we could call on as needed. In our time, we never figured out a magic bullet for how to operationalize that slowdown on a day-to-day basis, even as we did manage to do it for those big processes.

We don't regret allowing urgency to motivate us, although we regret our shortcomings in determining how to facilitate a sustainable pace of work. And we credit our quickness with our success at growing the organization as swiftly and successfully as we did. Prioritizing rapid action—dropping everything to draft an op-ed before the media cycle turns or to jump on an opportunity to "bird-dog" (that is, to follow around a candidate or other target to publicly challenge their positions) a campaign target when we learn they are speaking just a few miles away—allows for the small decisions and actions that add up quickly toward becoming a recognized and respected action-oriented organization. Our take wasn't "urgency or bust." We learned time and again that if we wanted to keep members with us, keep our base satisfied and healthy, we need to slow down enough not to lose them. But we also saw it as our responsibility as staff leaders to ensure we were doing all we could to strengthen the organization's reputational and financial standing. This wasn't an ideological commitment to one method or the other. As long as we could be impactful and hold together internally, we could move with deliberation or urgency. But we never did solve the conundrum of how to balance the two to everyone's satisfaction.

Leadership Development

Whether we are moving fast in order not to lose the media cycle or planning a campaign, none of it works without leaders. And lots of them. Movement building requires many layers of strong member leaders on the national and local levels. Leaders are not plucked out of a crowd; they are developed over time by organizers. As Ella Baker, the American civil rights organizing giant, said: "I have always thought that what is needed is the development of people who are interested not in being leaders as much as in developing leadership in others."[9] This is why central to any credible organizing project is a robust leadership development program. As part of JVP's overall organizing approach, we understood leadership development as the constant work of cultivating new leaders while simultaneously deepening the leadership of longer-term members. Ideally, leadership development animates everything from organizing to operations to fundraising. Leadership development includes honing members' practical skills, their political analysis, and their personal practice. While some aspects of leadership development focus on individuals, leadership development is very much about interdependence and team building. Organizing work is collective, not individual, work.

Beginning in 2011, JVP dedicated significant organizational resources to bringing together member leaders for weekend-long intensive leadership development institutes (LDIs). These heavily subsidized retreats, often over Shabbat, were spaces for ritual and community building as well as intensive workshops on topics ranging from community-campus collaboration, growing and sustaining your chapter, and strategic messaging and communications, to anti-oppression and political analysis development (for example, the Facing the Nakba curriculum).[10] Our initial approach to LDIs was to rotate around the country according to our regional divisions (Northeast, South, Midwest, West), and LDIs took place a few times a year. They were coordinated by the organizing staff alongside a steering committee made up of member leaders from the region. The sessions were facilitated by staff and members: often, staff brought the broader organizing brass-tacks skills trainings, and members brought the case studies and political analysis sessions. The sessions were extremely participatory and interactive, employing the tools from popular education theories such as Paulo Freire's *Pedagogy of the Oppressed*, which was a foundational political education tool for many of our staff and leaders. Our NMMs were in some ways mega-LDIs. Central to the schedules were leadership development sessions, as these were a key way to get hundreds of leaders trained up and conversant in the same organizing language and practices.

Chapter Development

To link the national staff to the chapters on the ground, we relied on a system in which new members or existing leaders knew whom to go to for the support they needed, whether drafting a press release or navigating internal conflict. We found that the relationships between member leaders and staff organizers could make or break the strength of chapters in key moments, especially for newer or more emergent chapters. Our larger and stronger chapters functioned like mini organizations of their own, with their own internal structures and roles. Staff organizers were not responsible for the day-to-day functioning of chapters; instead, they focused on the bigger picture of maintaining a functioning chapter and plugging chapters into the resources, campaigns, or opportunities from the national headquarters. Staff were available to member leaders to field questions and concerns or to provide support on strategy setting, media approach, and other core elements of successful organizing. During our time, organizers were assigned in various local and regional formations. Ideally, the lion's share of a staff person's time would be spent doing leadership development with member leaders rather than being pulled into national projects, though that was at times a struggle.

Chapters, like the people who comprise them, are always at different stages of development and strength. Some are scrappy and run by just a few dedicated leaders; others hum with multiple active working groups and have a full-time dedicated staff person; and every stage in between. There are multiple reasons why a chapter would be in any one of those stages: capacity of the member leaders; the makeup of the local community; relationships and chemistry between the members; strong local alliances that meant ongoing requests for participation; and, of course, a strong campaign or programmatic focus. Just as a leadership development model is attentive to creating and integrating opportunities for growth, that same attention should be brought to the development of chapters. Strategies for chapter development can mirror those for individual leadership development. Just as we gathered leaders for a weekend retreat as a key part of JVP's organizing strategy, we gathered chapters to do the same. Just as we created opportunities for mentorship for individuals, we did the same for the chapter collective. In-person gatherings, beyond the intensive skills building on offer, were an expression of our investment in members and chapters, and an opportunity for them to develop their own sense of the leadership roles they played in making JVP successful. These were immersive experiences during which, even if just for forty-eight hours, we would be a village unto ourselves, moving from mealtimes to intense political discussions, to role-playing strategies for new member engagement, to singing around a bonfire into the wee hours. Everyone who attended got to relish, even for a moment, living in a JVP world.

JVP's organizers found that different outcomes were possible, depending on not just the skills and passions of the members in the chapters but also on their context. For example, a chapter in a midsize city with a progressive majority, like Durham, New Orleans, or Portland, was able to move legislation on the city council level far more successfully than a chapter in a larger city like Philadelphia or New York. In contrast, a city like New York, with a richness of like-minded Jews, is a perfect venue to pressure high-profile targets like the ADL. On college campuses, our chapters were well positioned to do deep community building, of course, but also to be in coalition with allied movement organizations and to campaign together for divestment in a multivocal and unified strategy.

Early on in the development of our organizing infrastructure, Alissa and Stefanie toyed with various internal websites that were to serve almost as a JVP social media platform, but none really worked. We found that to get people's consistent engagement, we needed to be in their inbox or existing social media accounts, not trying to get them to log in to a site only to do JVP-related work. The most effective was just a good old-fashioned email list where chapters could share their work, ask for advice from other chapters, and brag about an event that went really well. In-person gatherings were chances to deepen relationships and put faces to names.

Amplifying National and Local Power

In 2018, the North Carolina Triangle chapter built a kick-ass local coalition that won the first major victory of the Deadly Exchange campaign, which seeks to end police exchange programs between the US and Israel. As national leaders, we were eager to trumpet the win nationally, but the chapter was juggling delicate alliances, issues of credit, and political positioning with the elected officials who had just voted to end US-Israeli police exchanges in Durham. In our eagerness to claim the victory, we stepped on their toes and put their relationships in danger. Even, or maybe especially when, we win, we still need to make sure we are being respectful of local priorities and not harming local relationships. Moments like those always brought into focus the tensions around national staff seeing chapters as an extension of the national organization, whereas chapters saw themselves as autonomous in their own right. Both are true. Clear channels of communications for the frustrations, explicit working norms and agreements, and holding to those boundaries as much as possible are keys to allowing the both/and of the national-chapter dynamic to not go sour.

As is the case with all organizations that have both national and local formations, as national staff we had to figure out how to hold political lines that cohesively reflect the organization's strategy, theory of change, and values. National staff are ultimately the guardians of the overall strategy and principles, but local chapters must be empowered to build strong relationships with their local groups. Attending to how the collective groups work together and communicate, and how prepared they are for mobilization at any given moment, are all essential to maximizing local power. In high-attention moments in particular—during an escalation of violence, or in the wake of huge campaign wins that need to be amplified through protests, die-ins, or civil disobedience at the doors of decision-makers and aggressors—being able to mobilize chapters quickly and efficiently is key to turning those moments into real forces for change. In such moments, the national staff often kept going full steam ahead, particularly when it came to digital or online organizing. We would launch entire campaigns that existed entirely in email and social media, with no connection to on-the-ground organizing. The participation of members in these campaigns was the same as that of the general public: signing a petition and circulating it on social media. On occasion, there would be attempts to bridge the online and offline worlds with an in-person action. These opportunities were always fraught because, though a chapter might be in the city of the headquarters of the campaign's target, the chapter was not part of designing the campaign. A national staff person or team would strategize how to turn up the heat on a target, so we'd ask a chapter to play a role—for example, by dropping a banner in front of the target's offices or bird-dogging during a public appearance of a key decision-maker. Chapters would usually agree to take part, sometimes expressing frustration with our expecting them to mobilize, often on short notice, for a national campaign unrelated to the ongoing organizing the chapter was engaged in. Chapters are doing all they can to make the most of the precious hours each of their core members has, outside of work and other commitments, to give to JVP chapter organizing, so using that time for a national campaign rather than moving forward the work of the chapter was a big demand. More broadly, it ran the risk of creating a feeling of being instrumentalized by the national staff, without the respect of being integrated into the campaign-building process. In sum: organizing is all about relationships, and those must be tended and protected at all costs for the long-term health and success of the organization.

One of the most tried-and-true tools to amplify national strategies, especially in moments of rapid response to violence on the ground or in the news cycle, is a toolkit that is a one-stop shop for chapters of any size. These toolkits included talking points, tips for taking good photos, ideas for rituals, or text for placards, making it easy to mobilize without being cookie-cutter in nature. Creating national actions that are coordinated and unified but not "astroturf" requires striking a very delicate balance. Success relies on a strong sense of political unity and trust that is only built through relationships over time. Our relatively highly structured organizational model offered the time necessary to build those authentic relationships and that trust. These toolkits also allowed small chapters to take part in national mobilizations in whatever ways they could, and larger chapters were often the ones designing the rituals and art that we shared out in these toolkits.

Communications with Visionary Hope

JVP's communication style and reach were an integral part of JVP's movement-building strategy and success in the Jewish world, in Palestinian solidarity spaces, and beyond. As the first architect of JVP's communications, Cecilie Surasky built out JVP's "voice" as one of visionary hope that articulated with heart and clarity our values and from that place inspired people to take action. We wanted people to know that the vision of the world we want was possible and that the path there needed to be traveled together. The strategy used emotions, stories, and strove to invite people in rather than castigating them for not knowing enough. This possibilities-oriented approach contrasted, on the one hand, with vanguardist, ideological messaging that focused on having the "correct" politics delivered in crude terms, and, on the other, with a more policy-wonky, detail-heavy orientation that is the province of more traditional advocacy groups. For example, while it was an ideological decision not to take a position on one state or two, it also freed us to focus on values rather than on specific policy formulations, matching our movement-building ethos. This values-led communications approach was mirrored in the BDS movement's tagline, "Freedom, Justice, Equality," the prerequisites to any sustainable and desirable endgame scenario. As supporters of BDS, this allowed us to continue to focus on principles rather than policies.

Part of JVP's strategy to ensure our communications landed as we intended them, full of hope and possibility, was to make them colloquial, speaking to our members as if we were chatting with them face-to-face. When we wrote emails, we got in the practice of addressing first drafts to specific people, helping us remember that real people were reading them on the other side, and that this was their movement and their work. It sounds hokey, because it is, but it worked.

Both traditional and social media work was critical to making JVP part of the public conversation in the Jewish world, Palestinian solidarity space, and beyond. We built out a reach on social media of easily a million people in total, enabling us to drive conversations and traffic. We intentionally built relationships with reporters and editors, becoming reliable sources, whether on background or on the record, reposting articles we appreciated, and offering specific, constructive feedback when we felt like the analysis missed the mark. We invested in a media database, allowing us to instantly send press releases and advisories to the right reporters. We found that sometimes just sending a few quotes from staff and member leaders they could grab for a story would do the trick to get our take included. We hired graphic designers to ensure our social media feeds, action visuals, and press materials were compelling. Our efforts were by and large successful—we regularly placed op-eds in Jewish and

Israeli outlets like the *Forward*, *Haaretz*, *JTA*, and others, while also placing op-eds in the *LA Times*, *Washington Post*, *Guardian*, and leading city and state papers around the country (though we were never successful with the *New York Times*). We were covered on NPR and appeared occasionally on MSNBC and regularly on *Democracy Now!* [11]

When JVP communications and organizing were working in sync, they reinforced and strengthened one another. We were able to funnel interest on social media into email engagement and eventually real-life chapter membership and individual action. Our campaigns relied on our ability to communicate moral urgency and thus mobilize thousands, which increased our real and perceived power. Making a big splash with an ad or a billboard or a well-executed action generated public conversation, inspiring more people to join. This was never truer than at moments of crisis, when we were able to channel grief, rage, and fear into action and thousands of new members. There were also times when JVP's communications and organizing felt like separate tracks. We had some successful online campaigns that barely engaged our membership, and sometimes we struggled internally to match our organizing priorities with what was compelling to a mass audience. But those times when our membership, our supporters, and the wide world of onlookers were on the same wavelength were heady moments when we could feel and experience the public narrative shifting before our eyes.

Grassroots Fundraising for Political Independence

Our successful organizing and communications strategies were the basis of our grassroots fundraising model, which, during our tenure at JVP, enabled the budget to expand from $400,000 to about $4 million. This growth was fueled by the waves of people stepping into solidarity with Palestinians as the brutality of

Israel's treatments of Palestinians, supported by a blank check from the US government, became too hard to ignore. The story of how JVP managed to harness the snowballing outrage of American Jews and others into this movement must be told in the context of both JVP's level of skill and organization *and* the political conditions that led many to support the Jewish organization doing this work.

In JVP's early days, the very idea of getting funding from foundations was laughable; our politics were seen as that controversial. As it turned out, that was the best gift we ever could have gotten, because by necessity JVP had to develop a different strategy for funding.[12] In the years before we joined the staff, this strategy was guided by Kim Klein and Stephanie Roth, who were national leaders in grassroots fundraising strategies; Cecilie Surasky, one of the first staff people, who was ambitious in her recognition of the need to invest in both visionary communication and the technological tools and infrastructure to make sure we were prepared for our next phase of growth; and tireless member leader Penny Rosenwasser. They helped JVP develop a model that relied on individual member contributions to build its budget. That meant using a combination of email list building (its infancy at that point), membership dues, and relationship building with major donors. Knowing JVP's primary goal was to organize Jewish communities, the challenge was lopsided, given the outsized resources of organizations in opposition to us. As a collective project, we felt politically committed to building up our resources to fight effectively. But that lived in uneasy balance with the understanding that the entire ecosystem of organizations devoted to Palestinian freedom needed to thrive. We knew, on the one hand, that there was not a scarcity of resources to be raised for our allies from Arab American communities and, on the other, that Islamophobia and anti-Arab racism were part of the reason we were growing faster than other Arab- and Muslim-led organizations. Especially at peak moments of crisis on the ground, our allies often noted that money flowed in unevenly to us. When we could, we would offer skills building and support to other allied formations, but this was an ongoing point of tension within the movement.

One of JVP's most successful practices was truly viewing fundraising as political work. Even as JVP's fundraising systems became more sophisticated over time, Ari Wohlfeiler, as development director, was able to imbue our staff, members, and donor teams with that understanding.[13] We knew that building up a broad base of donors was what would allow us to act boldly and independently, and that meant fundraising was not siloed or separated from our other work. We had a strict policy in place not to fundraise during times of war and violent escalations on the ground, but the truth is that a huge amount of money flowed in during those moments, which fueled our overall growth. Eventually, our base grew to about 20,000 annual donors, about a third of whom gave $250 or more per year. Dedicated member leaders as well as staff and board made up the ongoing fundraising team, including over seventy-five people (roughly thirty staff, twelve board members, and thirty-five members). Coordinated by the development staff, each person, depending upon experience and capacity, had a "portfolio" of between five and forty major donors whom they were in touch with multiple times a year. We invested in data analytics, which allowed us to understand what moved our base, and how to be responsive to segments of our list that needed attention. Staff and board were required to participate in fundraising, and members stepped up to be part of the team to keep the organization growing. We successfully built a culture that melded a movement orientation to member-based dues and donations with more traditional major donor cultivation.

The system was not without its challenges, particularly for the staff and board (members who opted in were self-selecting, so they tended to be comfortable with the system). Some staff were really nervous on the phone or apprehensive about asking for money, no matter the communication medium. Those who were not organizers sometimes chafed at being part of work that they didn't see as part of their core responsibilities. Staff who were not Jewish (especially those who were Palestinian) or who spoke English with an accent could find themselves in awkward, uncomfortable, or straight-up racist conversations with donors. These dynamics were not things we recognized immediately, but they became clear as part of the RJT process and as we built a staff with more varied backgrounds. What had felt at first like a radical response to funding barriers—and a way to maintain our political independence—also turned out to have its own drawbacks, rooted in our lack of attention to the race and class dynamics of asking for money.

As political currents shifted, foundations began to be interested in funding us, but their contributions always remained a small portion of the overall budget as a matter of principle. The large number of donors meant that we were not politically beholden to any one donor and could walk away from any individual who made demands on our agenda, without risking economic collapse. This gave JVP a level of political freedom unusual among nonprofit organizations and lent legitimacy to our self-identification as a movement organization. Many who have worked in our fundraising program have become evangelical about the model, enamored of the political independence afforded by the ability to fund your work through the grassroots. It has been gratifying to see a number of skilled fundraisers at JVP seeded into sister movement organizations in the time since. This fundraising model didn't just provide political freedom—it required and facilitated accountability, too. It would be a mistake to think of donors as different from members or chapter leaders. Many, if not most, were all three—and part of the fundraising team besides! This not only created a culture of fundraising within the organization but also meant that while JVP wasn't accountable to any individuals, we were accountable to the larger base, which would vote with their wallet en masse if our politics didn't remain relevant to them. The fundraising program leveraged, simultaneously, our massive list of supporters and the philanthropic culture established in the nonprofit sector and through the US tax code, which trained major donors to give at the end of the calendar year for tax purposes. It was routine for us to raise a quarter of our budget that last week of December.

This fundraising model was part and parcel of our organizing mindset and values, in addition to being the necessary mother of invention. Fundraising is also communications work. Most important were the relationships. The process of making sure the large solicitor team was ready for their conversations meant that our core leaders were up to date on the organizational analysis of the political moment, JVP's current standing as far as political power was concerned, and our political vision for the coming period. The fundraising team also spent a lot of time training people to be comfortable asking for money, normalizing the need for funding to accomplish the work that needs to be done. JVP's style was personal and visceral, and it broadcast a visionary optimism about what we could create together. It was an essential rung on our ladder of engagement—moving people from social media (which wasn't a force at all when we began), to the email list, from which we could invite people to in-person events, develop relationships, and identify those who were ripe to become active members or chapter leaders. It was in this way that many of our more than sixty-five chapters came into existence. Fundraising was never separated or isolated from everything else JVP did, and we cultivated a political understanding of the role of money to the success of our movement.

Fundraising was also extremely labor intensive. In later years, as JVP became known somewhat as a fundraising success story, other organizations began to seek us out to learn how to build member-driven fundraising programs. The team always emphasized that it is not a magic wand—that it takes years of investment in training, staff, relationship building, and the technological tools needed to track donors and solicitors, build powerful lists, and analyze your metrics. In fact, JVP had a head start in building our list— we were the first Jewish organization against the Israeli occupation that started fundraising at scale, so there was no competition when we began from other Jewish organizations seeking to raise money to do similar work. We also got in early enough that fundraising via email was still novel. So, the endeavor to build a similar fundraising program faces more challenges today, though it is certainly still possible.

The constant fundraising was hard on staff and compromised our ability to be as creative and generous with our partners as we would have liked. Especially because the budget continued to grow, each year there was more work to do. Even as the entire fundraising team was depleted at the end of the yearly fundraising cycle, we had to start over again right away. There simply was not another path to funding JVP's work besides this intensive cycle. The way that fundraising was entwined with our political work made for powerful growth and accountability. And, while the fundraising program increased in scale and sophistication over time, it never strayed much from the model that had been built out of necessity at the beginning.

Living in the Both/And

The business of organizational leadership is not for the faint of heart. To do it well, you must be flexible and decisive, open to feedback and able to let criticism roll off your back, able to hold the whole but attend to the component parts, to be both responsive and proactive. You have to give all you have to the organization yet not give so much that you burn out. When it works, it is magic, and it is also easy to get the balance out of whack. Leadership is also about embracing the both/and.

Living in the both/and can either be a recipe for constant tension or a way of making space to embrace contradiction. We aspired to democracy and organized internally as a hierarchy. Our impact came from the talents and passions of both staff and members. We were both a community and a workplace. While we can't claim to have always approached, or handled, the both/and with equanimity, we have come to the conclusion that being willing to live in the space of both/and is what enabled us to be as successful as we were at becoming a force to reckon with. JVP's early decision to intentionally build up staff and fundraising allowed us to grow dynamically, which translated into size and power rooted in the logic of a mass movement at a time when few, if any, other organizations on the left were able to do so. The continued unabashed building of infrastructure during our tenure, the pursuit of funding and staffing, and our commitment to base-building and leadership development at scale were key to JVP's achievements. We think being willing to live in the both/and was an important factor in leading us to the size, sophistication, and internal political cohesion that enabled us to meaningfully challenge the status quo in Jewish communities and beyond.

We believe movement building is the only way to realize the world all people deserve. The nonprofit legal structure is an expedient form, at this moment in the US at least, to scaffold the members, chapters, campaigns, and communications that make up movements. This means that every movement organization that is also a nonprofit is burdened with figuring out a unique structure and approach that makes sense given their mission, structure, and culture, while ensuring it adds up to the power needed for impact. This burden is also a blessing. When done well, base-building, leadership development, rapid response, long-term campaigns, communications, and fundraising stewarded by staff but actualized by members can add up to a powerful force that can't be replicated solely with a nonprofit form.

Organizing Strategy Reflection Questions

Movement Building in a Nonprofit

1. What are the contradictions between mass movement building and nonprofit form animating your work? How do you intentionally navigate holding or resolving those contradictions?

2. Does your organizing model allow for members to bring their specific skills and strengths into the organization? If not, how can your organization build out more ways for members to plug in that will attract varied personalities and constituencies?

3. How do your choices about how you structure decision-making impact your work in terms of pace, sustainability, input, and internal power dynamics?

4. Is the hierarchy in your organization visible and transparent? Are decision-making procedures clear to all? Is there internal clarity among all levels of the organization about who drives processes and decisions?

5. Do your funding sources restrict the political positions you take or the campaigns you pursue? If so, how might you expand your major donor program or peer-to-peer fundraising to allow for more political independence?

Chapter 3

Confronting Our Own Community

There is no doubt that the central emotional and political challenge of our years at JVP was the reality that Jews were not just our target constituency but also, often, our primary adversaries. Every day, in multiple ways, we were challenging and confronting our own community—of origin and of choice. In this chapter, we will unpack the details of those confrontations so others who are likewise seeking to organize their communities can hopefully find resonance and inspiration, not to mention the courage to continue the struggle even when it is hard! We will contextualize JVP in the broader Jewish world, the ways we struggled with insisting on our legitimacy, and how we found our power to move from the margins to the center of the American Jewish discourse on Israel/Palestine. Pushing boundaries within your community of origin by definition creates conflict and consequences for continued participation and inclusion in those communities. It takes a thick skin, circles of affirmation and support (like those built in the sort of political home we discussed in chapter 1), and a deep clarity of purpose to weather those relentless forces of rejection that risk unmooring even the most dedicated activists.

Launching Young, Jewish, and Proud

A significant turning point in the growth of JVP's influence was in 2010, when Prime Minister Netanyahu was in New Orleans to address the Jewish Federation General Assembly (GA). JVP's deputy director at the time, Cecilie Surasky, had the insight that the GA would be a powerful media opportunity. She surmised, correctly, that Prime Minister Benjamin Netanyahu would be a last-minute speaker, and the crush of media there could be a powerful opportunity to bring attention to the pain and grief that more and more younger Jews were feeling about Israel and its treatment of Palestinians. Part of that was understanding that legacy Jewish institutions like the Jewish Federation were deeply concerned about losing younger Jews, so having young, Jewishly engaged JVP members lead the action would add additional weight and symbolism. It also dovetailed with an internal priority of JVP's to consciously organize younger Jews. Stefanie Fox, JVP's organizing director at the time, emphasized the need to use the moment to build the kind of leadership in the group that would last past this particular action and really work with the young people, who had been carefully recruited to take part because of their deep connections to Jewish or Israeli institutions. This interplay between good communications strategy and deep organizing was emblematic of JVP's approach at its best. A third factor was working with trusted donors when exciting opportunities arose. A single generous donor, who was willing to take a chance on the experiment based on his prior experience and relationship with JVP via Cecilie, funded the week of learning and action.

After months of planning, the group spent a week in New Orleans at a leadership institute, getting prepared. Stefanie led the group along with JVP member Elaina Ellis, a poet, publisher, and performing artist (the pair would later together launch the JVP Artist and Cultural Workers Council). Together, they facilitated the group through a process of sharing personal experiences, meeting local Jewish and Palestinian activists, training each other in media, civil disobedience, and collective action, and talking for days about the principles that inspired them to come to New Orleans. They debated how to make the most impact and made an action plan. They used art, reflection, ritual, and communal care for each other and broader Jewish communities to prepare for the experience. There was an emphasis in the plan on speaking from love and pain, even if they had to yell to be heard.

JVP bought youth tickets to the GA for ten activists—five of whom would be protesters, each paired with another member who would document what happened. Roles were found for everyone, regardless of whether they were prepared to risk taking public action or not. The plan was deeply under wraps, with no one outside the immediate team knowing exactly what was going to happen. A breathtaking video still circulates of what ensued. In a cavernous, packed convention center, Netanyahu begins his address.[1] A few minutes in, as he takes a moment's pause, a young woman rises from her chair, unfurls a banner, and begins to yell, "The loyalty oath delegitimizes Israel, the loyalty oath delegitimizes Israel!" She yells it over and over again, until she is hustled out of the room after about a minute. The room eventually quiets down, Netanyahu makes a dumb joke, and the speech continues. But, a few minutes later, another person rises from their chair and yells, "The occupation delegitimizes Israel! The occupation delegitimizes Israel!" This time the crowd groans as he begins to speak, and, after he is hustled out after about thirty seconds, you can see a religious Jewish man ripping the banner with his teeth to great applause. A few minutes later: "The settlements delegitimize Israel!" The words can barely be heard over the roar of the crowd, which has now become a mob, and it takes only about three seconds before the young woman is physically engulfed. As a viewer, knowing we weren't done, it was sobering to think of the courage it took to be the last two protesters, as the rage of the enormous crowd continued to grow. But it was also clear that Netanyahu's speech was essentially ruined, as the whole crowd waited for the other shoe to drop. And it did. The fourth protester rose to shout, "The siege of Gaza delegitimizes Israel!" The sound inside is so immediate and so loud that the viewer only knows his message by the subtitles on the video. Finally—ironically and accurately—"Silencing dissent delegitimizes Israel."

It wasn't just that the team had planned a kick-ass protest. The careful planning of the documentation of the protesters so that viewers could get a visceral sense of the impact inside the hall made it an immediate moment. The video, edited and put out the same day, went viral and got extraordinary press coverage. It struck a nerve, capturing the sense (of excitement or dread, depending on your perspective) that the rising generation was alienated from Israel. For many years afterward, there was virtually no serious conversation about the future of young Jews in America that didn't mention this action and its message. The careful planning and execution symbolized an entire generation's refusal to support the oppression of others, much as, many years later, the Sunrise Movement's Green New Deal protest in Speaker Pelosi's office symbolized and catalyzed the strength of youth-led climate justice efforts.[2]

Rabbi Brant Rosen remembers the significance of this action clearly. A progressive activist in his congregation, Michael Deheeger, had long been on the fence about dipping into Palestine organizing. Michael called Rabbi Rosen and asked him to lunch after seeing the action of the Netanyahu disruption on his social media feed. At that lunch, Rabbi Rosen invited Michael to a congregational delegation to the West Bank he was leading the next month, and Michael bought his ticket the next day. Fast-forward a few months, and Michael attended JVP's first ever Leadership Development Institute for Midwest chapters. A few years later, he was hired as the Chicago chapter's first staff organizer. Thanks to the strong leadership development infra-structure already in place (discussed in detail in chapter 2), JVP was ready to integrate those who saw us in the headlines. This is just one story of hundreds in which young Jewish activists were pushed off the sidelines thanks to this action and became leaders of the evolving movement.

An enduring cultural touchpoint also emerged from that week. The time the group spent preparing for the week discuss-ing principles was turned into a piece of poetry that was both a statement of intent and a call to action.[3] Divided into four parts, We Exist, We Remember, We Refuse, We Commit,[4] it read, in part,

> We refuse to have our histories distorted or erased, or appropriated by a corporate war machine. We will not call this liberation. We refuse to knowingly oppress oth-ers, and we refuse to oppress each other. We refuse to be whitewashed. We will not carry the legacy of terror. We refuse to allow our identities to be cut, cleaned, packaged nicely, and sold back to us. We won't be won over by free vacations and scholarship money. We won't buy the logic that slaughter means safety. We will not quietly witness the violation of human rights in Palestine. We refuse to become the mother who did not scream when wise King Solomon resolved to split her baby in two. We are better than this. We have ancestors to honor. We have allies to honor. We have ourselves to honor.

Later, it was made into a moving collective video that is still being replayed and imitated more than a decade later.[5] It was one of the moments when JVP's organizing, digital and press savvi-ness, and finger on the pulse of the moment came together with a transformational power.

JVP's efforts to engage more "civilly" with the Jewish Federation and the wider circle of legacy Jewish institutions had not just gone nowhere, it actually led to their tightening of the boundaries of inclusion in order to keep JVPers out. Screaming to be heard was the only option, unless we were willing to shut up, which our members were not. So, these young Jews fortified themselves to confront their community with cries of love, pain, and rage. Thanks to their bravery, JVP was catapulted into a new era of growth and power, rooted in a sacred insistence to be heard.

Going to Get Our Cousins

With encouragement from Palestinian partners, JVP embraced our responsibility to organize American Jews. Because JVP falls far to the left in the spectrum of political positioning in American Jewish communities, our adversaries are multiple: the far right with whom we share no values and also have little social overlap except maybe around the family holiday table; the center, where some of us started but fled in despair; and the center-left/liberal Zionists, with whom there are many social connections that are apparent when we are out in the world, engaged in other kinds of social justice activities. JVP's ongoing experience of being a beleaguered minority in Jewish communities was exactly opposite to the reality that we were the largest organization in the metaphorical room of the Palestine movement. We have come to understand this phenomenon as a manifestation of what Olúfẹ́mi O. Táíwò describes in *Elite Capture*, in which he reminds us not to "treat the status of 'elite' as a stable identity, it's a relationship, in a particular context, between a smaller group of people and a larger group of people."[6] In other words, in Jewish spaces, JVP was a relatively small outsider, but in Palestinian solidarity spaces, JVP held more power than most.

JVP's theory of change is rooted in a belief in the power of the grassroots, of masses of individuals rising up together to upend the powers that be. While the Jewish community is not yet at the critical mass needed for anti-Zionist Jews to safely emerge from their closets wherever they work, live, and pray, this is beginning to happen, thanks both to Israel's steadily increasing right-wing extremism and to the more open atmosphere that our organizing has provided. JVP's dual ability to adapt to shifting terrain as well as to shift that terrain to make coming out more and more possible is one of our greatest strengths. It helped our organizing that many staff and members grew up and continued to be part of other Jewish communities. While these relationships could become fraught and fragile over the years, the tethers of connection meant that there were open doors, accessible contact information, and introductions that could be made to the decision-makers or influencers in Jewish communities. In fact, the redlines that legacy Jewish institutions drew were precisely to sever the ties that many anti-Zionist Jews have with other Jews.[7] By regulating who is in and who is out, what type of critique is tolerated or not, these red lines seek to exact a cost from Jews for standing in solidarity with Palestinians by denying participation in Jewish spaces. For example, liberal Jewish organizations organized a "Jewish Social Justice Roundtable," the purpose of which is to bring together a network of Jewish organizations that "strengthens and aligns the Jewish social justice field in order to make justice a core expression of Jewish life and help create an equitable world."[8] Presumably, it was organized to be a parallel to the umbrella organizations of the right-leaning legacy Jewish organizations, where coordination and strategy setting take place, primarily around a pro-Israel agenda. While their members include organizations that do work on Israel/Palestine, for example the New Israel Fund and T'ruah, JVP has been locked out of the roundtable.

Our role within the broader movement ecosystem was to organize Jews to support Palestinian rights. Organizing Jews means wrestling with when, how, and if to engage with synagogues and other collective communal organizations like local Jewish Community Relations Councils or Jewish Community Centers that exist in every city and are explicitly Zionist and actively supporting Israeli apartheid. Over the years, JVP's strategies for doing that shifted. When JVP was getting started, it was clear that our role was to shout from the margins, but, as our numbers grew and we became more of a real threat to the pro-Israel Jewish community, we realized that we needed not just to bang on the door but to actively make space for those we were reaching to come in. Public opinion was shifting toward us, we were succeeding at shaping the conversation on Israel/Palestine leftward, and with that came new responsibilities to ensure our organizing practices were welcoming and embracing of all who want to join us, and to deploy our power in careful, strategic ways. For example, we were very careful to not take to Twitter to bad-mouth, antagonize, or subtweet as an organization those we adamantly disagreed with but who we thought were movable or whose base would be receptive to our message, realizing that it was to our benefit to remain in good standing in order to ensure our message was not undermined. Even as we were being careful to temper our voice, those to our right (even if marginally) would seek to delegitimize us through an informal whisper network that sought to sully our reputation. Through our personal friendship networks we would hear that some were accusing us of being shrill, disloyal to Jewish communities, unstrategic, or worse.

There's no question that JVP, like other movements trying to massively shift and confront their own community, began as a small and despised minority. Even as those who were becoming disillusioned with the organized Jewish community came toward us when they saw us on their social media feeds, on the streets, or in the quad on campus, we were not always the best positioned to organize our fellow Jews directly. Because of the ways legacy Jewish organizations have been successful in demonizing us and our political positioning, many Jews are scared to be associated with us. Even if they might agree with some of our values or politics, they feel that identifying as a JVP member publicly comes with too much baggage. That was particularly true for rabbis and other Jewish communal professionals who feared repercussions for their careers.

Out of the Closet

By staking out a spot farther left than the liberal mainstream, paired with an ever-expanding base of supporters, savvy social and print media messaging, dozens of chapters around the country, and strategic campaigns, we were increasingly able to draw the conversation where we wanted it to go, no matter how vehemently resistant our adversaries were. JVP staff and members were learning and evolving in our own politics, as was the public discourse. From the time the two of us started at JVP, when we centered conversation around the occupation, until a decade later, when our framing included settler colonization, we were in a dynamic process of learning and pushing our own community as we learned and pushed ourselves. Effectively navigating the pushing of politics leftward, without overplaying one's hand or being too cautious, relies on the clarity of the values you use as the guideposts for your work. An articulation of your values serves as a metric for when to shift your political positioning. Relationships of accountability to directly impacted communities provide the goalposts for where the organizing is headed, allowing you to ensure your efforts are headed in that same direction. Those relationships of accountability can look like sending over a proposal for feedback, picking up the phone for a check-in, or more formal feedback gathering.

While pro-Israel Jewish institutions focus their advocacy and power building behind the scenes with decision-makers and elites, JVP was out in public, building grassroots power. Our public efforts sought to bring the fight into daylight, where we can build allies, shift public opinion, and demystify the struggle for Palestinian freedom. JVP's adversaries are notably loath to have this public debate, knowing that liberal American Jewish communities' own values collide with the actions, methods, and ideology of the Israeli government. JVP's fight was always to bring the conversation about Israel out from behind closed doors, where its defenders wanted to keep it. Many key mobilizations against Israeli apartheid happen in democratic forums, where ordinary people weigh in, according to their values. For example, the various mainline churches where delegates vote on resolutions at semiannual conventions, including resolutions directing their denominations to divest from companies that profit from the Israeli occupation of Gaza and the West Bank, including East Jerusalem. Or student governments that take actions directing their universities to divest. And, of course, progressive elected officials who are unafraid to publicly challenge Israel are increasingly winning seats up and down the ballot. In these forums, the power of grassroots organizing strength shines.

Organizing Gets the Goods

The most powerful tool in any organizer's toolbox is always their relationships. Everyone knows someone who is a Jewish anti-Zionist! The early gay rights movement focused on coming out, based on the idea that the more gay people are visible, the more people cannot demonize them—finding instead that they not only know gay people but also love them. The same is true in Jewish communities. Most, if not all, liberal American Jewish organizations have staff or members that are anti-Zionist Jews or on a journey in that direction. Over time, this changes the calculus for the leaders of those organizations, rabbis, and others who hold the position of gatekeepers in Jewish communities.

Organizing means building relationships with people, supporting them to align their values and their actions. Organizing means having the people to knock on doors, sit down for coffee with neighbors, hold teach-ins at their houses of worship, and make connections to and show up for allied movements. Where JVP lacked millions of dollars, we had connections with tens of thousands of people beyond our members whose values are aligned with ours. When threatened by a bear in the wilderness, you're taught to make yourself big. That's exactly what we do through organizing. We magnify our power, punching way above our weight, and, as our weight grows, we don't shrink back. There are both benefits and costs to playing this avant-garde role as part of confronting our own community. On the one hand, we benefit from being fluent in the cultural references and communal dynamics at play. This allows our strategies to be mindfully agitational and for us to wade confidently into thorny fights. We also benefited from being attention grabbing in staking out a position so outside the mainstream. Free from the haziness of subtlety, those we are trying to organize know exactly what we stand for, even if it is initially a bit too scary.

There are also costs, of course. The American Jewish culture we are organizing in is profoundly liberal. On the one hand, that means there is a certain fetishization of nuance that insists upon qualifying statements in every situation that speak to "all sides" instead of being attentive to power, which leads to watering down or undercutting a clear analysis or demand. We see this acutely in the call for BDS, which many liberals claim is too extreme an action to take against Israel. This liberalism is deployed to mask a commitment to the status quo and a form of ethnonationalism and deep-seated anti-Arab/Palestinian racism that is unwilling to give up its own privilege, even more frustrating when voiced by a Jewish American community that roots itself in values of equality. It conveys a belief in two equal sides in conflict, when it is clear that the actual power imbalance is extreme. As we have seen in calls to abolish police or cancel student debt, and as Reverend Dr. Martin Luther King Jr. admonished in his "Letter from a Birmingham Jail," liberals often balk at clear calls for accountability in place of incremental reform.

No More Secret Girlfriend

Even relatively progressive organizations, such as Bend the Arc, a US-based progressive organization focused on "domestic" politics, were worried about how their donors would react to any coalitions with us. So, for example, a nationwide "Chanukah for Black Lives" in 2014, which was a collaboration among a number of progressive Jewish groups, floundered because Bend the Arc didn't want to be listed on the website with JVP—even though the joint effort did not touch on Israel/Palestine. Things were even more fraught with liberal Jewish organizations, like J Street and T'ruah, which did work on Israel/Palestine but strongly opposed the BDS movement. In 2011, Rebecca was invited to debate BDS at the J Street national conference, to a warm reception. However, after that, J Street never directly engaged with the ideas behind BDS again, and we heard from multiple people that they had gotten so much pushback from donors about it that they never again hosted a proponent of BDS. Despite these formal separations, there were always personal relationships among all these groups. Some of these were because of the relatively small networks of organized Jewish communities and our camps, schools, and other institutions where JVPers grew up together with those individuals now leading Jewish organizations across the political spectrum. And in the course of our years on staff, just as JVP evolved, we watched as members or leaders of other organizations continued to evolve closer to our positions as well.

But there was also a phenomenon we came to call the "secret girlfriend." These were people embedded in all kinds of Jewish organizations, not just liberal ones, that had serious concerns about Israel's actions and their organizations' response to them. They wanted to talk to us to unburden themselves, and maybe to receive absolution, or be pushed to take action. Sometimes these relationships took hours of our time and emotional energy. They seemed worth it for the same reason that we were invested in organizing more generally—if there are people who are interested in what you're doing, you should talk to them! And since our communal relationships felt so tenuous, it felt satisfying and exciting to know that JVP was a place where people inside the Jewish mainstream world felt they could come with their doubts. But the key word was "secret." No one wanted to be public about their associations with us, even as they were drawing on our knowledge and patience. Often, those fears were career-based—that any association with JVP would put their jobs at risk. We also noticed that as we accumulated more power, those who were *just* to the right of us in Jewish communities would place themselves as gatekeepers, trying to manage our power for us. JVP would regularly be encouraged to remain behind the scenes under the guise of "strategy." Claiming our political positioning was too spicy or our reputation too tainted, we would be encouraged to allow a more center-left organization to represent the coalition. This is despite the fact that JVP was the only Jewish organization with a grassroots base or had for years been organizing around the issue and had much more depth of knowledge. Even the power we built wasn't ours to deploy.

The parameters of JVP's open tent shifted over our years there. In the early years, our members ranged from liberal to anti-Zionist. As we grew and our politics shifted, external conditions that JVP helped to create also shifted who was attracted to JVP. We paid attention to and embraced our "right" flank, knowing that it was insufficient to have "correct" politics if we weren't successfully growing our base. We sought to maintain our open tent and never imposed litmus tests on members, but once we had endorsed BDS (in 2015) and anti-Zionism (in 2019), the natural range of politics of our members and potential members also shifted—at the same time that other organizations, like IfNotNow, emerged as a place for those not yet comfortable with those positions. On occasion, we struggled to figure out the balance between our open organizing approach, how much of a personal toll we expected our members to absorb, and the fierce need to build something that spoke to the needs of our current members, not those who were on their way toward us.

No Pictures Please

This "secret girlfriend" pattern reached its nadir at one of our NMMs, in 2015. We had agreed to allow some people not to wear name tags and not be photographed, because they felt they couldn't attend otherwise, given the personal risks. We wanted to accommodate people's concerns and where they were on their personal journey, in the hopes that when they saw the vibrant, welcoming, and justice-centered culture we were building, they would want to join outright. These were mostly rabbis or rabbinical students, Jewish studies professors, and other Jewish communal professionals, all white and middle- or upper-class. They wanted to be there, but they also worried about repercussions they could face for attending, for their standing in or employment at Jewish communal organizations. There is truth to the fear that association with JVP in the mainstream Jewish world can label you with something of a "scarlet letter." Being publicly identified with JVP runs the real risk of being denied access to that world, all the more so if you are a person of color, poor, Jew by choice, or otherwise marginalized in the Jewish world, regardless of your political position around Israel.

Of course, we wanted Jewish communal professionals of every stripe to participate in our NMM, so we made room for them to come pseudo-anonymously and even provided fluorescent stickers they could affix to their name badges that said, "No pictures please." But those of us who planned the gathering almost immediately regretted the decision. The stickers created a sense of boundary, the specter of something untoward going on, as if what *we* were doing was somehow wrong. (If anything, the mainstream Jews who twist themselves into knots to defend occupation and apartheid were the ones with something to hide.) We had prepared for the meeting for the better part of a year, aiming to build a sense of trust, collective learning, and a few precious days when we could live out the embodiment of a vision of Judaism that embraces justice in all its facets. Should we really spend our time and energy and offer our effort to those who wanted to enjoy it without risk or responsibility? In the grand scheme of things, attending a conference is such a low-stakes activity that acquiescing to the request for protection from it felt like a capitulation to a definition of Jewish life that we were organizing to free ourselves from. The message it sent to the rest of the attendees who were there proudly was toxic, too, as if there was something to be ashamed of by being there, breaking our sense of being out and proud together and drawing strength from one another. It turned out we had emotional limits to what we were willing to embrace in our commitment to meeting people where they are.

There are repercussions for doing this work that are real for everyone who does it seriously. As leaders, given the stakes and the potential fallout, we saw it as part of our role to create a container in which it is possible to ask everyone to be just a little bit braver than they would have been otherwise. We don't want to deny the emotional and practical impacts of being denied access to Jewish communal spaces, jobs, and familial and communal comfort that Jews compromise for speaking out publicly in support of Palestinians. But there were limits to what we could accept in our tent, even in the earliest years. There was an expectation that our members would have a basic understanding of the ongoing, violent repression of Palestinians, even if the outcomes people believed in and political strategies to get there were different. And while our organizing program made room for people to deepen their understanding at their own pace, we always prioritized creating a sense of safety for anti-Zionist Jews, knowing we had no other home. Balancing safety with openness, without capitulating to a sense of fear that runs counter to movement building, is the tricky tightrope we had to walk. No more secret girlfriend.

Topping from the Bottom

Confronting your community is almost always a move to lead your community from below, because those with power are generally comfortable with the status quo. That's why successful campaigns involve bringing people directly face-to-face with the powerful: tenants who organize the community to do eviction defense; workers who mobilize consumers in support of their union drives. This community support bolsters those fighting for recognition. Without that sense of support, the feelings of ostracization and rejection can become all encompassing.

For the two of us, when we were able to dig ourselves out of those dead-end feelings, we were able to see that we were doing what we had set out to do: shaping the direction of progressive American Jewish life, at least regarding Palestine. This was a deep ethical imperative that stemmed from a sense of disappointment that our community was not living up to the very ideals and principles that many of us had learned were part and parcel of Jewish life, which fueled our sense of obligation to confront and change it. For human rights defenders, there continue to be real stakes for speaking out on Israel/Palestine, as doing so impacts careers and relationships in ways that have a chilling effect on activism. JVP was seeking to supplant the hollowed-out legacy Jewish organizations littering the American political landscape. This is not unique to Jewish communities—Black freedom-fighting and queer organizations likewise struggle with legacy institutions with retrograde politics that hold back the priorities and visions of the current population they ostensibly serve. These generational tussles are happening all over, so we can—and must—share strategies and tactics for successfully challenging the status quo.

Organizing Strategy Reflection Questions
Confronting Your Own Community

1. How can you continually assess your relative power inside your own community as conditions shift? How will you notice when your stance needs to shift from defense to offense? How does your messaging and the way you deliver it need to evolve as your influence grows?

2. How do you support your people to feel confident and empowered to confront your own community, given feelings of rejection they might be holding?

3. How are you pushing yourselves to evolve in your politics even as you are pushing your own community?

4. As you are building your power and influence, how do you maintain your integrity and dignity in collaborative work with those in your community you are trying to move and with whom you have substantive political disagreement?

5. Are you clear in your power-map analysis? Whom are you trying to move? To ally with? Who is your target? Whom are you trying to get out of your way?

Chapter 4

Fighting Antisemitism and Its Weaponization

U nderstanding antisemitism and the importance of resisting it in all its forms is a core obligation for all of us.
Unfortunately, the weaponization of antisemitism, specifically in
connection with anti-Zionism, is so widespread that it informs
just about every repressive tactic marshaled against our movement.
Those two realities must be held in tandem. There is no way to
fully understand the intensity of the challenge of shifting Jewish
communal support for Israel without understanding the role
antisemitism plays. This includes the history of anti-Jewish violence and genocide, the reality of anti-Jewish sentiment, and the
cynical manipulation of accusations of antisemitism to undermine
the movement for Palestinian rights. The strategies we must use
to dismantle antisemitism and its weaponization are instructive
for all movements. It is critical that movements build capacities
to fight systems of oppression while simultaneously not allowing
those fights to compromise our politics or our core values and
demands. Contesting dominant narratives—whether they be the
view that reproductive justice can be realized by protecting only
the rights of white, rich women; or that trans women ought not be

included in feminist formations; or that supporting Palestinians is anti-Jewish—is a crucial task. These narratives are so deeply embedded in the culture all around us that you have to be rigorously attentive. It can be exhausting, but you can't take your eye off the ball for a second, lest any inherent biases get in your way.

In this chapter we will dig into antisemitism and its misuses, clarifying some common misconceptions and misinformation of the history of Zionism as it relates to anti-Jewish hatred and violence. We will look at how the right and the center perpetuate a dangerous conflation of anti-Zionism with antisemitism, designed to undermine the movement for Palestinian freedom. We will also reflect on the defensive fights we got pulled into, as well as proactive strategies we implemented to try to go against the grain of pervasive narratives, tackling them head-on. Understanding antisemitism is no longer solely a moral imperative but also a strategic one.

Clarifying Our Terms

During the lead-up to the Presbyterian USA General Assemblies in 2012 and 2014, where votes were taking place on whether or not churches would divest their holdings in companies that profit from the Israeli occupation, Alissa would visit Presbyterian churches to discuss divestment. At nearly every church someone would raise their hand and ask, "What do I do when I get called antisemitic?" And Alissa would respond, "Well, are you?" Of course, critiquing Israel, supporting the divestment of your church's resources from companies that profit from the occupation of the West Bank (including East Jerusalem) and Gaza, and standing in solidarity with Palestinians are not inherently antisemitic. That said, it is very important for Palestine solidarity activists to interrogate their own prejudices. This is particularly true for Christians, given the theological and cultural antisemitism endemic in Western Christianity. Ideas such as supersessionism (the idea that God replaced the covenant with Jews with a covenant with the Church) and deicide (the idea that Jews killed Jesus Christ) are two of the dominant anti-Jewish ideas most Christians are exposed to. Antisemitism, like anti-Black racism, homophobia, and other toxic ideas, seeps into our psyches because it is part of our culture (for now). We are more vulnerable to false accusations of antisemitism when any anti-Jewish beliefs go uninterrogated.

Antisemitism is discrimination, prejudice, hostility, or violence against Jews as Jews. Antisemitism takes many forms, including physical violence, threats of violence, repeating or circulating antisemitic conspiracy theories and stereotypes, and other aggressions and microaggressions.[1] In the past decade in the US, we have seen all those manifestations come to life as right-wing extremists pulled nostalgic threads of Nazi-era racial pseudoscience mixed with Christian religious fundamentalism and hatred toward Jews. A key feature of antisemitism, ever since the inception of the term in the nineteenth century, has been to essentialize all Jews, considering us as a monolithic group or even a separate "race." This separationist theory had advocates among Christian Zionists, Nazis, and fascists, as well as Jewish Zionists, who internalized the idea that the Jews were a problem for Europe that should be solved through separation.

Zionism is a political ideology that advocates for Jewish settlement of historic Palestine. A form of Jewish nationalism that led to the establishment of the modern state of Israel, Zionism's early advocates were 1) mostly secular Jews, responding to the political, cultural, and social upheaval and oppression of Jews in Europe in the nineteenth century and the emergence of settler-colonial ideologies amid the proliferation of nation-states that were in vogue at the time; and 2) European Christians who were eager to accelerate Jewish colonization of the land as part of their eschatological theology, coupled with their political desires to cleanse Europe of the "Jewish problem." Today, Israel is governed according to the ideas central to political Zionism: the land of Israel is the historic and current homeland of the Jewish people, only Jews are granted the right to national self-determination, and Jewish-only settlement of historic Palestine is prioritized.

Anti-Zionism is political opposition to Zionism. Anti-Zionism recognizes that Zionism, by definition, denies all basic rights to Palestinian people and has entailed ongoing destruction of villages and towns, theft of land, and ethnic cleansing. Anti-Zionism understands that the founding of Israel is responsible for the ongoing Nakba, and that the idea and practice of a state that privileges Jews to the exclusion of all others is antithetical to Palestinian self-determination, to their indigeneity to the land, and, for those of us on the left, to our most basic principles. Jewish anti-Zionists span a political and religious spectrum, ranging from religious and secular progressives who view opposition to Zionism as an antiracist praxis, to ultra-Orthodox Jews who oppose Jewish dominion until the time of the Messiah, to anarchist Jews who oppose the very concept of nation-states, Jewish or otherwise, to Jews who see Zionism as harmful to Jewish values of justice.

There Has Always Been Debate about Zionism and Jewish Safety

From the inception of the Zionist movement in the late nineteenth century, there has been wide disagreement and debate inside Jewish communities about the idea that Jewish safety lies in a Jewish-only state. Part of the logic of the founding of the state of Israel, fifty years after Zionism had emerged in Europe, was that the world turned its back on the Jews during World War II, allowing six million Jews to perish. Zionist ideology from the beginning, including the writings of the founder of political Zionism, Theodor Herzl, had integrated the inherently antisemitic concept that European Jews could not assimilate and therefore needed their own state, which took on a devastating logic in the wake of the Holocaust. This idea that only a Jewish state could provide enduring safety for Jews was and continues to be deployed as a key strategy to ensure the success of the Zionist project. While for Zionist leaders it was a savvy and effective rhetorical tool, it has been earnestly taken to heart by Jewish people the world over. This endures as a narrative challenge for anti-Zionist organizing.

Deeply embedded in the Zionism that Palestinians live under is this awful idea that safety only comes from isolation and violent domination. The legacy of the genocidal antisemitism of the Nazi Holocaust continues to be wielded by the state of Israel to defend its indefensible system of oppression against Palestinians. And, as Palestinians and their allies raise our voices against the human rights abuses Palestinians suffer, we are charged with antisemitism. At this point, most everyone who speaks up for Palestine in one way or another has faced an accusation that their voice for justice and freedom for Palestinians is anti-Jewish. These bad-faith, false accusations of antisemitism are themselves a threat to Jewish safety, as they can muddy one's understanding of what is or is not antisemitism, leaving Jews vulnerable.

JVP, from the very start, has been guided by the exact opposite principle, that writ large we live in an interdependent world, that we all deserve safety, and that the way to gain safety is through solidarity. In practice, the communities we are creating are safer when we live by this principle—when we have the backs of our partners and they have our backs. From the founding of JVP, our members and leaders always took seriously the understanding and opposing of antisemitism as part of our work for justice in Palestine. In 2004, JVP, then a relatively small Bay Area organization, published a short book, *Reframing Anti-Semitism: Alternative Jewish Perspectives*, that aimed to deepen the understanding of antisemitism in the fight for social justice. In the years since, defenders of Israeli policy have increasingly used false charges of antisemitism to stifle the Palestine solidarity movement, along with attempts to redefine antisemitism to link it with criticism of Israel. JVP's 2017 book, *On Antisemitism*, offered a new approach, rooted in the political reality of the United States and offering a fresh analysis of the complexity of the intersection between antisemitism, accusations of antisemitism, and Palestinian human rights activism.[2] Importantly, the book included voices of Palestinian students and activists as well as the voices of Jews who are often marginalized in mainstream discussions of antisemitism, including Jews of color and Sephardi/Mizrahi Jews. With *On Antisemitism*, JVP attempted to model our vision of how oppression should be resisted together (an enduring theme for JVP). When it comes to solutions to the intermingled challenges of antisemitism, Islamophobia, and anti-Palestinian racism, we believe the best path forward is a multiracial, multifaith network focusing on dismantling the systemic, movement-wide manifestations of antisemitism in the context of other forms of racism, all of which are embedded in white supremacist, Christian Zionist, and neo-Nazi movements. This is what poses the most powerful and gravest threat to Jewish safety around the world.

We believe it is important to understand antisemitism in the context of other forms of oppression. This puts us at odds with those who insist that antisemitism is a phenomenon that operates fundamentally differently from all other forms of racism. Even as various forms of racism have unique dimensions, we believe this insistence is wrongheaded and dangerous, as it runs the risk of isolating Jews from other oppressed peoples instead of allowing our resistance to oppression, and fighting for the world we want to be born, to be united and complete. We share the view of writer, activist, and professor Keeanga-Yamahtta Taylor, who has noted, as when reflecting on the heightened intensity of the 2020 protests in the wake of George Floyd's murder, "History is cumulative, not cyclical."³ We take from this that we must learn from the past and allow that to inform liberation strategies for today, but not assume that current conditions are a replica of the past or that oppression is a static, ever-present part of the world. As we noted above, the initial and enduring claim that Zionism is the only answer to Jewish safety is predicated on this same logic—that the past will predict the future.

When Jews didn't have citizenship rights in Christian Europe, there were limits on what jobs Jews could have and where Jews could live. At the same time this was happening, white, Christian Europeans were colonizing other places around the globe, including what became the United States. The logic of discrimination against Jews was the same logic that justified colonialism—racism that privileged white, Christian Europeans, justifying the kidnapping, enslavement, control, and/or murder of Black and Indigenous people. It was precisely in those centuries that the version of whiteness that still has us by a stranglehold was being created and consolidated. This is the same idea behind Zionism.

The right embraces Zionism and hails it as a model for a Christian nationalist, white future. In 2018, when Israel passed the "nation state law" granting Israeli Jews "an exclusive right to national self-determination," this move was lauded by Richard Spencer, a leader of the alt-right in the US, who said, "I have great admiration for Israel's nation-state law." Spencer went on, "Jews are, once again, at the vanguard, rethinking politics and sovereignty for the future, showing a path forward for Europeans."⁴

Right-Wing Antisemitism

The Trump presidency thoroughly changed the perception of safety of Jews in America. The chants of "Jews will not replace us" in Charlottesville in 2017, and Trump's defense of those chanting as "very fine people," was a wake-up call, as Trump indicated that, instead of working to combat such ideas, his tenure would be one that emboldened and empowered attacks on Jews. Though the rationales of the perpetrators are varied in each instance, since the Trump administration, Jews have been the targets of violence in the United States in ways unseen for decades. Where we pray, shop, and live. With spray paint and assault rifles, machetes, and fists. In centers of Jewish life, like New York, San Diego, Pittsburgh, and everywhere in between—including in Alissa's grandfather's synagogue in Indiana, which was spray-painted with swastikas and pro-Nazi sentiments. The Trump presidency unearthed the fact that antisemitism still very much animates white supremacist movements, and the opening he gave them to express those sentiments freely has yet to be reined in.[5] Christian Zionists proclaim their love of Israel even when these groups are openly antisemitic. Trump, similarly, continued a multidecade bipartisan policy of blank checks—literally and figuratively—for Israel, even while he emboldened antisemites. Even more disturbing, Jewish American legacy institutions and the Israeli government itself have been willing to overlook the increasing displays of hatred as they elevate Trump with praise, putting Jewish people at risk in the process.

At the same time, twentieth-century systemic, state-sponsored antisemitism (such as restrictions on buying homes or attending college) has ended in the US, and white Jews, at least, do not face restrictions or lack of opportunities because of their Jewishness. This assimilation into whiteness for Jews is, of course, conditional, and interpersonal manifestations of anti-Jewish hatred continue.

As violent antisemitism from the right has ballooned since Trump took office, instead of finding common cause among Jews to fight back against violent, xenophobic, and murderous antisemitism, Israel and its defenders have used the opportunity to double down on the claim that holding Israel accountable for human rights abuses is antisemitic.[6] The antisemitism industry, led by the Israeli government in concert with the Israeli lobby in the US and around the world, is willing to sacrifice free speech, scholarly inquiry, academic freedom, and Jewish safety in order to shield Israel from accountability for its unjust policies toward Palestinians. The impact of this is effectively giving the right a pass on their naked antisemitism, as long as they continue to support Israel. This is often echoed by legacy Jewish institutions, which spend much more time attacking those who criticize Israel than on fighting antisemitism from the right.

While he was the president of the United States, Trump made numerous blatantly antisemitic remarks, including a parroting of the antisemitic canard of dual loyalty when, in a High Holiday call in 2019 with Jewish Americans, he told them, "We love your country" and "your prime minister," speaking of Israel and Benjamin Netanyahu. At a 2019 gathering of the Israeli American Council, Trump said, "A lot of you are in the real estate business because I know you very well. You're brutal killers. Not nice people at all. But you have to vote for me; you have no choice."[7] Israeli officials and Israel's defenders in the US made haste to give Trump a pass on his antisemitism because of his support for Israel's policies of domination and apartheid, neglecting the fact that allowing those comments to go unchallenged only serves to bolster the antisemitism of his base of white supremacists and Christian nationalists. In giving him a pass, they are shamefully risking the safety and well-being of Jews everywhere.

The New Antisemitism

Over the last several decades, a collaboration between right-wing Israel advocacy organizations and the Israeli government has worked to redefine antisemitism to include criticism of Israel and, in particular, to define anti-Zionism as antisemitism. This "new antisemitism" promotes a logic that since Israel is the "Jewish State" it is the "Jew of the World"; therefore, critiques of it often, or always, have an antisemitic bias.[8] The problem with this configuration is that it basically gives a pass to any action that the Israeli government takes. It is used as a tactic of repression, particularly to subvert the legitimacy of Palestinian voices. The irony of the impact of the "new antisemitism" is that, in its conflation of Zionism with the Jewish people, it further entrenches antisemitism. To conflate Zionism with all Jews—many of whom are anti-Zionists struggling alongside Palestinians for their freedom and equality—is itself a harmful assumption. It is premised on the antisemitic notion that Jews are uniform in our beliefs and political commitments, and that all Jews, no matter where we live in the world, are fundamentally loyal to a foreign government, and that the "real" home for all Jews is Israel.

The primary tool currently used by those advancing this "new antisemitism" is the definition drafted by the Europe-based International Holocaust Remembrance Alliance (IHRA), known as the IHRA definition. The IHRA definition is a key instrument that strives to cement the conflation of Judaism with Zionism, thereby actually promoting antisemitism by encouraging the idea of collective Jewish responsibility for all violence committed by Israel. This definition was developed in 2005 by the American Jewish Committee (AJC) for use as a tool for monitoring and data collection in Europe and, over the past decade, has been repurposed as a legislative template.[9] The definition itself is concise, but appended to it are a set of eleven examples, which include statements such as "Denying the Jewish people their right to self-determination, e.g., by claiming that the existence of a State of Israel is a racist endeavor."[10] This essentially compromises Palestinians' ability to narrate the reality of their own lives. Palestinians who talk about their direct experiences of occupation, exile, violence, and repression have found themselves afoul of the definition and have been accused of antisemitism. At the time of this writing, the IHRA definition is the current US State Department definition of antisemitism and has been signed into law by twenty-three states. There are active coalitional efforts to push back, with early indication of progress.[11] As of now, this definition remains an active threat to freedom of speech and academic freedom.

It is of note that the most powerful group advocating for this "new antisemitism" definition in the US is Christians United for Israel (CUFI). CUFI boasts more members than the entire Jewish population of the United States and promotes an apocalyptically instrumentalizing view of Jews, claiming Jewish emigration to Israel as a prerequisite for the second coming of Jesus Christ—at which point Jews must convert to Christianity or burn in hell.[12] There is hardly a more antisemitic idea than that! Yet, CUFI promotes making the IHRA definition the standard definition of antisemitism and has included it as a top priority in their legislative agenda in recent years.

Decoupling Zionism from Judaism

Accusations of antisemitism as well as their weaponization against Palestinians and those who support them are a linchpin in the battle for control over the narrative and action on Palestine. These accusations are used to bully, harass, intimidate, fire, and silence voices for Palestinian rights and are deployed in every point on the continuum of repression we outline in chapter 8. False accusations of antisemitism play a unique and destructive role in the movement for Palestinian freedom and to Jewish safety. The conflation of anti-Zionism with antisemitism is both false and dangerous, as the immoral actions of the state of Israel entrench anti-Jewish stereotypes and conspiracy theories, thanks to the encouragement of Zionist leaders who push people to see all Jews as responsible for Israel's actions and policies as well as for its "safety" and "power." Decoupling Jews from Israel and Jewishness from Zionism are therefore essential to the struggle against real antisemitism, toward realizing Jewish safety, and, of course, for Palestinian liberation. JVP's existence serves as a powerful contradiction and alternative to the power, intimidation, silencing, character assassination, bullying, McCarthyism, repression, and the ugly Islamophobia and anti-Palestinian racism of Israel and its defenders.

In order to shift the narrative toward support of Palestinian freedom and to combat antisemitism itself, it is crucial to distinguish between actual antisemitism against Jewish people and accusations of antisemitism used to shield Israel from criticism. As long as conversations about antisemitism include discussion of Israel, the legitimization of discussion of what constitutes antisemitism must expand beyond Jewish communities. Given the impacts on Palestinians who are accused of antisemitism simply for reporting their lived experience under Zionism, their perspectives are essential in the debate over what is and isn't antisemitism.

Fighting Antisemitism Together

One common thread in JVP's work—one of the secrets that help us keep fighting through the repression we face—is to do our work in the way we want the world to be, not as it is. That means always from a multiracial, multi-issue stance focused on collective liberation. The focus on "critique of Israel is antisemitic" has left Jewish communities sorely underprepared to effectively resist antisemitism together. Jewish communities have been too distracted by this single, usually falsely employed, definition of antisemitism to truly see how white supremacy, Islamophobia, and other forms of oppression intersect with and rely on antisemitism. So, JVP looked outside Jewish communities to find the partners we need.

In 2017 and again in 2020, JVP organized opportunities for a multiracial panel to publicly share their thinking and commitments to fighting antisemitism as it is manifesting in the US. In 2017, it was an event to promote our book *On Antisemitism*, with Linda Sarsour, Leo Ferguson of Jews for Racial and Economic Justice—which had also just published a new resource on antisemitism—and Lina Morales and Rebecca from JVP, moderated by Amy Goodman of *Democracy Now!*, at The New School in Manhattan.[13] Inviting Linda Sarsour was a deliberate decision. Although Linda is regularly viciously criticized by large swaths of the mainstream Jewish community, in reality she has been a steadfast ally of Jewish communities in New York and all over the country, including personally raising funds to repair vandalized Jewish cemeteries. As a Palestinian American who works in numerous multiracial coalitions, she has experienced both working in coalition with Jewish communities and being accused of antisemitism when she speaks as a Palestinian. Though we knew it would be provocative, we wanted to actively challenge the idea that only Jewish people could talk about antisemitism and its impacts. In typical fashion, the pushback was intense and swift. The *New York Post* editorial board labeled the event an Orwellian "fake panel . . . meant to promote Israel-bashing."[14] The *Jerusalem Post* editorial board slammed it as "a forum of 'antisemites on antisemitism'" that "makes as much sense as a KKK forum on civil rights."[15] The Anti-Defamation League's CEO, Jonathan Greenblatt, tweeted about the event: "Having Linda Sarsour & head of JVP leading a panel on #antisemitism is like Oscar Meyer leading a panel on vegetarianism. These panelists know the issue, but unfortunately, from the perspective of fomenting it rather than fighting it."[16] *New York Times* opinion columnist Bret Stephens also weighed in, likening Linda Sarsour to white supremacist Steve Bannon.[17]

We knew that the accusations against Linda are completely baseless, and to counter her marginalization is a key long-term goal. We couldn't sideline her powerful voice merely because our adversaries had decided to make her into a pariah. We know she has our back, and we wanted to continue to give her a venue to speak and be heard because she has a crucial perspective that serves to enlarge the conversation on antisemitism in the US. This is what we wish others in Jewish communities would do for us; instead, we were role modeling how we wished an open, reflective, intellectually honest conversation could happen both inside and outside Jewish communities. This panel became a microcosm of both the problems we face and also our counterstrategies. The apoplectic reaction from the Jewish world whenever non-Jewish people of color seek to ally with Jews against antisemitism is devastating in its shortsightedness and its racism.

For all the hate-mongering bluster the event precipitated, the event was an unqualified success. Hundreds poured into The New School auditorium, thousands watched the live stream, the questions asked in the Q&A were thoughtful and generative, and multiple news outlets covered the event (this would not have happened if there hadn't been such a virulent backlash). We were able to generate the exact conversation we wanted and even radicalized some people along the way who were horrified by the mainstream Jewish community's outsized response. This event made critical inroads in the conversation about antisemitism, situating the conversation as one that all communities must engage in—not just Jewish communities. Just as tens of thousands of non-Muslims streamed to the airports in protest when Trump's Muslim ban was announced, or when, in response to the murders of Trayvon Martin, Michael Brown, George Floyd, and too many other Black Americans by the police, hundreds of thousands of non-Black people took to the streets in outrage nationwide, we can expect the same solidarity. In the event of escalated violence or threats toward Jews in the US, shouldn't we want the same response from non-Jews? Of course we should. More important, these events show that we're already getting it.

A few years later, JVP saw another opportunity to push the conversation further, particularly on the issue of who can speak on antisemitism. Hosted through the 501(c)(4) entity JVPAction in December 2020, Peter Beinart, Dr. Marc Lamont Hill, Dr. Barbara Ransby, and Representative Rashida Tlaib gathered to discuss "dismantling antisemitism, winning justice." The pushback from the pro-Israel world to this event was similarly intense and hyperbolic: *Jerusalem Post* columnist Seth Frantzman wrote that the panel lineup "must be a story from *The Onion*."[18] And former *New York Times* columnist Bari Weiss tweeted that the panel seemed to actually be about "dismantling *accusations* of antisemitism."[19]

These events are a reminder that when you are up against adversaries that are resourced to the tune of hundreds of millions of dollars more than what you have access to, there are still ways to move the conversation where you want it to go. In planning these events, which JVP decided to do proactively, we knew that we were going to be sent headlong into the horrific spin and accusations of the right. The backlash often brings publicity and buzz, drawing more eyes and ears to your message. Yet, it also takes an emotional toll. It can be confusing to ascertain if it's all worth it. It is tricky to measure exactly how many people changed their thinking due to these events, if the exhaustion exacerbated the depletion of your staff, or if it was ultimately galvanizing. But those headaches and hardships need to be taken in tandem with the rewards. Through these events, the leaders we want to speak more publicly on our issues are challenged to articulate what they believe and why, when so many reporters are calling for comments or social media posts go viral. These events were an excuse to huddle and strategize together with organizations outside our most intimate circle, pushing ourselves out of our comfort zones. The confrontations serve as a reinforcement of the importance of coalition and team, a chance to remember that at the bedrock of our social movements are real, strong relationships. In the lead-up to and in the wake of these events, having to push yourself to keep at it, you get a reminder that you have to keep on showing up because you want to change the world and be changed yourself, not simply to demand of others that they bend to your will.

One of the six guiding principles at JVP reads: "Foundational to our work for justice and peace is believing people, organizations, and communities are dynamic. We create space for people to move and transform."[20] Even when it seems that things are stuck or at a dead end, this principle reminds us that we must, as a matter of our own integrity, leave room for dynamism. By creating spaces for that transformation to take place, you are given a chance not just to live into your principles but also to move forward your political goals—the most precious of wins.

Dismantling Antisemitism

We believe the work to realize Palestinian freedom requires dismantling all forms of oppression, including antisemitism. Especially as there are millions of dollars being spent to confuse us and desensitize us to actual antisemitism in order to shield Israel from criticism, a core challenge for our work becomes how to claim our rightful place as leaders in the fight against real antisemitism even as we refuse to accept the codification of the dangerously false equation of anti-Zionism with antisemitism. We believe that understanding antisemitism, as with all forms of oppression, is essential for all freedom fighters today.

Antisemitism isn't a virus, it isn't a tide, it isn't a force of nature, it isn't a permanent fixture of the world—it's a political tool that gets used to divide us.[21] And it is made by humans, so that means it can be unmade by humans. Antisemitism can end, and it must.

Organizing Strategy Reflection Questions

Fighting Antisemitism
and Its Weaponization

1. How well prepared do you feel to distinguish between real antisemitism and bad-faith attempts to shield Israel from criticism through false charges of antisemitism? What work might you need to do to educate yourself and your people in order to understand antisemitism?

2. Regardless of what movement you work within, how do you orient your organizing and political education to reinforce the need for solidarity and community safety for all people?

3. If you are organizing your own community against nationalism, how do you account for and respond to the myths and emotions that already exist within it in a way that allows you to build your base more widely? How can you structure your political education work to counter powerful flawed messaging?

4. What do you do to take care of yourself and your folks when faced with vitriol, attack, or backlash, especially when it is racist, antisemitic, Islamophobic, sexist, or transphobic?

Chapter 5

Nurturing
Movement Partnerships

While coalition work animated just about every facet of JVP's strategy and actions, the reality of working in coalitions and with partners is dynamic and messy—constantly evolving. This is another place of both/and: it's about building long-term trust and relationships, based on common values, and sometimes it's about bringing partnerships to an end. It's about having a clear approach and strategy and adjusting joint work to accommodate changing political circumstances, JVP's needs, and those of our partners. In this chapter, after looking at a peak moment of partnership, we will share four hard-learned best practices for coalition building: maintaining principled boundaries, learning from missteps, playing specific roles that may push you out of your comfort zone, and offering support without exerting control.

Vision for Black Lives Platform

The Vision for Black Lives platform was released in the summer of 2016 by the Movement for Black Lives (M4BL). An extraordinary document, developed over the course of more than a year by a coalition of more than fifty Black-led organizations, it presented a comprehensive policy vision from those leading the resistance to ongoing structural and state violence against Black people in this country. The platform encompasses detailed policy briefs and proposals in six broad categories, backed up by data, sources of organizational expertise, and legislative models. One paragraph of the platform addressed the oppression of Palestinians as a racial justice issue, endorsed BDS, and called what is happening to the Palestinian people a genocide. The response of Jewish communities, from liberal groups to the far right, was immediate and extreme. At a moment when the most exciting and powerful call for racial justice in decades was being released, almost every Jewish organization turned against the M4BL. Devastatingly, to this day there are reverberations from this stance regarding both funding and support. The reaction from the pro-Israel Jewish establishment turned the public conversation about the platform into one about Jewish communities and antisemitism instead of about the comprehensive and liberatory vision for Black people in this country that is needed, in the process erasing the existence of people who are both Black and Jewish.

Within JVP we knew immediately that we needed to help disrupt the emerging narrative coming out of the mainstream and liberal Jewish community. JVP endorsed the platform without qualification, and the JOCSM Caucus wrote a statement in solidarity with the M4BL. It read, in part:

> As a caucus we fully endorse the Movement for Black Lives Platform in its entirety without reservation. We do this first and foremost because it was created as "a response to the sustained and increasingly visible violence against Black communities in the U.S. and globally." This fact

must be foregrounded in all discussions of the Platform, which was created to protect Black Lives.[1]

This was a moment when JVP's Jewish identity was significant. JVP and the JOCSM Caucus's interventions made a difference. By intervening in the public debate, we were able, at least, to interrupt and complicate the harmful and inaccurate emerging narrative that the M4BL was ignoring Jewish concerns.

Since its founding, JVP has been a force to shatter the myth of Jewish consensus around Israel, and this was another moment to highlight that the concerns coming from legacy Jewish institutions were, in fact, not Jewish concerns but Zionist concerns. So, this moment was not just about showing up for partners under attack but was also an opportunity to decouple Judaism from Zionism, which was emerging then as a core political goal of JVP. Yet again, JVP prioritized our values—in this case, transnational solidarity and liberating Judaism from Zionism—over alignment with the mainstream Jewish world. Key moments like this one face every movement, and the decision—whether to try to push the paradigm of what is possible by going beyond current communal norms or to go only as far as you think your community will permit you to go—needs to be both guided by core values and based on strategic goals, your role in the overall ecosystem of a movement, and the stakes of the moment. In this case, JVP's standing in solidarity with the M4BL when the Jewish mainstream attacked it brought more Jews into our orbit. They were put off by the mainstream Jewish communities' hijacking of this crucial moment for the M4BL, as well as the tone policing and erasure of Jews of color. Even though in the leadership of JVP we knew this action would deepen the chasm between us and legacy Jewish communities—in fact, we were told so directly by leaders of some of their organizations—we understood that the reason we were building power was exactly for moments like these. JVP was building mass Jewish opposition to Zionism in order to leverage it in support of our allies. Therefore, our primary consideration was not legitimacy within the eyes of the mainstream Jewish community but whether we were successfully supporting our partners and allies with whom we share values.

Values are how to figure out who your partners are in the first place. Especially when working in a solidarity stance, there needs to be clarity about exactly whom you are accountable to. It is insufficient to just say "Palestinians" or "Black people" when you get to the brass-tacks work of designing campaigns. The partners you work alongside are those with whom you share politics, yes, but most important, with whom you share principles and political approach. The two of us think of values as the way you know which organizations and people you want to take political direction from and provide political support to. During our time at JVP, our values included a commitment to transnational solidarity; an anti-oppression and anti-apartheid framework; and dedication to full equality and grassroots leadership of Palestinians, as well as liberating Judaism from Zionism. In this instance, beyond those overarching commitments, we also saw a more specific set of shared values in the M4BL policy platforms: the urgency of protecting Black lives; linking the issue of justice for Palestinians to the issue of justice for all people; rooting organizing in clear, actionable policies won through leveraging grassroots power; building broad coalitions that develop clear vision and practical strategy through iterative discussion and debate; a deep belief in the possibility of transformation and the capacity for people to change; moral courage to speak your truth, no matter how unpopular it might be; and support for the Palestinian-led call for BDS.

Living your values is harder than it sounds. The day-to-day work comes fast and furious, and it can be hard to pause and consider how your everyday decisions reflect your values. As a smaller organization in which everyone has built the framework together, it was relatively easy for people to feel a sense of ownership. But, as we grew, we realized we needed to train ourselves and everyone else to practice a level of attentiveness to values as we made even routine decisions. By creating filters that centered our ultimate goals, we were able to integrate into our infrastructure a facsimile of the organic processes that characterized our decision-making when we were smaller and more centralized.[2]

In many ways, supporting the M4BL policy platform paralleled and was an extension of the decision to endorse the BDS call. We knew that there was a significant proportion of Jewish people who wanted to support the Palestinian call for BDS, which was not reflected by the actions of any Jewish institutions, just as, at times, large legacy LGBTQ institutions have not been attentive to trans rights, or large conservation organizations don't apply a climate justice frame. Because JVP is an organization founded to bring the once marginal voice of American Jews in solidarity with Palestine to the center, this moment felt like an affirmation and reminder of why JVP is needed. Endorsing the M4BL policy platform without reservation was not just the right thing to do ethically but the smart thing to do strategically, given our goal of organizing American Jews in solidarity with Palestine. In light of the majority of the American Jewish communities' repressive and racist response to the policy platform, our embrace of it stood out to those who likewise felt called to embrace it.

This remains one of our proudest moments. Reflection on how easy the decision was, based on our values, and how swiftly we acted, reinforces how important it is, in any movement, to have clarity and alignment on your values and red lines, developed in moments of relative calm. That enables you to act swiftly in moments of crisis. JVP used the political capital we had accumulated as a growing force in Jewish communities in a moment when it was needed, and there was no other American Jewish group that could play that role. In this case, our values guided us to the most precious of rewards: consciously sharpening our politics, showing up for partners who were under attack, and deepening relationships with the Black-led organizations leading the fight for racial justice in the United States.[3]

Coalition Work—Messy but Crucial

Not every story of partnership is as clear cut as our work to flank and support the Vision for Black Lives. It's hard to describe in exciting terms what it's like to work in coalition. Mostly it entails lots of meetings and check-ins. There's a reason for that: communication between partners in a coalition has to be clear, ongoing, and take into account the different roles and responsibilities everyone brings with them. In the most highly functioning coalitions we were part of, each partner brought different focuses, expertise, geographic reach, or constituencies to the table, making the whole larger than the sum of its parts. Smaller organizations benefited from gaining national reach, and, as a national organization, we benefited from the participation of groups that had less reach but deeper relationships and expertise in particular areas. In addition to coalitions that formed around campaigns or projects, we tended toward ongoing relationships with varying sets of organizations in the different organizing worlds we straddled. Campaigns were a primary vehicle for building and enacting these relationships, times during which we deepened those partnerships and really unleashed their power and potential. When we built out campaigns jointly with partners, it meant JVP was prioritizing intersectional framing, targets, and wins.

Whether in the short or long term, we found that we needed to be intentional and proactive about collaboration and coordination. We developed protocols for checking in regularly with core partners before taking work in a new direction. This ethos of collaborative work was part of JVP's solidarity praxis and an expression of our commitment to organizing. While JVP wasn't simply a solidarity organization, since we set our own strategies, we also strove to be consultative and receptive to feedback. At times, our efforts to get feedback were clunky, conducted in formats that made it hard for critical feedback to be heard; at other times, we could have relied on our previously articulated commitments or requests from partners without burdening them to offer ongoing feedback once a foundation of trust was in place. Despite these flaws, our feedback processes were fundamental to staying on track and integrating accountability into our work.

The very act of entering into coalitions was a manifestation of JVP's orientation that our work was most powerful when placed in the context of a broader left. We prioritized our relationships with Palestinian partners specifically, because we were a Jewish organization with an understanding that Palestinians have to lead in the fight for Palestinian liberation. This was made much easier by the existence of the BDS movement, which offered clear guidelines and conditions for effective solidarity. Given the ascendance of BDS as a core strategy to pursue in solidarity with Palestinians, coupled with the enormous pushback it received as it began to gain steam, the Palestinian BDS National Committee (BNC), the governing body of the BDS movement, became a priority partner for us. Our deepest and longest-term partnerships were founded on a set of shared politics that included support for the BDS movement; an anti-oppression analysis that included, in particular, opposition to settler colonialism, anti-Blackness, Islamophobia, and antisemitism; and a belief in the power of the grassroots to end complicity and realize change toward freedom, justice, and accountability. We had a set of national relationships with Palestinian-focused organizations in the US that remained relatively steady over time.[4] While we would come together in changing configurations for specific campaigns, projects, sign-on letters, or other efforts, the relationships were of long duration and steady enough that trust, history, and personal connections were built over time. This allowed us to be able to talk with fluency and familiarity about strategy, funding sources, emerging issues, and challenges. JVP also maintained a set of relationships with organizations leading other movements, including immigrant rights, the M4BL, Indigenous organizations, and anti-Islamophobia groups. On occasion, as in the Vision for Black Lives example, JVP was called upon to defend and protect leaders of these movements who were falsely accused of antisemitism or to signal-boost and participate in their actions and campaigns. These relationships allowed us to draw on the common values we shared and were the elements of what shaped up to be an emerging left bloc.

Coalitions don't just exist at the national level. Whether it was campus chapters taking up divestment campaigns targeting student governments or community chapters passing human rights resolutions in city councils, JVP chapters were part of local coalitions that combined their power to great success. National policies can have lasting and undesirable impacts on local relationships and coalitions. We found that policies that create as much space as possible for collaboration are essential, and reviewing them and onboarding local members outside of rapid response mobilizations is key. We also sought to work in coalition with values-aligned elements of the US Jewish left, though our relationships with the Palestinian rights movement and US Jewish communities were calibrated differently. With Palestinian organizations, we were always finding a place in a movement that was ultimately theirs. With other Jewish organizations, we may have had a more natural sense of ownership and place, but even our closest relationships entailed an inherent element of political challenge. In other words, we never really had a Jewish organization that we were in complete alignment with, which made it harder to build trust and ongoing projects together.

Joy Is Our Sorrow Unmasked

In 2017, at our NMM in Chicago, which takes place over Shabbat, we embraced the chance to live in the Jewishness so many of us long for, to revel in knowing the Jews we are surrounded by share our vision for a liberated Palestine. A rare and precious occasion! As part of the Friday evening opening event, we brought klezmer musicians in our membership together into an impromptu band to play celebratory music for us to begin the weekend.[5] The stakes of the weekend were not lost on us. For one, it would be the first gathering at this scale of the secular Jewish non- and anti-Zionist left, with more than a thousand registrants. The afternoon before it began, the Israeli Strategic Ministry issued a statement condemning our event because we were hosting Rasmea Odeh, a respected Chicago-area Palestinian American community organizer and longtime activist for justice, who was being deported by the US after a decades-long battle with the Israeli and US judicial systems. She was indicted in US federal court for failing to disclose on her naturalization forms twenty years earlier that she had been convicted of participation in a 1969 bombing on the basis of a false confession, obtained under torture in the Israeli military court system, which has a conviction rate of more than 99 percent. After many decades as a central community leader in Chicago, just a few weeks after our NMM she would be leaving forever. Our hosting her felt like an important opportunity to honor her before she departed, and we knew it would bring extra attention and scrutiny to the event and attract more Palestinians than our previous membership meetings had. Given our invitation to Rasmea, alongside other contemporary political luminaries including Nick Estes, Linda Sarsour, Diana

Buttu, Robin D. G. Kelley, Rachel Gilmer, Dima Khalidi, and Judith Butler, among others, our NMM took on more of a feel of a movement-wide conference than a space specifically for Jewish anti-Zionist cultural expression. But, for our membership, it was still the same unique and beautiful, infrequent chance to be together that had grown so precious to us.

As the klezmer music echoed through the hotel and we swarmed into rings of dancing as you might find at a Jewish wedding or bat mitzvah, many of the Palestinian attendees were taken aback. As we heard later, the dancing and singing landed for some Palestinians in attendance as an affront.[6] Here we were, finding joy and building community from a source that was ultimately built on Palestinians' pain of dispossession and struggle for liberation yet unrealized. This response from our Palestinian allies was both jarring and understandable. Much of the time, our work is backbreaking and frustrating, and we are joyful to have found each other in our shared commitment to Palestinian liberation. But we understood the uncomfortable truth that our joy in this context is built on the backs of Palestinians' suffering. When Palestinians continue to have their homes demolished, rights stripped away, movement restricted, and identities denied, among other vulgarities of apartheid, it is understandably difficult to stomach Jews rejoicing in the midst of it all. Ultimately, no matter how close we were as allies, partners, and comrades, this was a moment in which our different experiences couldn't be reconciled. That said, we recall making an internal commitment to ensuring that, going forward, gatherings focused on building Jewish community be held in JVP-only spaces rather than more movement-wide venues like this one was. In this work there are all too few moments of unqualified victory or sense of satisfaction. We have to create those for ourselves, in order to maintain our ability to keep going. This festive klezmer parade was a chance for us Jews, going against the grain of our own communities, to

feel a sense of joy, connection, and possibility amid our own chosen community. It was a chance to tap into the rhythms that sustained some of our ancestors, who likewise carved out moments
of joy in otherwise grueling lives. There were so many reasons to
be in our joy at that moment. These moments are the glue that
binds us together, recharging our batteries for the ongoing fights
and the inevitable pushback we will receive. Our rage and pain at
what Israel is doing led us to each other, and that is its own cause
for celebration. The poet Kahlil Gibran captures the spirit of the
kind of joy that we felt that night:

> Then a woman said, Speak to us of Joy and Sorrow.
> And he answered:
> Your joy is your sorrow unmasked.
> And the selfsame well from which your laughter rises
>   was oftentimes filled with your tears.
> And how else can it be?
> The deeper that sorrow carves into your being, the more
>   joy you can contain.

The sorrow the two of us feel at what Israel is doing, ostensibly
in our names, to Palestinians is the root of the power of the joy
we feel as we tap into our tradition in order to keep going in
the work to abolish Zionism, end Israeli apartheid, and liberate
Judaism from Zionism. It was because of the sorrow and shame
we feel at Palestinian dispossession that we could connect to
the joy of finding each other, comrades and fellow travelers who
share that vision, against all odds. As Gibran captures, our joy is
only known because of the immensity of our sorrow.

Articulating JVP's Accountability to Palestinians

JVP's legitimacy in the broader movement for Palestinian
liberation is largely dependent on Palestinians/Palestinian

organizations giving us their blessing. We got the buy-in we needed from Palestinian partners through sustained consultation. But that doesn't mean Palestinian groups have decision-making power in our organizational decisions. Those of us on staff would ask for feedback on our plans large and small, but there wasn't a specific or mutually agreed upon way that feedback was used. We relied on the ongoing exchange inherent to authentic relationships, our partners offered their feedback trusting we would take it seriously and integrate it into our work as made sense. One key reason the relationships usually worked was because, as a matter of principle, we did not seek to set political horizons or demands but responded to those that came from Palestinians. We also made efforts to center and include Palestinian voices where there were none, acting as a bridge to get Palestinians access to tables and rooms with more political power. This wasn't always emotionally comfortable, we didn't always do it perfectly, but by and large it was understood and appreciated by JVP's Palestinian allies.

Beginning in 2016, JVP set out to codify an articulation of our accountability to Palestinians as a set of principles that would serve as a guide for our organizing as part of our unique solidarity framework. Up to that point, organizationally, we had been operating on a set of commonly understood but not explicitly spelled-out principles. By 2016, we had welcomed thousands of new members, dozens of chapters, and many new staff, which spurred us to articulate clearly how we collectively understood something as fundamental as our approach to being accountable to Palestinians. This process was part of the organizational life stage we were in, needing to take things from being informal and unwritten for a small group to being formalized and shared with a wider group. Often, in organizing, principles and practices are transferred passively, but that runs the risk of the nuances slipping through the cracks and, over time, being lost. Especially when trying to create a consistent organizational culture, putting things down on paper is critical. That was the logic, as the process to codify our accountability to Palestinians began.

Consulting with Palestinian Partners

Naturally, the first step of drafting our guidelines for working accountably with Palestinians was to consult Palestinians! A staff team surveyed more than fifty Palestinian leaders and had conversations with thirty Palestinians whom we had worked with closely over the years, in the US, Europe, and Palestine. They offered feedback on the resulting first draft of our principles as it was in process. There were also multiple internal discussions among staff and board. The result was a document that included a forthright articulation of JVP's accountability to Palestinians for the first time. It read:

> Our accountability to Palestinian partners is an ongoing process: of deep listening, continual relationship-building and genuine reassessment. It is a set of discrete actions we take: it's how we check in, set strategy, share resources, and take action together. We take responsibility for our work and its impact and therefore do it in consistent communication and relationship with Palestinian partners who share our values for a future of equality and justice.
>
> Part of this process is being open to criticism and critique of our methods and goals, and a willingness to change our actions and plans in response. It also requires acknowledging the power dynamics of our relationships given the imbalance of power in the world at large, specifically the privileging of Jewish voices and the way that

White supremacy, racism, and Islamophobia underlies [*sic*] these dynamics.

Accountability insists we take responsibility for making decisions and for developing new strategies; it means we recognize the need to take accountable action and bring about change, especially within Jewish communities. We consult with our Palestinian partners on questions of strategy and impact but direct our own day-to-day work. Accountability means that we choose action over fear of making mistakes, and that we have a duty to do the best and most impactful work we can. Accountability is a network of relationships built at the many layers and components of our organization, relationships based on a process of continuous communication and trust that account for, and work to dismantle, unjust power dynamics.

Feeling pleased with the process and outcome, we shared a draft of the statement for feedback and discussion at the NMM in 2017 in Chicago. Presented at a workshop at the NMM, the document was not well received by a sizable segment of Palestinians in our circles who were in attendance. They were reluctant to endorse the recommendations and next steps in the working definition until we got feedback from a far wider set of Palestinian society—in Palestine and throughout the diaspora. The concerns raised with the document were about both substance and process. Some felt the circle we reached out to was too small and not representative and broad enough to reach a threshold of consensus or affirmation. Given the fragmentation in Palestinian community across political and geographic lines, there was concern that the approach amounted to choosing a side in a debate that was intra-Palestinian and not JVP's to refine or control. The points of contention included tensions between

Palestinians living in the diaspora and those on the ground in Palestine, those who employed a human rights framing or a more anti-imperialist approach, those who advocate for a one-state or two-state endgame, among others. There were also hesitations about the design of the survey and concerns that the process being led by JVP made it feel unsafe, or at least uncomfortable, for participants to share their real feelings. Some asserted that whatever feedback we got was just going to be tepid and not actually represent a real affirmation of our proposals.

Unwittingly yet unsurprisingly, intercommunal conflict inside the Palestinian American community was playing out on our doorstep. The sensitivities and insecurities of the lack of unified political leadership and organization among Palestinians in the US came to the fore. At a meeting in which we brought together Palestinian leaders to discuss the proposal, one person quipped, "Only JVP could bring this many Palestinians together!" The joke stung, as it was a reflection of the fragmentation among Palestinians and JVP's outsized power. Of course, the Palestinian community is not a monolith and has been riven by its own internal debates about desired tactics, strategies, and outcomes. JVP's attempts to codify our accountabilities illuminated not only those divides but also how our alliances impacted the movement ecosystem. While we had a core relationship with the BNC, they were based in Palestine, as was the civil society umbrella they brought together, so even the BNC was not sufficient to represent Palestinians worldwide beyond the specific issue of BDS as a way to demonstrate meaningful solidarity with the Palestinian liberation struggle. The fact that there is no unified body of leadership that Palestinians say represents them made JVP's solidarity harder to orient and more susceptible to criticism when it came to clarifying accountabilities.

As leaders, we had to actively make choices about which organizations we built trusting relationships with and which we asked for feedback, and the same was true for chapter leaders throughout the country working with local partners. Organizationally, we gravitated toward partners who shared our values and approach (a commitment to transnational solidarity; an anti-oppression and anti-apartheid framework; dedication to full equality and grassroots leadership of Palestinians; an understanding of the role of organizing), and those relationships deepened the more we worked together and built trust. The rationale for JVP's soliciting feedback from Palestinians ourselves, rather than collaborating with Palestinians on collecting feedback from the get-go, was that we didn't want to put the onus on Palestinians to do this labor for us. But the impact was that some Palestinians felt our process was just another way that JVP's outsized power and influence in the movement meant that we were controlling the boundaries of accountability, and that our choice of people and organizations to consult was skewing the result. This was yet another example of the ongoing balancing act JVP was navigating as part of our solidarity stance. We wanted input from Palestinians as to how, as allies, we should show up for them, while also believing that we should bring our own expertise into how we organize in Jewish communities.

As a leadership team, we decided to go back to the drawing board, and this time hired a consultant to take the lead, in collaboration with two Palestinian staff members, in the dissemination of a survey to Palestinian leaders of the Palestine solidarity/liberation movement about JVP's accountability processes. The second round succeeded in reaching a hundred respondents and resulted in a report that detailed various recommendations for JVP including that JVP focus on targeting Zionism explicitly, practical suggestions for sharing resources, and preferred practices for staff, chapters, and members for developing relationships with Palestinians locally, nationally, and in Palestine. This second process was not without its critics, either. Some Palestinians involved with the first round felt frustrated by the concerns raised and the insistence on doing the process over again. This is a reminder about the multivocality within the Palestinian community and was a familiar internal family feud, much like the ones we often found ourselves in with our fellow Jews!

Movement Partnership Best Practices

Collaborating with organizations inside the broader movement ecosystem is a delicate dance. With some organizations, the dance is fluid and seamless; with others, there is a lot of confusion as to who is leading and an inevitable stepping on toes. Here, we share some best practices for nurturing movement partnerships over time.

1. Intentionality in Your Accountabilities

As the above description of JVP's process of articulating our accountabilities to our most core partners illustrates, the process of being in an accountable relationship is nonlinear. The important thing is to approach the partnerships with intention. Upon reflection, the two of us have identified a set of lessons learned for approaching relationships of solidarity with intention.

As an overarching principle, the primary obligation is **attentiveness to relationships**. This may seem obvious, but it is important to reinforce. Maintaining relationships for ongoing communication and consultation to ensure that your work is in harmony with the work of partner organizations is the single most important element of maintaining relationships for the long haul. This requires being willing to work more slowly if it means bringing more organizations along with you, and placing relationships above immediate action.

Part of that attentiveness entails **conscientiousness about not attempting to set the political direction**. Even as you are stretching to enable your own community to push their politics forward, the political direction of the movement must be set by those directly impacted. This includes being careful to democratize your collaborations and partnerships to avoid unwittingly selecting the representative for the movement as a whole. Especially when there is not a clear entity offering movement-wide leadership, you need to be sensitive to not elevating one group as the de facto leader for the movement as a whole. This is part of the obligation to **stay in (or return to) your lane as part of the movement ecosystem**. At JVP, as one of the largest, if not the largest, organizations in the US movement, we often found ourselves taking on movement-wide campaigns that were not specific to our core goals. This tendency was both about our actual relative capacity as well as our at times arrogant assumption that we were necessary to make the campaign a success. Eventually, we realized that we not only were spreading ourselves too thin but also weren't spending enough energy on the areas where we could be the most impactful. In the process, by throwing our weight around, we were annoying at best or alienating of our partners at worst. Ensure that your campaigns draw up the strengths of the unique constituency you bring to the table, rather than being a campaign for any and all in a movement to join. When we did our best work, we chose campaigns to which we could make a specific contribution, which were powerful on-ramps for those new to the movement and provided tangible ways to ensure the conversation about Palestine was ongoing and organizing skills were being built.

The accountability process is iterative, requiring **soliciting, listening to, and integrating critical feedback** on an ongoing basis. There were plenty of tense moments with Palestinian partners over time—it is inevitable in any relationship, let alone one that is overlaid with the tensions and unequal power between Jews and Palestinians in the rest of the world. But, no matter what, we kept showing up to do the work. Our partners saw that we were not going to abandon them when things got hard, and that mattered. Especially when mistakes are made, it is crucial to seek to understand and repair through listening and then to integrate, in refreshed practices, the lessons learned. That process of feedback integration ensures that **your actions match your words**. When Palestinian leaders came under ruthless and relentless attack with false charges of antisemitism, we had their backs. It wasn't just about saying the right things but also backing up those words with actions. Our partners saw us stretching and pushing through the campaigns we chose and fights we picked, and that mattered a lot.

2. Principled Boundaries

The work of coalition building is the day-to-day work of movement building. For JVP, coalitional work was about values alignment with a broad range of partners and collaborators more than coalescing with a broad range of groups around a narrow political issue. In other words, we prioritized building relationships with other movements that shared our values rather than with organizations that shared our outlook on Palestinian rights but operated from a different set of values. This led JVP, for example, to ally with the M4BL but not with the Neturei Karta, an organization of religious anti-Zionist Jews who were also deeply patriarchal and homophobic. JVP was conscious of its role in the broader left, and the importance of building and supporting a broad left ecosystem that integrated Palestinian freedom into it.

During the 2015 strategic planning process, our team articulated a set of six guiding principles that endured throughout our tenure as guideposts in our work:[7]

- GRASSROOTS ORGANIZING, LEADERSHIP DEVELOPMENT, AND RELATIONSHIPS
- THE CAPACITY FOR PEOPLE TO CHANGE
- SOLIDARITY AND ACCOUNTABILITY
- RESPECT FOR THE HUMANITY OF ALL PEOPLE
- JEWISH COMMUNITIES CENTERED AROUND JUSTICE
- FLEXIBILITY AND TENACITY FOR THE LONG HAUL

While there was no fixed method for assessing alignment with other organizations on these principles, at baseline there was a commitment to not working with those whose approaches undermined any of these principles.

At times, JVP was at odds with organizations with which others in our movement partnered, and took action to cut ties. An example occurred in 2015, when JVP took the unusual step of cutting ties with the organization If Americans Knew (IAK) and its founder and leader.[8] IAK frequently appeared publicly with white supremacists, Holocaust deniers, and anti-Jewish and anti-gay Christians. Their positions were a clear and flagrant transgression of our principles, contradicting one of our core values: the opposition to racism in all its forms. IAK never disavowed, debated, or challenged the thinking of any of those people when they engaged in conversation or made any public commitments to no longer engage with those people. Because IAK at that time was often asked to speak or cosponsor events alongside JVP at movement conferences, it was essential to cut ties with IAK out of principle.

3. Learning from Missteps

In 2009, as divestment campaigns were just starting to take shape on college campuses, JVP learned an early lesson on the challenges of navigating how to step forward and step back as needed. At UC–Berkeley, those opposed to divestment claimed antisemitism and pointed to the hurt feelings of Jewish students who felt attacked by calls to divest the university's assets from companies profiting from the Israeli occupation of Palestine. At that time, Jewish voices for divestment were mostly unheard of, nowhere near as commonplace as they are today, so it seemed a smart strategy to foreground Jewish voices in support of divestment at the student senate hearing. As a result, much of the hearing was taken up by dueling Jewish voices. In the debrief meeting after a public comment session, the folks who were there learned that the impact of that decision was a feeling of frustration by our Palestinian comrades. In a sincere effort to support Palestinian calls for divestment, we inadvertently sidelined Palestinians' voices, making the debate about Palestine and Palestinians into a debate to be negotiated between Jews. The attempts to frame it as primarily a Jewish communal issue took us away from the core principle that Palestinians must be able to speak for themselves about issues of human rights and justice that affect them—even if it comes at the cost of Jews' feelings. Learning that lesson early on was valuable, as that experience became a cautionary tale that staff retold to ourselves and referenced with Palestinian comrades to gauge if we were erring on the right or wrong side of the line between subverting Palestinian voices and helpfully challenging a frame of "all Jews oppose divestment." Unfortunately, there is no actual gauge to alert us when we get out of range, so relationships of trust and open channels of communication with allies are necessary to give feedback as well as the need to develop our own internal sense of boundaries.

4. Playing the Role That Only You Can (Even When It's Uncomfortable)

At Presbyterian Church USA's General Assemblies, where church leaders gather biennially to set church policy, an uncomfortable pattern emerged. In the committee meetings in which resolutions relating to Israel/Palestine were being debated, the speakers' list during open hearings was dominated by Jewish voices. For hours at a time, Jews would take to the podium, one after the other, either to support or malign the resolutions being proposed. JVP members, invited by our allies—the Israel/Palestine Mission Network (IPMN) of the Presbyterian Church (USA), who had successfully organized to bring the divestment resolution that far—would speak up and applaud church members for finding the courage to align their values with their investments. Upholding a pro/con pattern, we were followed by representatives from the local Jewish Community Relations Council (JCRC), who would take the podium to claim that support of this resolution was a betrayal of the Presbyterians' Jewish friends and would compromise the delicate interfaith friendships they enjoy in their local community. These threats began before the convening; we heard from many pastors that, in the months leading up to the vote, rabbis and other local Jewish leaders would visit their offices to bully them into voting against divestment or risk being labeled an antisemite.

In 2012 at the Pittsburgh General Assembly, Rabbi Abraham Cooper of the Simon Wiesenthal Center got his turn at the mic and elicited a horrified gasp from the room when he told the committee that the young JVP speakers were "not real Jews." It backfired—the vote went against him in committee, and the divestment resolution moved to the plenary floor.[9] The spectacle was dizzying, and surely it was confusing for the delegates tasked with deciding whether or not to recommend divestment. It was a show we have come to think of as "intra-Jewish conflict theater," where the disagreements within Jewish communities were put on display as an awkward form of entertainment for the Presbyterians gathered to debate their internal resolutions. Jewish speakers from opposing sides would never speak to each other directly, but instead hurled insults or undermined the other's authority in front of this third party.

And, while there would also be Palestinians in the mix at the podium, the impact of this theater was to recast a conversation on solidarity with Palestinians through divestment from American companies profiting from the Israeli occupation as a question primarily about Jewish communities. Because of Islamophobia and anti-Palestinian racism (as we detail in the "continuum of repression" in chapter 8), leaving the debate to the mainstream Jews present, who claimed to speak for all, would mean forfeiting the possibility of Presbyterians taking a bold action that would have ripple effects of impact throughout the socially responsible investment world and other mainline Christian denominations. The human rights violations and the US financial backing for Israel's system of oppression were reason enough for US Christians to take up this issue on their own, but if they needed our voices to push them over the edge to vote their conscience despite the threats, it was important for us to be there to voice them, so we put on our show.

In retrospect, given the complex history and the ongoing experience of living under Christian dominance in the US, we feel there was indignity to this theater for us as Jews, bringing our intra-Jewish conflicts to that venue, unable to resolve them on our own. This theater also served to reinforce the problematic idea that Palestinian liberation is about Jews, when in fact it is about colonialism. But there is also a more redemptive way to look at it—that these venues offered us the chance to express ourselves and be heard by those willing to hear us, even if our fellow Jews were not.

5. Offering Support, Not Control

In 2011, the American Friends Service Committee (AFSC) and JVP noticed that Students for Justice in Palestine (SJP) chapters were growing in number on college campuses, and student leaders were seeking more training and support on campaigning.[10] As organizations with resources and staff experienced in organizing, we thought we could offer support to SJPs with their practical skill building as they ramped up their organizing and divestment campaigns. Campuses are incubators for profound organizing, where peers—across cultures and in the process of growth and expansion—explore ideas and practice building and exercising power. The movement for Palestinian rights has a long history on campuses, beginning in the 1950s with the formation of the General Union of Palestinian Students (GUPS). At the onset of the Second Intifada, in 2000, SJP chapters began to form, revitalizing a student movement that had lost momentum in the 1990s, coalescing over the coming decades into National Students for Justice in Palestine (NSJP), a collective of organizers that support more than two hundred Palestine solidarity organizations on college campuses across the country. Beginning around 2010, JVP chapters began to form on college campuses, as did Jewish organizing spaces intentionally forming in partnership with preexisting SJP chapters. Over the course of the first two decades of the twenty-first century, student activism on campus became a key battleground for the fight for Palestinian rights.

Beginning in fall 2011, JVP and AFSC teamed up to fund and lead weeklong training sessions for student leaders, collaborating on agenda setting and logistics, sharing the costs for the gathering itself between our organizations. At first, the trainings were focused on bringing the "We Divest" campaign (targeting retirement fund giant TIAA-CREF to divest from companies profiting from the Israeli occupation) to campuses, but, over the years, they expanded to mounting all types of BDS campaigns.[11] Staff from JVP and AFSC brought together students from campuses coast to coast for workshops to build their skills around topics such as group building and sustainability, Divestment

101, BDS and nonviolence, legal issues, communications and media, intersectionality and joint struggle, dealing with racism and Islamophobia, and strategies for sustaining divestment wins. It was also a space to build relationships and connect across schools, with a focus on linking campuses regionally for coordinated action during the academic year. NSJP leaders were part of developing the program alongside AFSC and JVP staff. We also brought in leaders from partner organizations to co-facilitate the workshop sessions according to their expertise.

In 2013, the group of organizations involved in the trainings evolved into a more formal structure to support student organizing. These organizations included the core set of groups we worked with on an ongoing basis: the AFSC, Palestine Legal, Institute for Middle East Understanding (IMEU), US Academic and Cultural Boycott of Israel (USACBI), and National Students for Justice in Palestine (NSJP). Each organization was in touch with student organizations in their own ways, so it made sense that we should meet on a regular basis to share what we were working on, to notice patterns across campuses, and to be a support to students. This "campus BDS support group" organized itself primarily to be a resource for students but also to be an efficiency for ourselves—by having one coordinated meeting, we saved ourselves hours of emails, texts, and phone calls. Each of our organizations was being asked to support the crises and opportunities on college campuses, and we were reaching out to one another ad hoc and without coordinating, so we decided it made sense to set a regular meeting time when coordination, strategizing, and delegation of responsibilities could take place. This was one of those times that an ecosystem approach really worked—each organization brought a particular focus, expertise, and role to offer the students that made it a convenient one-stop shop for all of us. As larger national organizations in the movement, it was also a way for us to share resources, including financial resources, with smaller groups that needed it. Moreover, it was a reflection of the larger Palestinians rights movement's prioritization of student work, a recognition of the centrality of student work in moving forward policy and culture change toward Palestinian freedom, and the importance of weathering the backlash students were increasingly experiencing on their campuses.

Four years into the Student Leadership Training and shortly after we coalesced as a campus BDS support group, a critique was brought to us by a handful of student leaders, voicing their frustration with what felt like an inappropriate overstep by professional nonprofit organizations into grassroots, student-led organizing. At the NSJP conference in 2014 at Stanford University, those of us in attendance from the coordinating group were summoned to a meeting during a break in programming. Student leaders voiced concerns that it was not the place of nonprofits to decide the strategies for student leaders or to decide on their behalf what training or education they needed. These critiques provided a chance for reflection on how we were approaching student work and to check our assumptions about what students do and don't know. It was a clear moment when the friction became apparent between being a movement and being a nonprofit.

The campus BDS support group had approached this project with the idea that we could help students ramp up their organizing by sharing lessons from historic divestment campaigns and our collective expertise. Through this call-in we realized that students want to lead creative processes and, in fact, often do want to reinvent the wheel, figuring out for themselves how to best do their work. It was an important reminder that their goal was not to be the most efficient but to do the work together and in a way that made sense for their group at that time. When we came in with a toolkit and a game plan, even if our intent was to be helpful, the impact was eclipsing their creativity and leadership.

NSJP had grown and built up a coordinated structure, and its members were ready to do the training and coordination on their own. The campus BDS support group shifted in response to this feedback. We developed more of a stance of "we are here if you need us," with a list of specific supports that students can reach out to us for if they want. We retooled how we related to student organizing, figuring out how to be a resource to those who needed support and wanted it from us, without overstepping student leadership. The training program continued for a few more years with support from our organizations, financial and practical, but led by students.

It is a delicate dance to navigate the boundaries of where each organization that is part of the movement can play the unique role they should play, while recognizing that none of the organizing we are doing happens in a vacuum. Students rightly demanded autonomy for their work but also needed the support of organizations to weather the intense pushback that they were increasingly experiencing. This campus BDS support network had a lot of the hallmarks of successful coalitions: a regular place for coordination and accountability, clear roles for all participants, and a structure that allows for each participant to play whatever roles they can, as their capacity allows. Coalition participation is not a one-size-fits-all endeavor. Some organizations will just show up, some will dedicate multiple staff people and thousands of dollars, some will pop in to do intensive support work when needed, and everything in between. We found that making room for that ebb and flow and variation was the key to unlocking a thriving and successful group collaborating over many years. The campus BDS support group's role evolved as these conditions did—issuing statements condemning the harmful tactics being deployed by Israel's defenders and providing strategic and emotional support to students. The coordination and cooperation across the movement in such a tangible and ongoing way felt like a real embodiment of JVP's principles and strategy coming together, making the most of JVP's particular expertise in our flowering movement.

The Reward Is Worth It

Our work in intentional collaboration with partners meant a constant reconfiguration of the way we used our voice, deployed our political power, took risks, and set organizational policies. It required constant vigilance, adjustment, deep listening, and mutual trust to continue to function over the long term. At its best, the reward is a thriving, multifaceted, mutually supportive movement, pushing together to realize freedom for us all.

Organizing Strategy Reflection Questions
Nurturing Movement Partnerships

1. Are your values and guiding principles articulated in such a way that they can be referenced and relied upon to clarify who should be your partners?

2. When you enter into coalitions, what work do you do to establish shared values and principles and to establish norms of communication and decision-making? Is everyone clear about what role they play in the coalition and why they are a part of it? What do you each need to do to build more trusting, authentic relationships?

3. What are your obligations or commitments to your long-term partners?

4. How do you articulate the difference between short-term joint work with ongoing partnerships? Are there unique political considerations for those occasional alliances, separate from those for long-standing partnerships?

5. If your organization has disproportionate power and visibility in relation to organizations run and led by those directly impacted by the issue you are organizing around, what practices do you have in place to share your knowledge and resources?

6. If you are a smaller organization in coalition with larger organizations, how will you approach entering into coalitions so that your own needs and goals are also met?

7. Who from outside your closest inner circle of partners do you want to feel both included in your decision-making processes and satisfied with the outcome?

8. If you are part of a solidarity movement, how do you balance affirming your own group culture and traditions with the priority of supporting the people whose liberation you are fighting for? Especially if your own people are complicit in this oppression, how will you build meaningful partnerships while maintaining your identity?

Chapter 6

Growing While
Sharpening Our Politics

W hen the two of us think back on our years at JVP, what
we are probably proudest of are the ways that we continued to sharpen our politics while also continuing to grow. This
is not an intuitive or conventional understanding of the way that
movement building usually goes. As movement organizations
get bigger, they often become more cautious. For us, the opposite
was true. It took both deliberate strategies and a bit of nerve,
considering the messages of concern—some in good faith and
some less so—about the potential for our internal collapse if we
pursued positions that were beyond where anyone else had gone.

There were numerous factors that made it possible not just to
sharpen JVP's politics but also to disseminate our values, organizational culture, institutional memory, and strategies and tactics
as we moved from being a small group, in which everyone knew
everyone, to an organization with dozens of staff, more than
sixty chapters, and almost twenty thousand members across the
country were working—sometimes fractiously, sometimes ele-
gantly—toward the same goal. This section looks at several key
inflection points when JVP made crucial political decisions and

built out new programs for maximum impact and growth. We look not just at the moments of decisions themselves but at the processes and principles behind them. Our hope is that examining them will be useful for others grappling with how to expand the reach of your organizations and movements without losing your principles.

Endorsing the Palestinian-Led Call for Boycott, Divestment, and Sanctions (BDS)

The story of how JVP came to make the decision to endorse the BDS call is emblematic of one of the elements of our time at JVP: even as we grew larger, we continued to challenge ourselves to sharpen our politics. We continued to evolve our understanding of the Palestinian freedom struggle, our responsibilities to it, and our role in moving it forward, even in the face of harsh opposition. We are particularly proud that JVP was able to make a significant and risky political shift without the organization falling apart, even as there were significant political differences in our membership. This achievement flies in the face of the conventional wisdom that, in order to grow, organizations must move to the center.

It is hard to exaggerate the red lines around supporting BDS in Jewish communities. Hillel, the national organization that is meant to be a home for Jewish students on campuses across the country, developed guidelines in 2010, long before JVP endorsed BDS, that were specifically formulated to exclude JVP members, based on our limited support of the tools of boycott and divestment.[1] The impact on JVP's status as part of Jewish communities, and the depth of the gut-wrenching personal struggles required of individual members to make this decision, would both be tremendous. At the time of this writing, JVP remains one of the only US-based Jewish organizations, and certainly the largest, that has endorsed the BDS call. For various financial, political, and emotional reasons, no other US Jewish group has yet found the courage or conviction to stand with Palestinians as they are asking the international community to do. The decision itself and its ramifications are what the public saw, but underneath the political nature of the decision was an edifice of carefully articulated values, interlocking structures of the roles of board, staff, chapters, and members, and a commitment to holding our political home together even as we made hard decisions.

JVP embraced economic-pressure campaigns even before it became a national organization, in about 2006, and began building a relationship with the Palestinian BNC), which governs the BDS movement, and partnering with organizations that were following the BDS call starting in about 2009. The realities of our broad, messy, beautiful collection of passionate members, who each brought their own stories and relationships to how they viewed BDS and JVP's strategic role and tactics, meant that it took us until 2015 to endorse what is known as the "full" BDS call, targeting not just the occupation but Israel's regime of oppression itself. JVP was committed to economic pressure as a tactic for ending the occupation, even predating the call for BDS by Palestinian civil society organizations in 2005, in part because our members and leaders had been part of successful economic-pressure campaigns in labor and civil rights organizing. As early as 2004, at that time as a small, Bay Area–based organization, JVP embarked on shareholder activism to pressure Caterpillar for its role in sustaining the occupation through producing special militarized bulldozers for Israel. But that was still far from embracing the full call, which also entailed aligning squarely with the Palestine solidarity movement and supporting the Palestinian right of return, in contrast to just about every other Jewish organization in the United States.

In the ensuing years, JVP ran BDS campaigns that were limited to targeting companies that profited from the occupation. The BNC continued to welcome us as part of the movement, as long as we didn't undermine the three demands stated in the BDS call (end the occupation and tear down the wall; full equality for Palestinian citizens of Israel; and right of return for Palestinian refugees) and didn't undermine campaigns that targeted Israel's settler-colonial regime itself.[2] During these years, we fiercely defended campaigns led by others that went beyond targeting the occupation, even though those campaigns were beyond our self-imposed limits. JVP leadership took our time reconsidering our in-between position. The press and Jewish organizations who opposed us already assumed that we supported the BDS call in full. Meanwhile, many of our closest allied organizations, especially those led by Palestinians, were feeling less and less patient with our position. Throughout those years, for example, our friends at Adalah-NY would invite us to join cultural boycott actions and events that we couldn't say yes to according to the guidelines we were operating under. They were always very kind about it when we said no, but they didn't stop asking, either. That form of gentle pressure, reminding us that we were disappointing our close allies each time we stuck to our own rules, was great agitation and a reminder to us of the costs imposed by our self-imposed limitations.

Many JVP members felt impatient with the limitations imposed on our campaigns at that time, while some others were concerned that, if we went farther, we would lose whatever legitimacy we had in broader Jewish communities and our ability to organize and recruit members from within them. Our rabbis, students, people working to build relationships in Congress, artists, well-known members of our advisory council, and all of our other constituencies each had their own positionalities, fears, hopes, and potential personal consequences to take into account.

To face those contradictory concerns head-on, beginning in 2011, JVP embarked on an organization-wide process to evaluate our BDS policy. This began at our NMM in Philadelphia in 2011 and went on for another three years. The process included conversations with our allies, organization-wide webinars, chapter conversations, and surveys of members. Within our membership, which was only eight hundred people in the spring of 2014, a survey showed that 75 to 85 percent of our membership was eager to endorse BDS. We also asked questions in that survey about how fast we should move, explicitly posing the question of what our balance between thoroughness and swiftness should be in making our decision, on which members were almost evenly split. While there was a clear strong majority in favor of endorsing BDS in some way, the 15 to 20 percent who had concerns were largely longtime members and generally those who had closer ties to other Jewish communal institutions or identified as Zionist themselves. Strategically, there were worries about whether we would lose our ability to work within Jewish communities. There were also those who shrouded ideological concerns and reluctance to let go of Zionism in strategic concerns.

Toward the end of this process in 2014, Israel brutally assaulted Gaza, killing more than 2,200 people, including more than 500 children, injuring tens of thousands more, and destroying homes, mosques, and schools, lending further urgency to our deliberations. Our chapters and members were out in the streets, doing creative direct action and sometimes risking arrest. It felt like the right level of escalation considering the unconscionable death toll in Gaza. In our chapter town hall during that time, which was part of the BDS decision-making process, the chapters pushed us to be braver after we brought forward a proposal to endorse all the elements of BDS but not in the clear language they preferred. During the height of the attack on Gaza, our Bay Area chapter was asked to endorse an action to "Block the Boat"—to join a coalition of all the local Palestine solidarity organizations planning, with support from labor unions, to block an Israeli ship that would be docking at an Oakland port during the height of the war. The blockade action was an enormous success, resulting in the boat's not docking in Oakland. However, at that time, participating in actions that did not distinguish between the occupation and Israel was against our national policy. The chapter was divided, some feeling discomfort with some of the language of the action, and others thinking it was imperative to join the coalition and be present on the streets with allies, especially at a moment of incredible moral urgency. From the perspective of the national organization, our LT was concerned about the implications of one of our largest chapters endorsing an action clearly beyond our current guidelines in the middle of our process of reviewing the policy, so, as a result, we did not allow the chapter to be official partners in the action, though large numbers of chapter members did participate. The unique status of the Bay Area chapter—as JVP's founding chapter and with a concentration of staff headquartered there—meant that the actions of the chapter were more closely monitored than elsewhere around the country. In fact, in other chapters where staff weren't present and the relationships with staff weren't so intertwined, chapters at times endorsed events beyond the guidelines without repercussions.

The decision to forbid the chapter to formally cosponsor the action had far-reaching implications that continued to reverberate for a number of years. While, from the perspective of the national organization, it was a necessary short-term cost in order to get to the long-term gain of endorsing the BDS call, from the perspective of the Bay Area chapter, the cost of the decision imposed by the national organization was intense and long term. By not showing up in a moment when our allies asked us to, the chapter had to spend enormous energy to rebuild relationships with organizations, especially with those that were Palestinian led, with whom they wanted to be in strong partnership. And the irony of not responding to an immediate request from a Palestinian-led coalition while trying to move to a position of fuller solidarity with the Palestinian call for BDS was not lost on any of us. In contrast, our restraint at the national level allowed the BDS policy deliberations to continue to move forward with the full trust of the membership in the process. And ultimately, the decision to endorse the full BDS call did not cause an organizational crisis—both because it was an accurate reflection of where the vast majority of our membership wanted us to be, and because the minority who didn't agree largely felt part of a process where they were seen and heard. Endorsing the call was a moment of consciously sharpening our politics and going all in to support our allies and partners. Looking back, we are proud of the painstaking internal work we did to allow us to fully embrace BDS from that time forward.

It was both the patience and flexibility of the BNC and changes in our corner of American Jewish communities—in part, we believe, due to JVP's efforts—that allowed us to eventually endorse the full BDS call. Until that time, JVP was welcomed into the movement for Palestinian rights as an ally because the BNC was clear about its principles and parameters for participation and offered great leeway in the kinds of campaigns that fell under the BDS rubric. Global solidarity movements, in particular, are well-served by being offered principles and frameworks for action, with a lot of flexibility for local adaptation. Three operational principles advocated by the BNC in its global BDS campaigns were gradualness, sustainability, and context sensitivity. The BNC had itself learned from the call for BDS against apartheid South Africa about how best to structure a global solidarity movement. We honor the ancestors of our movements—and make smarter strategy—when we remember, learn from, and adapt successful movements from our collective past and present. In fact, BDS works in large part because it is the clearest call for solidarity and accountability that exists for those of us who are not Palestinian. It offers a clear path to taking action within a simple framework that is infinitely adaptable to end the complicity of institutions, corporations, and, eventually, states/governments. As a Jewish organization working for Palestinian rights, it is of utmost importance to have those kinds of guideposts to inform our work.

Patient Processes

Especially as an organization that includes members who have different histories, motivations, priorities, and preferred strategies, we have found that there are two factors that are most important in successfully moving a political decision forward. The first, as recounted in the initial section of this book, is remembering that we are in this together—that if we build and nurture a sense of community, then we will have the trust and relationships to move forward, even when, inevitably, not everyone agrees with every decision we make. And, of course, it is also a matter of recognizing which moments demand that we use the accumulated political capital we have gathered to make a crucial difference. In those hardest moments, having a political home is of critical importance. The second is having a disciplined, thorough, patient process for internal conversation and gathering input when we are making big decisions. The process of coming to endorse the BDS call was rooted in our internal process, which was intense and comprehensive, as well as in reframing our orientation to the movement. Yes, we were building the broadest possible movement of Jews fighting for justice for Palestine, but our obligations were not just in or to Jewish communities but also to our allies of all races and religions working alongside us—primarily to Palestinians leading the movement for their liberation. The BDS movement's roots in universal values, evident in the way that, over and over again, its members have spoken out against antisemitism as part of their categorical and consistent opposition to all forms of racism, enabled us to feel full trust that our partners have our backs as well.

The endorsement of the BDS call was informed by a process of grappling with and clarifying JVP's primary obligations and alliances. While we've always done our best work as a part of coalitions, this process helped to cement a framework for JVP to be embedded in a larger movement—primarily for Palestinian liberation but more widely within the shared values of the left.

The process and outcome of the BDS decision became a road map for how we made political decisions that had internal and external consequences. We want to pull out the strands of what worked and what was challenging in those moments, because these kinds of inflection points face every movement and movement organization. As organizations and movements grow, the cost of making these decisions can also appear to grow—the bigger the ship, the more energy required to turn it. Consequences can include the potential to lose members, funding, and the ability to speak to a wider community. But it's also important to remember that the cost of *not* shifting can have equivalent consequences, leaving you behind the political winds, alienating portions of your base and your closest allies, and losing the possibility of bringing in new members. In fact, if our politics hadn't evolved, it would have been a worrisome sign that they may have stagnated and dulled. There are a lot of lures to maintain the status quo, whether overtly, from foundations or major donors whose support may hang in the balance, or indirectly, from reluctance of the board or staff leadership of the organization to invite drama and agita into the organization. It's important to remember that growth is not for its own sake; it's to build power to keep pushing. Sharpening your politics, including by moving them leftward and more in line with the demands and aspirations of directly impacted communities, is a manifestation of political courage. In our world, it turned out that endorsing the BDS call in full was actually what made us stand out and attracted more members to us.

JVP's specific position in the Jewish world is relevant here. Throughout our history, one of our key roles has been agitating and challenging our own community—but also organizing them into the movement and welcoming them once they were ready. We've been conscious of being the avant-garde—or we could call it a continuation of the Jewish prophetic tradition—as a small minority within our own community that speaks uncomfortable truths and, as such, paves the way for larger swaths of the community to grapple with them, too, while also being a magnet for wrath and attacks when speaking out is a threat to the status quo. For movements ranging from the climate justice movement to white antiracist organizing to disability justice, to name just a few, this is a familiar position. We learned that making this type of decision takes patience, process, time, and bravery. It requires you to be flexible and to evolve, while also holding the containers and spaces that brought and nurtured members into the work to begin with. It requires an infrastructure and approach that can design systems to accommodate a range of positions and positionalities while remembering core values. And it requires a constant self-discipline, an awareness that what is true in the present will not necessarily be true in the future, and that your organizing can be the vehicle for the visionary expansiveness that is key to building new worlds.

Becoming Anti-Zionist

JVP's successful process to endorse BDS in 2015 created a blueprint for how to take on difficult political decisions within JVP when there was a range of opinion among the membership. By *successful*, we don't just mean the decision to endorse but also the rather remarkable result that JVP lost, at most, a negligible number of members when we formalized and made the decision public. By 2015, JVP had become large enough to have a number of constituencies who brought different concerns and represented different positionalities from within Jewish communities. To take the two most obvious poles, students who are just in the process of beginning their lives and the paths they will pursue have very different factors to consider than rabbis, who, by definition, are embedded in a number of Jewish communal institutions and have congregations, pastoral relationships, professional associations, and jobs to consider. By moving slowly enough to have time to consider the decision not only as a political strategy but also as a position that would affect our members' lives, we were largely able to hold our community together. It was an internal educational process that required trust and patience and was absolutely worth it.

When JVP announced our decision to endorse BDS, we didn't know what would happen. We didn't know if we would lose significant funding, membership, or access to Jewish spaces (which was already pretty minimal). It was a significant risk, and there were certainly voices both within and outside JVP that warned us that this would destroy any standing we had in Jewish communities or in (big-D) Democratic Party circles. As we write this, it is easy to forget the chutzpah it took collectively to make this decision. But, as it turned out, our fears were unfounded. JVP gained additional respect and closer relationships with allies in the M4BL and other racial justice groups, and an influx of new members who were attracted to the clarity of our politics. We were able to stop tying ourselves in knots over our self-imposed boundaries on BDS campaigns, and our chapters were able to freely enter coalitions with their local allies and work powerfully together.

So, we knew we wanted to take the same approach when we started on the long process of looking at our position on Zionism, which began in collective political education and reflection in 2014, before we had even made the decision about BDS. With that decision behind us, we gained a bit of confidence that we could organizationally weather any decision we ended up making. In truth, in adopting the BDS call, we had already moved decisively toward an anti-Zionist position, and from our experience with the BDS decision we knew that acting boldly could be powerful. Most staff were ready to make the decision and felt it was morally and strategically important to do so in our role of pushing Jewish communities to keep moving.

We recall being acutely aware of our responsibility, both in the Jewish world and to our Palestinian allies and others, to help shift debate in Jewish communities and beyond, including by helping to legitimize anti-Zionism, which has been systemically vilified and equated with antisemitism. We knew, as the largest grassroots membership organization working in solidarity with Palestinians (and probably one of the largest Jewish grassroots membership organizations period), that our positioning would have the power to shift the terms of the debate.

JVP had long considered itself an "open tent" organization, but, up to this point, had been specifically neutral on Zionism. Being an open tent meant that JVP did not have a litmus test for self-identification in relation to Zionism. If JVP's values, principles, and campaigns spoke to you, you were welcome. This, in and of itself, was a pretty radical position when JVP was founded and remains so today. In practice, in the years since, the proportion of JVP members who identified as anti-Zionist had grown. This was due to a number of factors, including external political conditions: a much stronger left in general was emerging by 2016, and JVP's appeal to anti-Zionist Jews increased after we endorsed BDS. In addition, a number of other Jewish organizations working against the occupation emerged in the wake of the war on Gaza of 2014, including IfNotNow, Open

Hillel, and the Center for Jewish Nonviolence. In what felt like a real flowering of the movement ecosystem, Jewish Americans who wanted to get involved in Palestine solidarity now had a number of organizations to choose from along the left-to-progressive spectrum.

In 2014, JVP leadership formed a committee through an application process that included board, staff, and members and was designed to represent the breadth of JVP members' positions. Over two years, that committee planned an organization-wide curriculum, held over Zoom. More than seven hundred members participated across the seven sessions, which also included opportunities for written reflection and chapter conversations between the sessions about how JVP's approach to Zionism impacted JVP nationally and locally. An online zine collected member testimonies about their encounters and histories with Zionism. The process also included a survey of individual members; discussions at the 2017 NMM; chapters submitting notes of their internal discussions; conversations with invited constituencies who had particular concerns, including rabbis, artists, students, and members focused on work in Congress; and feedback gathered in various forums and methods from JVP staff, the JOCSM Caucus, members of our advisory council, and Palestinian allies.[3]

The process mirrored JVP's overall approach to organizing. As we discuss elsewhere, our organizing program was built out to allow our member leaders to bring their specific talents and skills and for us to take aim at the multiple pillars supporting US support for Israeli apartheid. Likewise, these processes created ways for members to weigh in however they were most comfortable. For those that are writers or artists, there was the zine; for those who like to study and debate there were the Zoom sessions. For those only comfortable among known, trusted comrades, there were chapter or constituency-focused (rabbis, JOCSM, and others) feedback and discussion sessions. For those who are not core organizers but are supporters, there were surveys. Ensuring that members, no matter their temperament or comfort, could participate, and that multiple attempts were made to get genuine feedback and encourage participation, facilitated members' embrace of the result. The decision was not the only output from this process; connecting members in this way yielded a much tighter web of connection. That web is the bedrock of the organization and does require ongoing attention! These processes create the perfect opportunity for that maintenance.

Notably, there was not unanimity on the committee about an exact position to take. The feedback gathered showed that there were two main tendencies within JVP: anti-Zionists and non-Zionists. The hope was to affirm both, but given the amount of Jewish communal hostility toward anti-Zionism, it was most important to affirm the presence and leadership of anti-Zionists within JVP. It was clear that chapters needed to be free to enter into local coalitions with anti-Zionist organizations. And it was clear that, as an organization that valued base-building above all else, it was important to keep the tone of our statement welcoming and free of litmus tests. There was further consensus to focus any statement on the inevitability of Zionism's end, and therefore to focus on Jewishness beyond Zionism, with a message of liberatory hope. With this brief, the JVP board, with guidance from the LT (the executive and deputy directors) made the decision to make an unequivocal statement opposing Zionism. Then, the work of crafting the statement began, with the input the committee had gathered as the guidance for what to include. When it came to drafting the actual statement, the intention was to integrate the feedback in tandem with the values and organizing approach that had gotten JVP this far: removing barriers to organizing, primacy of base-building, leveraging the political power JVP had amassed, and prefiguring the future we are organizing toward. For certain, this statement was a statement of values for JVP, but it was just as much an intentional confrontation with the mainstream Jewish world.

The final statement began with a quote by Jewish lesbian elder Melanie Kaye/Kantrowitz z"l, "Solidarity is the political version of love" (which resonated so much with us that we used it as this book's title).[4] The first three sentences of the text read,

> Jewish Voice for Peace is guided by a vision of justice, equality and freedom for all people. We unequivocally oppose Zionism because it is counter to those ideals.
>
> We know that opposing Zionism, or even discussing it, can be painful, can strike at the deepest trauma and greatest fears of many of us.

Again, JVP lost very few members when we went public with our statement, and we continued to attract new ones. In some ways, the statement simply reinforced how JVP was already perceived by most people. It was also a liberatory moment, one that Palestinians appreciated for offering them some cover (while perhaps wondering what had taken us so long!). Almost immediately, the Jewish world began to engage in the conversation: J Street put out a long statement explaining how they differed from our approach but also reinforced our message that anti-Zionism had long been part and parcel of Jewish communal life; *Jewish Currents* commissioned a roundtable of notable thinkers to react to our statement, and *+972 Magazine*, long an outlet read widely across the anti-occupation to anti-Zionist left, commissioned a feature to explain to their readers what had brought JVP to this moment of decision.[5] As time went on, and anti-Zionism became more and more targeted by right-wing forces as antisemitic—in response to the power of the Palestine solidarity movement; in particular, as a way to delegitimize Palestinian lived experience—JVP's ability to act as an effective ally and partner was enhanced by this decision.

The BDS and Zionism decisions were both made as part of deeply intentional processes with a primary focus on ensuring we didn't get out ahead of where our members were ready to go. Our members needed to go on this journey together, to hear each other's strategic thinking and emotional considerations. They needed to share their fears. They needed to deepen their analysis and understanding of Zionism and of the importance to our Palestinian partners in boldly and clearly challenging it. It's worth noting that the painstaking discussions and processes JVP experienced internally were completely opaque to those outside JVP looking in, particularly those in the Jewish mainstream, who already saw JVP as supporting BDS and as anti-Zionist. That outside perception only reinforced our commitment to a thorough internal process.

We recall its being about intentionally moving the goalposts and bringing others to meet us. It was about our deciding for ourselves who we are and what we stand for, and taking these steps together as an organization. JVP's readiness to step out on BDS and Zionism signaled a sense of strength and power to ourselves and to onlookers. It was about getting bigger and bolder and forcing wider American Jewish communities to follow the conversation where we wanted to take it, and ensuring our base of supporters was prepared for the fights and challenges that would inevitably ensue. That—more or less—is exactly what happened.

A Slow Approach to Congress

Just as JVP used deliberative decision-making processes to make conscious political shifts, we used the same principles when developing new areas of our work. This was true of the evolution of JVP's engagement with Congress—from nonexistent until 2014 to the eventual launch, in 2019, of JVPAction, a 501(c)(4) organization that can lobby elected officials. Building out new programs requires political analysis, power mapping, and an honest look at capacity. As with big political decisions, we found that these conditions were best met when, as an organization, we took the time we needed and consulted as broadly as possible before jumping into new arenas.

Matching Strategies to Relative Power

A lesson that we learned collectively as we were growing was that we had to match our strategies and tactics to our relative power. There was no use making "demands" that we did not have the power to compel our target to respond to. That required being realistic about how much actual power we had and—digging even further back—talking about power at all. The discussion of power and power building can be a fraught one in left movement spaces. Leftists tend to be wary of the idea of power, which corrupts, which needs to be bent toward justice, which historically has abused dissenters and oppressed the weak. Yet, movements that take change seriously need to engage seriously in theories of power building. And, as the labor organizer and writer Daisy Pitkin has noted, power has many different forms—while we reject authoritarian power by force, we rejoice in power built through solidarity.[6] While often associated with oppression, power can also be liberatory if used in the pursuit of meeting the needs of marginalized people. Unions and other membership-building organizations have always done this.

When the left more broadly has less power—as in the 1990s when JVP began—it can tend toward bearing witness instead of fighting for change. In other words, the temptation can be to focus on naming your opposition to state policies and practices and showing that there is dissent instead of forcing the state to change. The antidote is to believe in and work toward building enough power to force change by even the most stubborn actors.

The reality is that, in DC, power cedes not to the power of persuasion but to the persuasion of power. After all, this accumulation of people power is the logic behind and prerequisite for the success of boycott and divestment campaigns—or just about any mass movement.

Over JVP's life span, we have taken on numerous short- and long-term campaigns, mostly through the BDS framework, with the intention to build our base, educate the public, and win meaningful victories. We began to build our congressional advocacy work when we identified that we had a broad enough base to make an impact, well before there were any overt supporters of Palestinian rights in Congress. Of course, when we say "we" in this context, we mean a broad and shifting team of dedicated staff, member leaders, and board members who developed this work over years.[7] This process illustrates the evaluation and balance of power building, effectiveness, process, and action that is at the heart of the lessons we seek to convey to those of you reading this book. From the time that, as a local Bay Area organization, JVP made the decision to invest in staffing in order to grow, we consciously chose to prioritize strategies that could shift power, create new realities, and contribute effectively to ending US complicity in Israeli apartheid. Rather than trying to work within frameworks that could improve conditions within the narrow confines of current political reality, JVP's founding generation onward understood that the parameters of what was possible would have to shift. That led to a fundamental commitment to movement building and growth. With other movements that had made the impossible seem possible as a guide, such as the civil rights movement and the movement to end support for apartheid in South Africa, JVP's analysis was that if you didn't have money, you would need truly significant numbers of people to turn the tide. That meant that no matter what we were doing—building chapters, engaging the media, designing campaigns, engaging different constituencies—it was all actually part of the same goal: building a membership broad and deep enough to be influential enough to change the language, reality, and, eventually, US laws and policies that propped up and enabled Israeli occupation and apartheid.

But that didn't mean JVP was ready to lobby lawmakers. It can be incredibly tempting, in any movement, to decide to try to meet with local legislators or, more likely, their staff. After all, they are a natural target, as the people who pass the laws. Their job is to meet with their constituents, so, in most cases, it is possible to get some sort of meeting, which feels like an accomplishment. If you're a small group without any power (as JVP was at the beginning), the meeting process goes something like this: you take a number of weeks or months to get a meeting with a low-to-medium-level staff person. Your group spends a lot of time preparing materials, talking points, and choreographing who will say what. You go in, you say your piece. The staff person listens or argues, depending on a combination of their personal sympathies, level of professionalism, and their boss's politics. What is doubtful, in this stage, is that the meeting makes any difference at all in the legislator's positions. Perhaps as a long-term project, developing the relationship and their knowledge that you exist is productive. But, as a strategy for change, these meetings had a negligible impact.

Within JVP's leadership, we didn't have any particular numbers in mind as to when it would be the right time to embark on congressional advocacy. We knew that we needed to be able to represent a significant constituency over a significant number of districts in order to have any real impact. If we couldn't have an impact, we didn't want to waste our time on energy-sucking efforts that might lull us into feeling like we were making progress without any real power to change anything. The broader base-building and discourse-shifting work, we believed, would ultimately change the calculus for these decision-makers. So, we made a conscious decision in our earlier years to double down on our focus on base-building, campaigns, and shifting the over-arching narrative. After the 2014 war on Gaza and the corresponding surge in JVP's membership, we started to rethink our stance. We had grown to about sixty chapters, and our supporters list had reached about two hundred and fifty thousand. Our thinking shifted as we realized that we might be ready for the next stage, that we actually did have the ability to engage in the field of real power, where decisions were being made.

As was our practice in JVP, it took many months to consider the pros and cons of expanding into a new arena. In the process of the discussions, a few things were clarified: the principle of prioritizing base-building and powerful campaigns would not change, and we would not alter or soften our positions to appeal to elected officials (even if, for the visits, we would put on business attire and leave our placards and bullhorns at home). In fact, the Congress program would turn out to be a source of base-building strength in its own right, a virtuous and energizing circle of harnessing our street energy and communication strengths to change the conversation and possibilities in DC.

During the deliberations, there were fears and pushback among staff, board, and members that, by embarking on this course, JVP would inevitably shift our center of gravity toward Washington just as it was a moment of enormous energy and growth across the country. There were also worries that JVP would start to act like a typical DC-focused advocacy organization, tailoring our demands to what was possible. Having seen it happen time and time again, we knew these fears were legitimate. As it turned out, by referencing that fear regularly in internal conversations, the articulation of fighting against that pattern itself worked as an accountability system to safeguard against it. But, alongside those fears were feelings of enormous opportunity to build out our congressional work as an extension and expression of our movement-building work.

We recall feeling a strong imperative to channel the growth we had experienced—which, after all, was mostly due to the horrific conditions on the ground, most recently in Gaza—in the most powerful ways possible. Based on our theory of change, we knew that Congress would probably be the last institution to change and that we were starting at an extreme disadvantage. But we did feel that we would be able to build relationships with representatives who, we would ensure, would know that we had enough of their constituents with us that they would need to take us seriously. And we were excited about the possibility of extending our BDS work to the "S" in sanctions, in ways that were otherwise impossible. We could build from there.

As at other times that JVP embarked on a new campaign, strategy, or program, the process of getting started on national legislative work was labor-intensive and arduous. It's hard to write or talk about building out processes and structures. It's not as sexy as the highs and lows of campaign work, and it's harder to make into a good story. We've often reflected that one of JVP's "secret sauces" has been how much attention we paid to building our infrastructure and investing in buy-in processes before taking action. In this case, even once we'd made a formal decision to embark on congressional advocacy and hire a staff person to lead it, we had work to do in setting out the parameters of how to approach the work for our chapter leaders. From the beginning, the Congress work was built out by a strong mix of chapter leaders, board members, and staff. We started to build a council of local leaders, who met regularly to talk through strategy and receive training on how to approach building relationships and credibility with their congresspeople.

One early practice, in keeping with our concerns about not getting co-opted into a DC mindset, was a resolution about how to talk about BDS with the congresspeople who were just starting to get to know us. We knew that JVP was not yet in a politically strong enough place to be able to ask members of

Congress to support BDS. Some of our leaders, understandably hoping to avoid looking too naive or outside the consensus as they built these relationships, asked if they should avoid talking about BDS in their conversations. The decision about how far to push in these kinds of conversations is a common one in activist organizations that target Congress—do you talk about abortion access in limited ways or as an overall part of women's health care? Do you discuss eliminating ICE entirely or try to win citizenship for an attractive category of immigrants like the young Dreamers? These questions are not necessarily binaries, and it often makes sense to carve out a specific campaign ask that will build toward a bigger one. But, in DC, the truth is that the norm is often working within the boundaries of the status quo.

The leaders of the Congress work were clear that it was important to start to normalize for congresspeople that they had interested, well-informed, and, not incidentally, Jewish constituents who supported BDS as part of the movement for Palestinian freedom. At the same time, we wanted JVP members to feel as confident and proud talking about BDS to their congresspeople as they did in the streets and in campaigns. So, a practice was developed of mentioning support of BDS as part of our standard spiel of introduction, with the ask being that congresspeople be willing to listen to accurate information from BDS proponents, especially Palestinians, and not to condemn it out of hand. Staff reinforced with JVP members that they shouldn't tailor their actions or hold back on their energy in the street for fear of offending the sensibilities of elected officials. JVP was taking on the role, essential in any movement, of trying to change the parameters of what's possible, creating transformative power shifts as well as real material change, in terms of US funding. When JVPers went to the offices of elected officials, the electeds learned that they had to take us seriously, because we had the power of numbers of their constituents behind us. At town halls around the country, electeds faced persistent, composed, and eloquent questions about their positions on Palestinian freedom, which were often met by wild applause throughout the room. This was in part because large numbers of JVP members had shown up but was also evidence of spontaneous solidarity. Elected officials got a visceral, firsthand sense of the degree of support for Palestine in their districts.

There is something about getting closer to power—getting closer to both that possibility as well as the enormous distance between that and actually winning—that makes legislative work challenging. It demands a willingness to balance urgency and reality and to constantly evaluate when to push and when to recognize a win, even a minute one. It requires a lot of longterm patience, a mix of hope and cynicism, and a willingness to engage in the contradictions of painstaking and authentic relationship building with elected leaders who are not our friends. It also demanded a commitment to self-evaluation, as our team constantly mapped who in Congress was a champion, a potential champion, neutral, or immovably against us. A grassroots organization like JVP that stays tied to both grassroots and spiritual and communal work is well situated to do long-term hegemony-shifting work, because you don't have to rely on legislative changes as your metric, which keeps you from limiting the horizon of your vision. The ability to be present with this emotional and spiritual disjuncture and be in relationship to power was strengthened by the variety of work that JVP was doing simultaneously. There is an ongoing tension in this balance, but it made us stronger to grapple openly with the commitment to that variety of tactics.

#SkipTheSpeech

By 2015, JVP had a functioning member committee and staff to lead the congressional work. When Republicans invited Prime

Minister Netanyahu to address Congress during the debate on the Iran deal and in the middle of Netanyahu's reelection campaign, the invitation broke protocol in multiple ways. By bypassing President Obama entirely, it was considered not only an insult to the president but also an unprecedented effort to have a foreign leader sway a US foreign policy decision, while also allowing Netanyahu to use Congress as a venue for his reelection campaign. Our impetus was to test and publicly prove that support for Israel in the person of Netanyahu had become controversial. JVP and allies were able to successfully ride the coattails of a more liberal critique, centered on the insult to President Obama, and utilize the attention brought by the unprecedented invitation to inject a much further left critique into the public discourse about it. While organizations from the ADL to the Reform movement to J Street suggested politely to congressional leaders that Netanyahu postpone his speech, JVP and allies demanded strong and clear action from Congress.[8] Once again, we were seizing the opportunity to blow past the boundaries by which other Jewish legacy organizations constrained themselves. Not only did this draw a bright line between our approach and those of more status quo lobbying groups, it was also a clear success.

For the first time, JVP members around the country all focused on Congress as a target. In coalition with allies, 110,000 letters and emails were sent to members of Congress from their constituents, two thousand members made phone calls, and members in thirty home districts delivered petitions to their members of Congress while staff delivered the same petition to sixty-five members in their DC offices.[9] JVP placed op-eds in the leading state newspapers in seven states as well as in the *Washington Post*, plus letters to the editor in dozens of smaller papers. Ultimately, fifty-nine members of Congress skipped the speech, including the heads of the Congressional

Black Caucus and the Progressive Caucus.

This was an early proof of concept for JVP's working theory that the movement for Palestinian rights was now broad and strong enough to be able to have a significant impact on the debate. The controversy also illuminated the growing rift between the Jewish American community and the Israeli government, as well as the growing partisan divide on Israel.[10] As with successful work against anti-BDS legislation, we were still clear-eyed about JVP's relative power. Both our successful work helping to defeat anti-BDS legislation at the state and federal levels and #SkipTheSpeech were key moments when coalitions could form with overlapping interests. Organizationally, we learned that we could effectively agitate to push a call for action into the public eye, and that we could play a specific role as a Jewish voice in the debate that supported and encouraged lawmakers who had the courage to push against the Israel lobby. Yet, we knew that it was the labor unions and the ACLU—in the case of the anti-BDS laws (which we detail in chapter 8)—and the Congressional Black Caucus (CBC) and more legacy Jewish groups, who were also worried about the impact of Netanyahu's appearance on the bipartisan consensus on Israel, who drove the legitimacy of the critique. At the same time, the sheer number of JVP members who acted made us indispensable to the coalitions we were a part of, overcoming prior concerns from groups (like more liberal organizations) about being publicly associated with us. The result was a sharper critique of US policy in support of Israel than was usually possible in such coalitions. In real time, JVP's growth, organization, and understanding of how congresspeople made their decisions was building our power and impact without compromising our values. We collectively held on to all these lessons as we continued to build out our congressional work, all the way through launching the 501(c)(4) and beyond.

Sharpening Your Politics as a Driver for Growth

The continuing evolution and expansion of operational modes in no way diminished JVP's political positions or street energy—especially considering that JVP took on an anti-Zionist position the same year we launched JVPAction.[11] The deliberation and intention with which we slowly built out our Congress program paid off by allowing us to feed off our ongoing growth and create new pathways to power, without giving up our fundamental principles or modes of work that made us strong enough to do so.

Successfully growing your organization while at the same time sharpening your politics is a delicate juggling act of smart strategy, relational organizing, and clear principles all working in tandem. The decision to endorse the Palestinian call for BDS, becoming anti-Zionist, and building a program to make headway in Congress all relied on one another. JVP's work in DC could have run the risk of becoming too reformist had we not already endorsed BDS. Our articulation of ourselves as anti-Zionist would have been just lip service if we hadn't translated that into meaningful solidarity by affirming Palestinian civil society's call and launching potent campaigns. And the political education and leadership development that happened along the way were essential to being impactful and effective as we began our work in the belly of the beast in DC. When we think about why these moves worked in our favor, our approach prioritized being well-timed, to bring the maximum number of people with us, and threaded the needle between being overly vanguardist versus attached to the status quo. We were able to move past the barriers of what felt possible without slipping into a fantasy divorced from an assessment of our strengths. We understood that being correct was insufficient if we weren't also building a base and amassing real political power.

And we give ourselves credit for being willing to evolve and adapt as internal and external circumstances shifted. Within JVP, we never assumed that because we had taken a position at one time we should not change it later. That may seem like an obvious point—but too many organizations and movements can get frozen in their current strategies and mistake them for principles. Instead of our political positioning compromising our ability to move in more mainstream political spaces as some might have assumed or feared, our decisions solidified our partnerships, clarified our ambitions, and freed us to engage in our work confidently and unabashedly clear about who we are.

Organizing Strategy Reflection Questions

Growing While
Sharpening Our Politics

1. As your base, influence, and resources grow, how are you leveraging that toward sharpening your politics and pushing the conversation where you want it to go?

2. What safeguards do you or could you put in place to ensure your political risk-taking instincts endure as your influence grows? How do you balance caution in taking political risks and pushing discourse forward with realizing practical wins in coalition that strengthen relationships and build power?

3. When making big political position shifts, how do you—or can you—measure whether or not your base is with you? What would it take to move people along if they're not ready, or to be willing to take the risk to lose a vocal few if the majority are with you?

4. What kinds of participatory processes do you have, or could you create, in your organizational culture that bring the perspectives of the widest spectrum of your base and stakeholders into your decision-making?

5. How do you assess how a leftward shift in position will impact relationships and standing with allies, partners, and funders? How do you adequately assess whether what is significant to your circle of primary accountability might be opaque to the outside world? How can you integrate that

assessment into your decision-making?

6. As a grassroots organization, how can you assess if more formal political engagement (501[c][4]s, PACs) will amplify and strengthen your grassroots work?

Chapter 7

Transforming JVP's Approach to Racial Justice

"White, Ashkenazi Jews are the power structure in Israel and the supermajority of Jews here in the US, so our organizing of ourselves against the grain of that is compelling to me. I think that foundational perspective on our work ended up undermining my ability to see the moral, ethical, and strategic value of actually being an antiracist organization and what it would take to get there. The mistakes I made surprised me. I expected more from myself. I had led antiracism workshops for white Jews over the years, including for members of JVP staff (before they were staff). One staff person who was part of one of the workshops I led said to me, in 2018, during a staff meeting discussing the critiques from the JOCSM caucus and our response, "You taught me how to think about being antiracist. I expected so much more and better from you." Ouch! But also, as she should! I did not fully appreciate how it might feel to Jews of color to have an organization that is pushing the boundaries so fiercely and intensely on Israel but falling into the same traps and shapes as every other Jewish organization.

If I were them, I would have also been really, really pissed."

—Alissa

"I felt an overall sense of my own frozenness and defen-
siveness throughout that time. This defensive crouch made
it hard for me to be truly open to what we were hearing or
to approach it with the creativity or confidence that I felt in
other realms. I thought I had a pretty good sense of my strategic acumen, my relationships, and my ability to balance
the different priorities, crises, and difficult situations we
found ourselves in almost daily, while continuing to move
the work of the organization forward. I hadn't yet been in a
situation where I didn't have the capacity to figure problems
out. I really didn't understand the limits of my own capacity, that what we needed was beyond it, or even how to ask
for help for a long time. I was scared to give up power in the
process. I was scared about what would be said or concluded
about us as leaders, and I was scared we would be pulled out
of what we had determined was the priority agenda."

—Rebecca

Starting in 2015, JVP staff leadership was challenged by
a group of members and staff who were Jews of Color,
Mizrahi, and/or Sephardi (JOCSM) to align our internal racial
justice practices with our external commitments, a common
experience of left organizations over the last decade.* In the
words of Shirly Bahar, Danny Bryck, and Sydney Levy—three

* The JOCSM caucus was known as such from 2015 to 2019, which is the period
of time we focus on throughout the chapter. In 2019, members of the caucus
renamed it the BIJOCSM Network. We refer to both names in the chapter
depending on the context and timing.

BIJOCSM (Black, Indigenous, Jews of Color, Sephardi and/or Mizrahi) JVP leaders and staff members at various times—in *Jewish Currents*, "Jews of color have been in leadership at JVP since its early days in the late 1990s, but it took the formation, in 2015, of a member-led Jews of Color and Sephardi and Mizrahi Jews (JOCSM) Caucus to demand accountability from an organization that had worked to hone its anti-racism with respect to Palestinians, but had yet to reckon with its practices regarding BIJOCSM."[1] In this chapter, we pull back the curtain on our experience addressing the challenges they brought, which built from the formation of a BIJOCSM Caucus to a comprehensive racial justice transformation (RJT) process, which sought to encompass almost every aspect of our work, from our internal communications to work with chapters and member leaders, campaign selection, HR policies, and beyond. This process, which, of course, was happening while all the other challenges, campaigns, and fast-moving world events that we dealt with day to day continued to unspool, was both one of the hardest and most essential of our tenure.

The emergence of the caucus and ensuing RJT process was undoubtedly the biggest test of leadership during our time at JVP. While that process is by its nature ongoing, we refer to it here as starting in 2015, when pressures from our membership, as well as our external movement alliances and changing political factors, challenged and moved us to address issues of white supremacy and racism within our own structures. It was a period in which the two of us struggled personally to make profound changes. Saying the "two of us" here is complicated; as we discussed in more depth in chapter 2, we had a collective Leadership Team (LT) of four people during this time. We can only speak to our own reflections on this process, and we imagine our comrades on the team would each tell the tale somewhat differently, but we want to acknowledge the particular awkwardness here of speaking as half of a team. Of course, this retelling reflects our retroactive reflections and not the JVP of today.

There is no neat narrative to summarize this initial phase of RJT, as antiracism is not a destination but an ongoing practice. As we did with all sections of the book, during our writing, we reflected on the RJT process with a few of the staff and members who were there along with us, but the conclusions are our own. We attempt to convey the (at best) "two steps forward/one step back" nature of these processes, in all their nuances and complications, and to be honest and reflective about our experience, while acknowledging that, yet again, we are retaining the power to narrate. As is always true when reflecting on mistakes, what is important is the impact, no matter the intent.

The caucus, which became the BIJOCSM Network in 2019, contributed innumerable key interventions over the years. As leaders of the BIJCOSM Caucus noted in *Jewish Currents* in 2023,

> Over the past eight years, we have celebrated Mizrahi and Sephardi culture and resistance, and have given minoritized Jewish voices and Black and Palestinian comrades a platform to express their unique and undervalued perspectives. We organized a letter by Latinx Jews calling on the Trump administration to close the camps where immigrants are detained on the southern border, spoke up in defense of a Palestine-inclusive Ethnic Studies curriculum in California, led a celebrated "Black Lens on Palestine" webinar, and supported local, national, and global Sephardi/Mizrahi cultural work, among other initiatives.[2] We have expressed solidarity with non-Jewish African refugees in Israel threatened with deportation—an ethnocratic policy that parallels the denial of the Palestinian right of return—and opposed the use of Blackface in Jewish communities.

We have also defended the Movement for Black Lives against false accusations of antisemitism aimed at silencing their support of Palestine.[3]

Even from this brief review, you can get a sense of the breadth of the intellectual, cultural, and political work that the BIJOCSM Caucus contributed to not just JVP but the left more broadly.

Emergence of the JOCSM Caucus

The growth of the Palestinian freedom movement post 2014, which unfolded the same summer as Michael Brown's murder in Ferguson and the emergence of the M4BL, led to expanding alliances with and obligations to people of color–led movements in the US. JVP consciously built these alliances nationally as chapters developed local relationships of solidarity with Black, Muslim, Indigenous, and immigrant–led organizing formations. By naming the connections between white supremacy in the US and Israel and the growing awareness among white Jews of those dynamics, JVP was able to expand the base of support for Palestinian rights in progressive circles. It was a pivotal moment of anguish, growth, and a sense of responsibility to meet the urgency of the moment, and a redoubled commitment to a left that shared analysis, principles, and solidarity in action. As leaders we had always understood the Palestinian struggle as a racial justice issue. The system of repression and control that Israel holds over Palestinians based on their identity as Palestinians is a racist system. That frame helped the LT develop a clear lens of how to understand not just the Palestinian movement but other antiracist movements as well, and was the basis for JVP's alliances, approach to Congress, and, later, the decision to become anti-Zionist.

As a Jewish organization in solidarity with Palestinians, JVP from the beginning lumped Jews together into one, big, inherently culturally white and Ashkenazi bucket in that framework. As a group, Jews have more collective power than Palestinians, even in the US. Given that JVP was a relatively small part of the Jewish community, it made sense that JVP would have more power speaking in a single, countercultural voice. Staff and members had made limited and flawed attempts throughout the years to do political education around Mizrahi/ Sephardi Jewishness, to broaden our conception of Jewishness in general and to more broadly transform the dynamics of being a vastly majority-white organization with an all-white leadership. We recall attempting to address questions of racial diversity in our organization as a political analysis question, but we had not looked deeply at internal practices or the way the institutional shape of JVP was replicating white supremacy and Ashkenazi dominance. Episodically, we included references to Mizrahi or Sephardi culture in our email communications, developed and disseminated a "Jews from the Middle East" fact sheet in 2015, and held educational sessions for our leaders and chapters to discuss racial diversity in the Jewish community.[4]

Despite these discrete efforts, as leaders we did not prioritize taking fundamental actions to transform the organization from a white organization to a multiracial one. Until the push from Jews of color members, many of whom experienced harm from being in the organization at that time, we did not take on the work to make the structural overhaul that was needed. In all honesty, as leaders we both at times felt and communicated a sense that the work of becoming a truly antiracist organization was, although important, a distraction from our core mission and already adequately subsumed in our work for Palestinian rights. The limited efforts toward antiracism were not prioritized by staff or board leadership and therefore did not bear much fruit.

At the time of JVP's founding in the late '90s and early 2000s, questions of identity in the US Jewish community did not loom publicly as large as they do today, and early JVP leaders did not make cultural identity central to how they approached the work of forging a space for Jewish voices critical of Israel. That being said, one of JVP's cofounders and JVP's first board chair are both Mizrahi Jews, from Iraq and Lebanon respectively. Sydney Levy, JVP's third staff person, who is Latinx and Mizrahi, played a longtime leadership role building JVP's campaigns and movement partnerships as a member, a longtime staff leader, and one of the founders of the JOCSM caucus. JVP, as a Jewish organization, focused, at least initially, on demonstrating there is a critical and growing mass of Jews challenging the status quo of unconditional Jewish communal support for Israel. Coupled with the common inclination of white-dominant organizations not to address race proactively, representing and centering the cultural and racial diversity of Jews never became a top priority as JVP grew until Jews of color forced the issue.

As an identity-based organization, JVP didn't pay enough attention to the intersecting identities that are included under the umbrella of Jewish identity. Over the past fifty years Jewish communities in the US have become increasingly racially and culturally diverse, which has only been recognized by the organizing efforts of Jews of color themselves. This necessarily complicates a Black-white binary in Jewish identity that dominated, for example, Jewish participation in the civil rights movement, broadening Jewish cultural markers beyond bagels and Yiddish, and challenging the common notion that all Jews are white, European immigrants to the US who fled persecution. Each of us could give you a rousing talk about all the systemic ways legacy Jewish institutions and the Israeli state project have sought to homogenize Jewish communities in the US and throughout the diaspora in service of Zionism. Despite, or perhaps because of, this intellectual understanding, we failed to see how we were participating in homogenizing Jewish communities through the "big bucket" approach. JVP's burgeoning relationships with Black- and POC-led movements only underlined our negligence. We were always careful and attentive to racial dynamics with our Palestinian partners, seen as a trusted ally when it came to making linkages across movements, taking risks, and pushing boundaries. Our fluency in antiracist practice when it came to broader social systems magnified just how insufficient our internal practices were, no matter how good our intentions.

In 2015, during the opening plenary of our NMM in Baltimore and in the immediate context of the murder of Michael Brown and the emergence of the M4BL, Rebecca said for the first time publicly that we understand the fight for Palestinian rights as an antiracist fight, and JVP as an antiracist organization. While it got rousing applause when she said it, over the coming days at the conference the statement continued to be discussed, unpacked, and ultimately challenged by Jews of color in our membership. Looking back, we understand how Rebecca's declaration of JVP as an antiracist organization was hypocritical at best, when there was ample evidence that we had not actually dealt with racism in our own house. Our staff, board, and membership were overwhelmingly white and Ashkenazi; we regularly used Ashkenazi cultural references as Jewish references; we would bifurcate Blacks and Jews, invisibilizing the existence of Black Jews. There was inadequate organizational support for staff of color in navigating the complexities and hardships of working inside a white-dominant organization. HR processes that failed to integrate a commitment to racial equity meant that when white staff were promoted or staff of color were reassigned, those decisions landed with all the weight of white negligence. Staff of color were vulnerable to the racism of members in the chat of Zoom calls, while soliciting donors on the phone, or during chapter visits and leadership retreats. The culture we created at JVP prized synergy, so conflict and disagreement were not welcomed or channeled as they could have been. Until changes were made as part of the RJT process, staff of color had no place to bring their challenges and grievances, leaving them saddled with the extra burden of needing to advocate for policies and protocols for addressing workplace harm on top of tending to the emotional impact of that harm. Given the white dominance of the organization, racial dynamics on staff, and the culture of the organization, it was premature and hubristic for JVP to claim to be antiracist—even if JVP was successfully practicing antiracism in some external realms.

After the NMM in 2015, a Jews of Color and Sephardi/Mizrahi (JOCSM) Caucus was formed, both to build support among the small number of members with those identities and to challenge and hold us accountable for the ways we had fallen short. Over the coming years, the patterns, absences, and biases that had been baked in JVP's structures were brought into the daylight by the JOCSM Caucus. The nascent caucus named their concerns, all of which were direct results of leadership decisions the two of us had a hand in making. The overarching themes were "nothing about us without us" and "we're more than diversity and inclusion." Specifically, these included how to approach hiring and how to use more precise language when it came to describing JVP's membership, solidarity model, and relationship to antiracism. In our striving to demonstrate JVPs multiracial bona fides, JVP fundraising and communications would fall into the trap of tokenizing people of color in our membership and staff by including pictures of smiling multiracial people in our emails, for example, which sent a very misleading message about the current makeup of the organization.

As Rebecca's NMM plenary talk exemplified, in trying to make antiracism central to the organization's mission, we moved too fast, skipping important steps of centering the leadership of Jews of color in our membership and staff. The budget was the purview of the ED, deputy directors, and board, so the caucus could make requests but not decisions. Over time, the caucus brought specific budget requests that would allow them to lead portions of work to organize BIJOCSM current and potential members, develop their own relationships, and deepen and disseminate their analysis to the wider public including through a blog. How we responded to these requests became an indicator of how seriously we were taking JVP's institutional response to their critique.

Getting Outside Help

As time went on and attempts to manage the relationship between the LT and the caucus floundered, deeper divisions emerged, and our personal relationships began to fray. As we later learned, this is a very common pattern when white-led organizations first begin to grapple with challenges around internal racism. As the LT began to integrate the framing offered by the caucus more systematically into our staff and board discussions, it became clear that we needed to undergo an organization-wide transformation of our racial justice practices and seek to structurally address our white cultural norms. That is how our racial justice transformation (RJT) process was born. The first step was getting outside help. The consultants JVP contracted with began with interviewing dozens of us and compiling a report, which named the core challenges to organization-wide racial justice transformation:

- The difficult relationship between the JOCSM Caucus and the LT and the profound and sometimes incapacitating impact it has had on the organization and its capacity to live its antiracist aspirations.
- The ways the dominant organizational culture operates to marginalize people of color and Sephardi and Mizrahi Jews, in chapters as well as on staff.

- Pervasive middle- or upper-class cultural norms that over-value intellectual knowledge, privilege agreement, and view conflict as negative.
- Infrastructure development that has not kept up with recent growth, revealing weaknesses in supervision and leadership development for people of color and the need for prioritization, focus, and slowing down for racial justice transformation to occur successfully.[5]

The RJT process, which for its first and most intensive phase focused on internal staff dynamics, began with a multiracial team that crossed internal hierarchies. That team first built up its own skills and comfort in talking about racism and later expanded to work with the full staff, the board, chapters, and members. It included skill-building sessions on communication toward inquiry instead of advocacy; navigating conflict; policy and procedure development to mitigate bias in hiring and hold members accountable to antiracist practices; and developing an enduring commitment to building the structures that will ensure accountability for the practice of antiracism.

No Neat Narrative

The RJT process was one of slow progress, backsliding, and constant learning. At every level of the organization, we continued to practice what we were learning, continued to make mistakes, and continued to adjust. We, as leaders, made many, many mistakes, some of them over and over again, over the course of the period we were grappling with, and responding to, these challenges. Staff and members of color continued to experience harm throughout the process. Just as in all racial justice work, we are talking here about unfinished processes, both in ourselves and organizationally. There is no neat bow to tie up this narrative in a pretty package.

If there is one thing we have learned from the process, it is that it is not a destination but an ongoing commitment that must be baked into the organization's structure, governance, policies, and culture. We are very aware that, while we experienced this process as messy and difficult, for members and staff of color it was a process of ongoing pain and disappointment in our ability as leaders to fulfill our intentions to change the cultures and practices of the organization as a whole. Since so many organizations and formations have these same challenges, we feel it is important to acknowledge just how hard it was for us to shift from understanding antiracist principles and practices to implementing them fully. So, it's not that we consider the two of us experts in how to address internal racism or structural white supremacy in white-led organizations. However, we do think we learned some things along the way that may be of use.

While the specifics of the following lessons are drawn from JVP's particular experience, given what we know from other movement (and non-movement) organizations, we imagine that these lessons are widely applicable in a variety of contexts. In the spirit of the organizing reflection questions at the end of this chapter, you may want to read these with an eye to how they apply to other movements, groups, or organizations that you encounter.

OBSTACLES

White People Controlling the Process

As an LT, we felt we accepted the overall critique offered by the caucus and understood that it needed to become an organizational priority. Where we fell short was in *how* in practice that could be accomplished, and some nonalignment with the details of the caucus's critique. The organization was led at the top by white Jews, and we had ultimate decision-making power. At the end of the day, we were in control of the process. We were in control of the budget, of staffing, and of programmatic priorities. As long as we were in leadership, we can understand why this fundamental truth undermined any sense of real change. Given that these power questions were always present, we could at a minimum have been transparent about them and ideally worked to address them. We could have been more creative and open about how to address our white power structure even within our structured and hierarchical staffing model.

Many of the white Jewish people in the leadership of the organization, including the two of us, felt a sense of loss and disorientation in realizing that we had to grapple even in JVP with issues of race and power. This came out of personal histories where we had struggled to find our places as white people in antiracist movements. Being at JVP, where the role of our Jewishness was clear, had been empowering and even exhilarating. Realizing we would have to continue to grapple even within JVP with the contradiction of our privileged race and class positioning was at best sobering, and at worst evoked our resentment and resistance.

Challenges of Implementation

Over the years, organizers had reported that working conditions could be unpleasant—long hours, mistreatment from members, and other issues. These issues were the direct result of the organizing culture that we in leadership had created and expanded over time. Because organizers are frontline workers who have more direct contact with members than leadership, the frustrations that members had with leadership would be directed at organizers. As more organizers of color began working in the field, they began to report that they experienced racism, aggression, and entitlement from some white members. Staff of color's insistence on members' oppressive behaviors being unacceptable led us to make changes in the overall organizing program that addressed conditions that organizers, white and BIJOCSM, had experienced as well (it was eye-opening to realize how much we tolerated being treated disrespectfully!). Just like any other body of people, we had members who were steeped in antiracist practices; we had members who, like all of us, needed support to adjust their practices; and we had members who didn't demonstrate respect or trust for the actual person of color they were working with. For example, organizers reported comments such as "You don't know how to do your job," or "I am right, you are wrong." These are harsh statements for anyone to hear, but because of the uninterrogated ways that racial dynamics were playing out in the organization, these comments coming from white members to organizers of color magnified the harmful impact.

The initial stage of the RJT process was entirely staff focused. As the next step, an ongoing RJT team was established to continue the work. One of the first projects the RJT team took on was a train-the-trainers program, in which the RJT team trained a subset of staff to facilitate RJT trainings for chapter leaders, who would then train their chapter members. The idea was to start to disseminate what we had learned and address the issues with microaggressions, bigotry, and boundary pushing that were emerging from the field, as well as increasing our members' skills and comfort organizing across race, class, and experience. In tandem with these trainings, we rolled out to the chapters and larger membership a recalibration of the expectations of chapters in terms of how they could interact with our organizing staff, including stronger boundaries for when there were disrespectful interactions. This included a newly articulated set of "ground rules," which included guidance like "making requests rather than demands," not dominating the conversation, not sharing nonpublic information, and refraining from "cross-examining," repeated interrogative questioning with escalating hostility and intensity. JVP staff sent an email to the membership announcing the new guidelines; held a Leadership Development Institute focused on rolling out the RJT curriculum in local chapters, which led to some chapters convening internal learning and discussions; and made changes that ultimately led to an organizing department overhaul in 2019.

The staff team made a good faith effort to change the unhealthy aspects of the organizing culture, but making it stick would have taken sustained time, attention, and resources. We created some systems, like special wellness benefits and improved conditions for staff travel, but, like the principles and plans shared with chapters, they were not thoroughly implemented. As white leaders, we didn't prioritize that ongoing process in a way that could have made that transformation a reality.

Getting Stuck in Deference Politics

The two of us have reflected upon how often we found ourselves not knowing how—or having the trust—to express principled disagreement with the caucus or other staff of color. Rather than practicing honesty and transparency so we could work through our disagreements, we were guarded and appeasing in our interactions. This behavior is not just common but pervasive in white patterns of attempting to deal with our racism. By the time we, as white Jews, became moved to action, there was already a lot of hurt and damage that had been done to the trust and camaraderie between white Jews and Jews of color and Sephardi/ Mizrahi (JOCSM) Jews in JVP, as well as between Jewish and non-Jewish people of color on staff, including Palestinians. We relied way too heavily on how thoroughly we thought we were welcoming and accepting the critique of the organization and of us as leaders, thinking that was enough to create a healthy relationship. This didn't give enough space to the hurt and the differential in power over resources, access to information, and responsibility for the organization as a whole. Because we carried guilt and shame for getting us to that point, we failed to articulate our disagreements or set the necessary boundaries once the process began. We tried to move toward solutions too quickly, before repair work had been successful.

In our larger membership there had always been small numbers of Jews of color and Sephardi/Mizrahi Jews. Not all of them joined the caucus, for a variety of reasons. Just as there is no one Palestinian perspective, not all Jews of color or Sephardi/Mizrahi Jews share the same views. But this furthered our sense of confusion about how to proceed. We didn't want to reproduce a classic divide-and-conquer move of splitting communities of color and working with those who were willing to work within the current JVP culture, thus delegitimizing the "troublemakers." But we also didn't want to ignore or delegitimize the JOCSM JVP members who were not part of the caucus, leading to further frozenness. Even as we were aware of this potential dynamic, we may have played into it, relying on those JOC who for their own reasons were not prioritizing challenging the internal JVP culture to justify our choices.

Balancing Urgent Priorities

We felt internal and external pressures about our choice to spend considerable time and resources on dealing with our internal racial justice issues rather than spending all of our time organizing directly toward Palestinian freedom. Unlike our other organization-wide processes, this one was primarily internally facing at first, so a lot of the work we were doing was opaque—not just to our supporters but also to our core chapter and council leaders.

This created a perception that JVP was turning its attention away from Palestine as we engaged in a process that, at root, was about strengthening the organization as well as the movement for the long haul. There is no doubt that some of our campaigns, media strategies, and organizing practices were given less attention as we turned our attention to the RJT process. There were legitimate political questions and subsequent disagreements about how to allocate our resources and energy among the RJT work and ongoing campaigns and projects among leadership, board, staff, and members.

At times we worried that we were putting disproportionate energy and attention to becoming the "perfect movement organization" rather than innovating our organizing strategies to end Israeli apartheid, a concern that has been echoed in discussions about how to build strong movement organizations in the years since. While, of course, it is not either/or, there are a finite amount of hours in a work week, and, within the LT, we often disagreed on how much attention to give to one or the other on any given day. If we had publicly named these tensions and created principles for how we were going to manage them, we might have engendered more trust in the process. Because we subsumed them within our private LT conversations, this also meant that, as individuals, we had neither accountability nor opportunities to take on individual roles in the process.

What We Wished We Knew Before

It'll be like peeling an onion.

As we addressed more deeply in chapter 2, structures are crucial. Because we all live in a world imbued with racism and sexism, and we are all affected by them both consciously and unconsciously, in order not to drift toward bias or even the status quo, it is essential to create systems that are designed to negate these tendencies, including measures of accountability. Be prepared for the process to be like peeling an onion—after you address one layer, you'll find there is always one further to go as you move toward the core.

The result of our large number of hires in 2014–2015 was that our staff was more homogenous than ever. In fact, we had a staff joke about the "Alanas" (sometimes Elana or Ilana)—there were five on staff by 2016, all of whom were white and Ashkenazi. We remember being slightly smug about it at first, thinking this was a reflection of our Jewish bona fides, but in truth what it really meant was that JVP was hiring from a very narrow pool—white, Jewish, class-privileged women in their twenties and thirties. The joke quickly became very much not funny. Until that point, JVP's hiring practices had relied on an unarticulated sense of "fit" that played directly into biases toward cultural sameness and led to a majority of white, Ashkenazi staff, even as there was a stated intention and hope to recruit multiracial applicants. We recall bragging that within the first few minutes of an interview we could tell if the person would be a good match for our staff culture. Of course, what that really meant was that our unconscious biases, games of "Jewish geography," (talking until we found connections through mutual friends, camps, schools, and the like) and desire to keep our cozy (to us) culture intact was not only leading us to make hiring decisions based on these factors but also limiting our pool of good candidates.

Through the help of a consultant, Stefanie Fox and Ari Wohlfeiler led a process through which we learned how to revamp our hiring processes. That didn't solve the problem of racism in the organization, but it was an important step that illuminated the structural interventions needed. For example, we learned to spend more time building out a pool of candidates beyond our known circles, to think carefully about the competencies we expected in any position to make sure they weren't excluding categories of people, and to use scoring matrices in our interviews to bring rigor to our evaluation instead of relying on snap judgments of people, which would inevitably be biased. We trained ourselves not to make small talk in interviews so as not to be swayed by the communal connections we did or did not find in those conversations. To keep ourselves accountable to the process, we committed to hard numbers about who needed to be included, and in what percentage in every stage of the hiring process, before we could go on to the next step. An example of that would be keeping a new job description open until we had at least twelve viable candidates, at least a third of whom had to be POC or JOCSM. The accountability practices we learned to use in hiring are helpful for operationalizing racial justice commitments with other organizational practices. For example, if you are starting a new program to reach out to an underrepresented group in your community, holding yourself to not running the program until 20 percent of participants are from that group would be a way to ensure equity.

And it worked. By 2017, about a third of JVP's staff was not white and Ashkenazi Jewish, and included Palestinian Americans, Black Jews, Jews of color, Mizrahi/Sephardi Jews, and other people of color. This led to a whole new stage where we came to comprehend that changing our hiring practices was just the beginning of the project to address racism in the organization. Then, the next layer of issues became visible. Because of the longer tenure of white staff, the newer staff of color were being supervised by people with limited experience in supervision generally and in supervising across race specifically. This led to some staff of color expressing that they felt they received insufficient support or feedback to succeed in their work. New staff were not prepared that the RJT process would be part of their role and workplace. Jews of color on staff were thus often thrust into middle-person roles, between a rock (their employers) and a hard place (their community of JOCs). Staff of color were still expected to adjust to the culture that had been built around white staff and experienced racism and harassment from some members. We recall understanding, then, that this process would be like peeling an onion—each time we took a step forward, we confronted issues closer to our core.

You can't do it on your own.

It is rare, if not impossible, for organizations to manage these transformations on their own. It is important to get outside help, which can help hold up a mirror to an organization's reality, design structures and processes to move forward, and offer coaching support when challenges arise, as they inevitably do. This is not the time or place to skimp. Investing serious resources (JVP allocated $50,000/year for the first two years) will allow you to make comprehensive and long-term commitments, as well as signaling the seriousness and commitment with which the organization is taking the process. Given the inevitability that movement organizations will get pulled toward rapid response or urgent campaigns in response to outside events or alliances, having a team that can offer an ongoing structure of accountability is crucial.

One thing we really internalized over the course of the process is that, as white people in leadership, we are always going to have blind spots due to our positionality and identities. This did not absolve us of the responsibility to be reflective and rigorous with our own practices, but it does mean you have an obligation to be always mindful of how to address and counteract those blind spots, including by trusting and welcoming the information shared with you—that you might otherwise miss—by those with less power and different positionality. Our reluctance to bring in a third party sooner was a manifestation of our belief that we could do everything best on our own, an idea that likely came from a mixture of our whiteness, class privilege, and related hubris, and an internalized sense that our work was so complicated and sensitive that no one could understand or would want to get enmeshed with it. Because we have been fighting Zionist forces so intensely and persistently, it likely gave us an outsized sense of confidence that we could tackle anything that comes our way. We simply didn't have what it took to get us out of a mess of our own making.

One note of caution (speaking as people who ourselves have done consulting work) is that typically consultants are hired by leadership, so they see themselves as primarily accountable to leadership. This can compromise members' receptivity to the consultants' findings and recommendations and, in some cases, the findings and recommendations themselves. The process of working with consultants is not a panacea. For staff, the outside support was essential to the feeling that the work was being prioritized, was being handled with skill and expertise, and was going to yield substantive shifts in JVP's culture and workplace. On the other hand, the caucus, which inspired the RJT process, was at that point pretty alienated from the organization, including from staff of color. Unfortunately, the process only exacerbated the tensions between some staff of color and the caucus, as well as between the LT and the caucus, instead of healing them.

As leaders, be prepared to apologize and take action.

Immediately accepting the critique was just the first step in taking responsibility. Again and again, we had to reflect on mistakes we made, apologize and account for them, and take clear steps to ensure we didn't make those mistakes again. In October 2018, at our annual full staff retreat, at the suggestion of our consultants, we apologized as the LT to the staff for the ways in which we had failed them and JVP as a whole. We read aloud a memo we had spent several days preparing, alternating who was doing the reading to acknowledge our collective responsibility. We went into great detail about the specific ways that we had failed, including not only our limitations as a white and Ashkenazi team but also our lack of transparency with the staff about the process, not acknowledging the very real power differentials between the LT and the caucus, and the lack of scaffolding or protection we offered to staff when they were left to manage relationships on their own. The offering worked as intended, breaking something open for everyone, allowing a level of communication, honesty, openness, and hope that was absolutely priceless. We shared the memo we had prepared with the caucus as well, as part of our emerging practice of being more transparent about our thinking. But, given that we hadn't created the same container of trust and collective work with them, and didn't speak to them directly, we understand it didn't provide any sense of healing for anyone beyond the staff who were there for the conversation.

Every corner of the organization

Don't expect to spend some concentrated time addressing racial justice and then move on, having "fixed" it. Even to maintain the advances you make when actively shifting your approach can be challenging because of how deeply entrenched racism is in our world. Without metrics, accountability, and resources, you will inevitably backslide to the status quo. And things continue to shift over time. There is always deeper to go, and/or outside factors or internal mistakes will continue to offer moments of challenge. If you can build your resiliency and skills to welcome these challenges as opportunities to continue to evolve instead of responding to them defensively as a distraction, they will become integrated into the ongoing shifts and flexibility of any dynamic organization.

One of our key takeaways about JVP's RJT process was the importance—and difficulty—of taking seriously a commitment to antiracism in every part of an organization for the long term, from HR policies to communications materials, fundraising strategies, consultants and staffing decisions, board selection, campaigning, and programming. For an organization like JVP that has chapters and individual members, the work of implementation throughout the organization is particularly challenging. There's no corner of society untouched by the legacy of white supremacy, and that includes movement organizations. This reality creates an organizational culture that privileges white ideas, beliefs, and practices, expecting people of color to assimilate into those white norms. This was true of our organizing culture, internal staff culture, and relationships with chapters. We are very aware of our role as white leaders in creating this culture and, despite our best intentions, our inability to transform JVP in all the ways we needed to.

As an LT, even before we turned our attention to white supremacy, we had a sobering run-in with sexism and JVP's pay scale that became a helpful touchstone for remembering how entwined our practices were with the external world, despite our personal political commitments. Around 2015, after JVP's hiring spree, to the LT's shock and horror, we found that men overall were making more than women and non-binary people at JVP. We were a women-led organization that took our feminist practices seriously—yet we were vulnerable to the ways in which sexism so deeply permeates our culture. We identified many reasons this had happened: as JVP's budget and profile grew, more men applied for positions, and pay scales had shifted as JVP grew, so men were entering positions at higher salaries; men applied for jobs that traditionally had higher salaries across the sector; and men negotiated more aggressively for salary adjustments. As the team in charge of the budget, the LT spent time and money to equalize pay rates across job categories, fix the inequities, and establish strict salary bands so that we couldn't fall back into the same patterns, but it was a sobering lesson in the ways that the structures we are steeped in impacted us even if we as individuals held deeply felt feminist values.

We were able to respond to gender inequities rapidly and confidently but white, Ashkenazi dominance in our culture and organizational practices was a different story. As in the case of the gendered pay scales, we hadn't had any safeguards in place to resist the structures and systems that were part of broader Jewish communities and society in general. Unlike the case of the pay scales, which we adjusted quickly once the problem was identified, we lacked the perspective and confidence to address racism internally in an effective way.

It is not your job to finish the work, but neither are you free to desist from it.

This period at JVP was one of confusion, tension, and lack of unity for staff, board, leadership, and members. Yet, it was absolutely essential to wrestle us into a new era of JVP's life when we better understood our responsibilities to reflect the reality of US Jewish communities as they actually are, and to integrate the political thinking of our BIJOCSM comrades into our analysis. And we must admit we still look back on it in some frustration and sense of having unfinished business. JVP's work in this realm continues. Even if we know, intellectually, that it was not a matter of "finishing" the work of antiracism, emotionally, our mistakes still rankle. And we are haunted by the reality that many members of the caucus and staff paid a steep price in difficult working conditions, with feelings of disappointment and even betrayal over the way we led JVP through this time.

The BIJOCSM Caucus constantly challenged us, in the best way, to deepen our analysis. They brought a sophistication and depth of thought to making the connections between communities in the US and in Israel/Palestine, the often unknown and uncelebrated cultural and political contributions of Mizrahi/Sephardi Jews and Jews of color in Israel, and the linchpin role these communities could play in forging a coalition to truly challenge Zionism. They gifted JVP with the urgency to finally address long-standing issues and to move toward doing a better job of representing who Jewish communities actually consist of, and how to work toward aligning our internal and external politics.

Organizing Strategy Reflection Questions

Racial Justice Transformation

1. What kind of ongoing training and support do you provide to your members on antiracist practice and unlearning white supremacist cultural norms?

2. Do you have a set of community agreements for how staff and members are expected to treat one another? What accountability mechanisms do you have in place to help identify and mitigate the ways white supremacy will inevitably enter your organizational practices?

3. Do your leadership bodies reflect the constituency you are trying to organize?

4. For organizations with staff: What systems do you have in place for ongoing evaluation, feedback, and improvements around your antiracist practices at the staff level? How do you ensure that staff, board, and members all move forward together on racial justice practices? Do you provide ongoing training for staff and board to build their skills at leading in multiracial organizations and supervising across race? Do you provide dedicated time and space for POC staff to be together?

5. For white leaders: What support do you have to identify your blind spots and make commitments to structural shifts as needed? What resources are you willing to allocate to ensure the process has adequate support if you enter into one? How will you communicate your commitments to the rest of the organization, so you can be held accountable?

Chapter 8

Weathering Repression

In 2010, about a month after the successful action interrupting Prime Minister Netanyahu at the Jewish Federation GA in New Orleans detailed in chapter 3, JVP–Bay Area (BA) was holding a meeting at a senior center in Berkeley. While the meeting was in process, it was interrupted by about a dozen activists from Stand With Us, a right-wing Israel advocacy organization funded at least in part by the Israeli government. This disruption came on the heels of escalating attacks on JVP–BA members throughout the previous months, including being aggressively recorded at demonstrations, being told by counterprotesters that they were going to find out where members lived, and calling them *Kapos*.[1] JVP's Oakland office had also been graffitied with violent slogans. Wearing an Israeli flag as a cape, a Stand With Us protester pepper-sprayed two JVP members in the face and eyes when they tried to nonviolently block her from aggressively videotaping the meeting.[2]

A multitude of tactics and strategies are used to repress support for just about any movement for justice that seeks to overturn the status quo. Abortion providers, abolitionists, or campaigners against megacorporations will recognize the tactics of repression we outline here. While the targeting and points of vulnerability named here are specific to the movement for Palestinian freedom, they are part and parcel of a common playbook that we see across movements. If there is one thing to remember about their impact, it is this: *they were designed specifically to have a chilling effect on movement building.* Cumulatively, they create an atmosphere of fear, raising the cost of doing movement work. Very often, these tactics are building blocks that reinforce and build upon one another. In the case of the Palestinian freedom movement, the Israeli government has funded or played a role in most of these tactics. Our hope is that by naming these strategies we can demystify them to allow ourselves more room to imagine strategies to anticipate these attacks and inoculate ourselves, and those we want to join our movements, against them.

We explore repression and its impact in three parts. First, we outline what we are calling the "continuum of repression." This is the reality of what every person involved in the Palestinian movement, and many other movements, has to contend with. It is impossible to understand the Palestinian freedom movement's internal and external dynamics without understanding this ongoing onslaught. Next, we explore the "impact of repression," which looks at how the severity of the attacks fall most heavily on Palestinians and people of color, but also can affect anyone who participates in the Palestinian movement. From a movement-building perspective, these tactics of intimidation and harassment take a toll on organizers that must be taken seriously if our movements will stay strong for the long haul. Finally, we share stories of "resilience in the face of repression," which we hope will inspire or at least neutralize the feelings of despair that come when the repression feels overwhelming. We have learned that the best antidote to despair is creating more connections through strong relationships, campaigns, and organizing that prevent you from ducking into a defensive crouch, giving you the courage to steel yourself as you go headlong into the next fight.

The Continuum of Repression

Social Pressure

For Jewish people, whatever your family's unique migration story—through Palestine or marred by trauma at the hands of the Nazis or being forced out of your home in Iraq or Morocco—opposing Zionism can feel like rejecting or disrespecting ancestors. The message is often sent overtly (and sometimes more subtly) that it's not okay to critique Israel or air Jewish "dirty laundry" publicly, and to do so is treasonous. These messages are particularly reinforced in Jewish day schools, at Zionist summer camps, and at most synagogues. It is not an easy sell for organizers to convince people to put themselves in a situation where family ties may be strained, or to risk awkward family get-togethers or being disinvited altogether. For those who are white and middle or upper class (a substantial portion of JVP membership), who are used to access, affirmation, and a fairly frictionless daily life, the chilling effect of this level of pressure is real and can push people back into the closet. When people do make the leap, it is critical to create a soft landing place for them, as we covered in chapter 1.

This phenomenon is not unique to Jews. Non-Jews also experience social pressure from friends and colleagues, exacerbated by the very uses of antisemitism outlined in the previous chapter. The chair of one foundation that gave money to JVP told us ruefully that he was hearing criticism from people he met at cocktail parties about the foundation's support of our work. The understandable, and laudable, desire not to be labeled as antisemitic

can have strong social force, which is one reason it is so important to push back against conceptions of antisemitism that are
based on critique of Israel, and to create welcoming communities
where people can be at home with their politics.

Harassment

The internet is not known for its subtlety. Even so, those of
us who speak out for Palestine know all too well the cesspool
that the comment sections of a social media post can quickly
become. The anonymity lends itself to vociferous name-calling
and threats. But it doesn't end there. Hate mail comes in all
forms—emails, snail mail, phone calls, text messages, Twitter
("X") comments, spray paint, flyers, posters. These attacks are
often directed to the person who made the allegedly objection-
able comment, but sometimes the harassment is brought to the
doorstep of a third party—the university dean, the boss, the faith
leader. The cumulative impact of being called dreadful names,
being threatened with rape or death, takes a serious toll. Many
of us doing this work hold fast to the "never read the comments"
rule and have tools to silence a lot of what we don't want to hear
(thank you, caller ID, email filters, and other settings). Even so,
the vitriol gets through the cracks. The harasser's goal is to create
a sense of surveillance, of threat and discomfort, to deter you
from speaking out for Palestine. It is designed to feel menacing
and all encompassing. A shrug of "haters gonna hate" only takes
you so far, especially when we know that both bots and humans
are being deployed specifically for purposes of harassment and
intimidation when anyone speaks out.[3]

A number of organizations, funded at least in part by the
Israeli government, exist solely to intimidate, harass, and bully
people, students in particular, who are active parts of the movement. These are largely anonymous and thus difficult to hold

accountable. They work to ensure that the profiles of movement leaders are search engine–optimized so that they are widely seen. Canary Mission, for example, publishes anonymous, slanderous profiles of activists, mostly students, who then must contend with initial post-college job searches that are handicapped by prominent accusations of antisemitism, which is particularly dangerous for those who are Palestinian, Arab, Black, or Muslim (or any combination thereof). Israel has also used the profiles created by Canary Mission to block individuals' entry to Israel.[4] Other notable organizations in this category include StopAntiSemitism.org, which chooses one target at a time and directs social media mobs to go after them; Stand With Us, for whom online smear campaigns are just one tool in their vast arsenal; and NGO Monitor, which focuses on targeting organizations. These tactics will be familiar to trans, LGBTQ, and people of color online, who often find themselves the targets of directed social media mobs.

Pressure from Large "Legacy" Organizations

There are a number of "legacy" Jewish organizations that trade on their perceived bona fides in fighting antisemitism to advance a right-wing agenda when it comes to Israel. These include enormously resourced and influential organizations like the ADL, American Jewish Committee, and the Simon Wiesenthal Center. It is important to note that all of these organizations are self-appointed arbiters of Jewish communal opinion and, increasingly, do not actually reflect the majority of Jewish perspective. The ADL, for example, publishes a "Top 10 Anti-Israel Organizations" list every few years that smears organizations working for Palestinian freedom and has doubled down on its commitment to equate anti-Zionism with antisemitism.[5] The #DropTheADL campaign has amassed materials on its history of attacking social justice movements, including for Palestinian liberation under the banner of civil rights.[6] These organizations are tightly coordinated, working from the same messaging and tactical playbooks.[7] Often, when an organization or politician uninitiated to the internal Jewish debates on Israel/Palestine steps out in support of Palestine, they will be greeted shortly thereafter by an onslaught of lobbying pressure by the ADL, the local Jewish Community Relations Council, and other organizations to backtrack. While we don't know exactly what is threatened or promised in these backdoor meetings, we know it is effective. As discussed in chapter 5 in reference to the Presbyterian Church (US)'s decision to support divesting from the Israeli occupation, local synagogues and Jewish organizations were recruited into pressuring local Presbyterian leaders to reject divestment or risk losing their interfaith alliances.

Organizations such as the Zionist Organization of America (ZOA), Christians United for Israel (CUFI), and Stand With Us, which have a more overt right-wing reputation, are also extremely well-resourced, often directly from the Israeli government.[8] These organizations then use their weight to bully institutions to decline to host events for or accept donations from, or even to fire those supporting Palestinian freedom, punish thought-leaders who speak out, and try to control the public narrative by purporting to speak for the Jewish people as a whole.[9]

Islamophobia/Anti-Palestinian Racism

The rise of a broad-based movement fighting for Palestinian freedom in this century has coincided with the sharp rise in institutional and cultural Islamophobia in the US in the post-9/11 "war on terror" era. Jewish Zionist institutions flourished in this anti-Muslim era, finding common cause with those newly concerned about the role of Muslims in society. They pivoted swiftly to conflate fear of Muslims with the need to "defend Israel" and further align the military and political interests of Israel and the US. The demonization of Muslims furthered Israel's interests and created a new bogeyman for the far right in the US.[10] The "war on terror" was taken up by pro-Israel groups as an insurance that Israeli security would be prioritized and the US's "special" relationship with Israel would endure. Many Jewish groups that include Muslims in their interfaith initiatives only do so with a strict litmus test that requires the groups they work with not to speak out too strongly on Israel.[11]

The "Muslim ban," one of the first executive orders made by Trump in early 2017, banning travel from several mostly Muslim countries, was a stark reminder of how Islamophobia animates US foreign policy. The Muslim ban did not come out of nowhere; it came from decades of racist, Islamophobic, and xenophobic policies and discourses around national security, the "war on terror," and immigration from both Republican and Democratic administrations. The Trump administration's policies were new, and arguably more extreme, but were built on existing infrastructure, overwhelmingly impacting those who are fleeing homes ravaged by the US military around the world.[12] The ubiquity of systemic Islamophobia in our culture in the US amounts to a form of active political repression. Muslim houses of worship are surveilled, people who appear Muslim are treated with suspicion, and all of this creates a culture hostile to organizing and movement building (to say the least). It's a testament to the profound commitment and courage of Muslim and Palestinian organizers that they keep fighting despite the dangers they face.

Online Censorship and Deplatforming

Palestinian organizations and those who support them face ongoing censorship from major social media and other crucial communication platforms including Facebook/Meta, Twitter ("X"), Instagram, YouTube, Google Maps, and Zoom. They also face barriers to using Venmo, PayPal, and other online donation platforms, often on the pretext of accusations of support for terrorism, another example of how Islamophobic narratives impact wide-ranging policies. As these are key global communications and fundraising tools, this lack of access can absolutely sabotage individuals' communications and businesses, as well as the effectiveness of Palestinian organizations, making it harder to raise awareness of Israeli human rights violations.[13] They also have real-world consequences, as Palestinians have been arrested for incitement for their posts, and Palestinian Americans have received home visits from the FBI for similar reasons.

The Israeli government plays an active role in advocating the removal of social media posts that document Israeli human rights abuses, with its Cyber Unit bragging in 2021 of a 90 percent success rate in getting posts pulled from Facebook/Meta.[14] For Palestinians, whose voices are routinely absent in mainstream media reporting, social media represents an essential tool for Palestinians' experiences under Israeli apartheid to reach a wide audience. By losing access to posting privileges, the realities of apartheid are further hidden from public view—which is precisely why Israel advocates so strongly in this field.

Lawfare and Anti-BDS Laws

A number of right-wing legal organizations, which collaborate and coordinate with the Israeli government, use politically motivated, bogus legal accusations to try to intimidate, shut down, embroil in legal battles, and impose fiscal and reputational costs on organizations promoting Palestinian rights. "Lawfare" can take many forms, including litigation, regulatory complaints, trying to withdraw charitable tax status, and pressure campaigns to cut off funding. Though the legal maneuvering is rarely successful, the chilling effect on and financial cost to organizations are profound. These tactics are a concerted threat not only to Palestinian civil society and solidarity organizations but also to organizations supporting a range of movements, as these tactics are tested on the Palestinian rights movement and are in the process of being adopted more widely to repress activism in support of abortion rights and climate justice, for example.

Since about 2014, attempts to legislate against Palestinian rights have proliferated at the state and federal level. These usually take the form of anti-BDS legislation or attempts to codify antisemitism to include criticism of Israel (that is, the IHRA definition discussed in chapter 4). As of 2022, almost 250 bills have been introduced in thirty-two states, though only about 20 percent have passed, and those that have passed have often been overturned by the courts for being unconstitutional.[15] Organizations such as the ACLU, Palestine Legal, CAIR, and the Center for Constitutional Rights have been instrumental in fighting these laws on free speech grounds, and the fights against them have helped more moderate Democrats to understand and defend the right to BDS.[16] These legislative attempts are meant to act as a deterrent against pro-Palestinian activism and are also a strategy to divert the attention of organizations working for Palestinian freedom from proactive to defensive work against these laws. These types of laws are also of grave concern for their use as a model to attack other movements, such as the climate justice movement, with similar tactics.

Spying and Surveillance

Palestinian rights activists in the US have long been the targets of surveillance and spying, dating back at least to the 1960s.[17]

There is evidence that companies such as the Israeli Black Cube and NSO's Pegasus have been used to surveil activists and attempt to entrap them in activities that could delegitimize or embarrass them. These efforts contribute to the overall intimidation that activists and organizations face and require attentiveness to personal and online security measures that can be expensive and unwieldy. Individuals and members of organizations almost routinely receive death threats and threats of violence that require individual and communal defense systems, all of which takes an enormous psychological, emotional, and physical toll, as well as incurring actual costs for physical safety measures. What's more, the reality of surveillance can foster damaging cultures of suspicion in organizing collectives that must be carefully guarded against.

Terrorism Designations

US government designation of organizations as terrorist or terrorist-supporting organizations has long been politicized. In the case of Palestinians, that intensified in the wake of 9/11 and the passage of the PATRIOT Act. Designation often reflects racist and Islamophobic policies and practices and US foreign policy biases. The impact of being designated a terrorist organization is severe and can include the freezing of all assets, deplatforming from social media, and criminal and civil penalties for the organization's leadership. The cloud of the Holy Land Foundation Five case, when the largest Muslim humanitarian aid organization was categorized as a terrorist-supporting organization shortly after 9/11, culminating in the criminal convictions and prison sentences of decades for its officials, continues to have a chilling effect on Arab Americans in particular.[18] The Holy Land case was directly related to Israel, as the accusation was of material support for Hamas, and two Israeli agents were

allowed to testify anonymously in closed courtrooms as part of
the persecution, among other injustices around the case. More
recently, Israel has also used terrorism designations to attempt to
undermine the work of leading Palestinian human rights organizations, jeopardizing their legitimacy as well as their ability to
raise funds and operate at all.[19]

The Impact of Repression

The repression experienced by Palestine solidarity movement
activists is not unique to the Palestinian freedom movement. In
fact, the tactics deployed against us often presage tactics used
on other movements. Successful, grassroots, global movements
rise to topple regimes of power and domination. Those regimes
and their defenders will, in turn, do their best to quash that
rising tide. Just because this is expected does not mean it is
not devastating or unsettling to those on the receiving end.
These strategies, while deployed against all those who stand
with Palestinians struggling for their freedom, from university professors to city council members to school teachers and
rabbis, are primarily aimed at Palestinians. They target specific Palestinian organizers and community leaders but also the
Palestinian people more broadly, with the intention that the
costs they exact will serve as deterrents to future activism. Of
course, when these attacks are brought against people of color,
as in the M4BL policy platform debacle outlined in chapter 5,
these attacks reverberate with the pain and force of the generations of brutal repression of Black organizing for liberation
and dignity.

While the most intense attacks are against Palestinians and
other people of color, white people in the movement are not left
unscathed. The threats to Palestinian life or livelihood, threats of
deportation, incarceration, and, all too often, death, come with

the full weight of both the US and Israeli legal systems, military, and ongoing strategic coordination between them. The toll for Jews can be painful but is fundamentally less extreme. We raise here the emotional and political impacts on Jews, because it is both where we have the most experience and because the cumulative impact of these repression strategies amount to a serious barrier for Jewish participation in advocacy and organizing toward Palestinian freedom. Toppling those barriers to participation is a core obligation of ours as organizers. At the same time, we are very aware of the disproportionate attention and support that the two of us get when attacked, compared to the impact on our Palestinian comrades. On every level, Jewish American and Israeli dissent receives more public attention and affirmation than Palestinians who have been saying the same things for decades. This is true on every level—from the public attention when Israelis are killed, compared to the attention given Palestinians, to the attention and coverage of Jewish or other non-Palestinian human rights organizations naming Israel as an apartheid state, after decades of Palestinian human rights organizations being ignored when asserting the same, to the differing levels of attention, concern, and action for individual Palestinian and pro-Palestinian Jewish students on campuses across the country. These dynamics are not unique to Palestinians and Jews. For now, and until we transform our society, the same biases exist wherever the power differentials do.

Jewish and Muslim and/or Arab communities live in starkly different communal systems in relation to the US government. The US has enacted multiple fundamentally Islamophobic laws, programs, and policies that are designed to eat away at trust, cohesion, and communal influence in Muslim communities by threatening deportation, imprisonment, and other punishments for associating with "terrorism." At the same time that these laws were being developed, pro-Israel Jewish communities were enjoying decades of complete carte blanche to develop extensive fundraising apparatus and communal organizations. Cumulatively, the funds raised add up to millions if not billions of dollars of support for Israel's military, lobbying on behalf of Israel in the US, and for propaganda to promote Israel in Jewish communities, including through the infamous all-expenses-paid trips to Israel for Jewish young people. So, when, for example, the Second Intifada began, in 2000, the pro-Israel Jewish establishment was prepared, organized, and coordinated to defend Israel, while organizing for Palestine was at a low ebb. It has never been a fair fight.

"Armenian Foundation"

As an example of the kind of forces JVP found ourselves up against, we share here for the first time a sophisticated attempt to discredit us, in the same time frame and with similar methods as the Israeli firm Black Cube was later revealed to be using.[20]

In 2017, some potential new donors reached out to JVP, offering a grant of $100,000. They identified themselves as representatives of an Armenian foundation that had been funding mostly humanitarian projects but were looking to move into supporting social justice in the Middle East because of the historic presence of Armenians throughout the region, including Palestine. Against the backdrop of ongoing public attempts to delegitimize our work, for example through the Reut Institute, the ADL, and Israeli Ministry of Strategic Affairs (which was very public about its attempts to tarnish and sabotage BDS networks and supporters), we were skeptical of new and unvetted connections.[21]After checking in with a couple of allies, including other funders, we found that no one had heard of them and they did not seem to exist in any funder databases. But we were also intrigued—$100,000 would be significant to our budget. After a few conversations and an initial proposal, they called Rebecca to float the idea of offering us "in-kind services" in addition to money, through an opposition research firm. They began to suggest, subtly at first, that they could use extralegal means to dig up dirt on our opponents, including individuals. After an in-person meeting and several phone calls, they finally began to use language that was clearly proposing illegal activities. Realizing that this was an attempt at entrapment, in that last conversation, Rebecca kept reiterating that we didn't want to use any illegal means or illegal information in our work.

After that call, Rebecca sent an email again reinforcing that we weren't interested in the "in-kind services" part of the potential grant—and we never heard from them again. Although we will probably never have proof, it seems fairly clear that we were the target of an op to discredit us. It was around the same time when stories about the Israeli firm Black Cube started appearing in the press—in particular, the accounts of attempts to entrap actor Rose McGowan to discredit her accusations of sexual abuse by Harvey Weinstein. It all sounded dreadfully familiar. Of course, this story is a partial reflection of the various ways that JVP and other movement organizations have been targeted over the years. It is also a reminder of the ways that chasing funding can be damaging to an organization's focus and clarity. If something looks and feels too good to be true, it probably is. There are no shortcuts for raising money to run an organization in sustainable, healthy ways.

This incident is very much in line with what respected veteran reporter Yossi Melman wrote in the Israeli newspaper *Maariv* in 2016: that the Israeli Ministry of Strategic Affairs had committed millions of dollars to defeat the BDS movement, including for "Black Ops" such as "defamation campaigns, harassment and threats to the lives of activists" as well as "infringing on and violating their privacy."[22] The range of activities undertaken at the time of the article included a de facto travel ban on BDS cofounder Omar Barghouti and a call for the "targeted civil elimination" of Palestinian BDS leaders. As always, the severity of threats toward our Palestinian comrades was of another order of magnitude, compared to what we faced.

Personal Toll Is Real

While we were at JVP, we thought the constant attacks were rolling off our backs. In reality, they took a very serious toll on both of us. Because the threats were often coming from inside our own community, they came with a unique kind of pain. At the same time, because we have a greater understanding of the communal dynamics at play than when attacks come from one community to another, we anticipated them and even understood, perhaps too intimately, the narratives our adversaries were working with. Narratives that labeled us as traitors, even as we see our work as in the best interest—physically and morally—of all of us.

One reason we felt these attacks weren't impacting us was because we personally enjoyed so much support and affirmation inside of JVP, and because our own Jewish legitimacy protected us. After all, no one could tell us we weren't Jewish enough: Rebecca was raised in a synagogue her grandparents founded, had a bat mitzvah at age thirteen, and went on to marry someone both Jewish and Israeli. Rebecca is currently on the board of her synagogue in Brooklyn, where both of her children, likewise, had their bat mitzvahs while she was ED of JVP. Alissa was educated in a Jewish day school, pursued Jewish studies in college, participated in multiple Jewish leadership development programs, and is also a rabbi. Together with our white, Ashkenazi status, there are not many more Jewish bona fides to collect. These traditional markers of Jewish American identity were a protective armor that shielded us from any corrosion of our own sense of entitlement to our Jewish identities or sense of belonging within Judaism.

We're very aware that for our members and coworkers who are part of interfaith marriages or families, are Jews by choice, had little formal Jewish upbringing, have a non-Jewish parent, are people of color, or some combination of the above have a different set of emotional challenges to overcome. Given the racist, classist, sexist, and unnecessarily narrow way that many Jewish legacy organizations gatekeep Jewish identity, we understand that the accusations and lack of communal support hit differently for those members and coworkers than they do for us. These communal dynamics are part of why the work of building a political home is so important. We want to create an expansive and embracing Jewish community for all those who want to be a part of one. Yet, even for the two of us, after leaving JVP staff positions, we realized that these constant attacks had taken much more of a toll than we would have anticipated, as we were barreling through them to keep going. It was emotionally, spiritually, and physically taxing to endure the fairly constant stream of harassment, rejection, and communal excommunication—not to mention ongoing attacks in social media, emails, voicemails, and, at times, in print. After all, the intent behind them was to make the price of our work too high to continue. These attacks were a visceral reminder every day that portions of our own community wished violence—whether literal or metaphorical—upon us, and that took a toll on us both, even with our strong sense of Jewish belonging.

That is not to say we have been unsupported when these attacks come. But even when petitions and statements of solidarity were made on our behalf, these attacks can still create a chilling effect for those who are thinking about speaking out. There's no doubt that those witnessing the repression, even passively, internalize a message of warning that keeps would-be allies and supporters on the sidelines because the price is too high.

Resilience In the Face of Repression

Thinking about and living with the tactics arrayed against movements can be sobering and even immobilizing. Here, we share two short anecdotes that illustrate how JVP and allies not only fought back against repression but also turned those attacks into opportunities for deepening relationships and practices. Sometimes the best form of resilience is not even reframing but simply winning!

Pushing Back against Anti-BDS Bills

State anti-BDS bills were starting to pop up all over the country in 2016. This was a deliberate strategy instigated by BDS opponents—Israel and a coalition of Christian evangelical Zionist organizations and legacy Jewish institutions—that would codify by law the repression of political speech on BDS. Our sense is that this tactic had multiple purposes: first, to create a public narrative that BDS was antisemitic and existentially dangerous to Israel before most people had ever heard of it or could understand its origins or demands. Second, to distract the movement and push us into a reactive stance instead of pursuing proactive legislative and electoral goals. Third, at a moment when the movement overall was accelerating grassroots support for time-honored economic strategies to advance Palestinian rights, opponents still held disproportionate power in legislative settings and used that power to make wins either outright illegal or shrouded with potential controversy, state investigation, or financial impact, which created an intense overall chilling effect.[23]

At the same time that JVP leadership was deliberating around the creation of a viable national strategy against the threat of anti-BDS laws, local formations were also reacting, in the immediate term, to multiple local threats of state anti-BDS bills. In New York, Pennsylvania, and Maryland, JVP's chapters were forming coalitions and fighting against state legislation. In the process, they were learning the ins and outs of state government, building relationships between chapters in the same state, building relationships with state legislators and their staff, and working in tandem with more established groups, like the ACLU, that were taking strong free speech–based positions against the anti-BDS bills as unconstitutional. When these coalitions were able to defeat the bills (though sometimes legislative wins were negated, as in New York, when, in 2016, Governor Cuomo passed a bill by executive order instead), chapter members got a taste of the potential power of legislative organizing and how even attacks like these can be opportunities to build a compelling public narrative. In this case, the idea that anti-BDS laws are a repressive assault on free speech and that the right to boycott is fundamental gained significant ground through these fights.

It was also a reminder of the key role that having a Jewish organization in these coalitions played, both from a moral perspective and from the "man bites dog" curiosity of the press. Underlying assumptions that Jewish communities almost unanimously supported these bills, which were loudly led and echoed by legacy Jewish organizations, were challenged when JVP members were actively involved in fighting the bills. The process of our fighting anti-BDS legislation was part of the public narrative shift of demonstrating that Jewish communities don't actually speak in one voice on this issue. Meanwhile, Jewish participation and leadership helped fight spurious accusations of antisemitism and reframe the conversation as a human rights and free speech issue, not one of bias against Jewish people. These fights continue to this day.

Network against Islamophobia

The way JVP approaches solidarity with targeted communities is itself a strategy to mitigate the pain and isolation of the repression and rejection we feel from our own communities. We show up in the way that we hope to be—and have been—shown up for. And, in the process, we are enriched by building our analysis, our skills, and our relationships for the long-haul fight we are in that will take various permutations and take aim at different targets. A great example of this virtuous cycle was JVP's Network against Islamophobia (NAI). Through the leadership and initiative of two member-leaders, Elly Bulkin and Donna Nevel, who are longtime activists, educators, and writers, JVP launched the NAI with them in summer 2015.[24] This project was a natural extension of the work we had long been doing to combat Islamophobia in Jewish communities, in US politics, in the media, and in our own communities. The NAI was created to sharpen the political analysis and the tactics we were using, as well as to deepen relationships with Muslim community leaders locally and nationally. It was especially powerful for local chapters who chose to make it part of their ongoing work. NAI served as a resource to JVP members and others interested in organizing against Islamophobia and anti-Arab racism and to be a partner to the broader, Muslim-led movement against Islamophobia.

In December 2015, JVP held our first Chanukah actions against Islamophobia, led by sixteen JVP chapters throughout the US, with the release of the original "Stop Profiling Muslims" and "Refugees Are Welcome Here" posters designed by JVP artist council member and movement artist Micah Bazant.[25] The poster was produced in collaboration with the JVP artist council and inspired by one of its members, writer and activist Aurora Levins Morales, who had the idea for a poster supporting Syrian refugees, inspired by the "Assata Is Welcome Here" posters of the '70s.[26]

Poster by Micah Bazant

Each chapter held public actions that illustrated the public harms of Islamophobia with giant, beautifully designed menorahs. The visual eloquence combined with the perhaps unexpected convergence of a Jewish group shining a light on Islamophobia as part of our holiday ritual ensured public interest and press coverage. As we discussed in chapter 1, weaving together the Jewish holiday cycle with our political commitments was a primary way our chapters took action. The actions were simple. Each night of Chanukah, Jews would go to a public place, holding nine signs, which, together, are in the shape of a Chanukah menorah. Each sign contains an injustice that we recommit ourselves to challenging. Those principles were:

1. WE WILL NOT BE SILENT ABOUT ANTI-MUSLIM AND RACIST HATE SPEECH AND HATE CRIMES

2. WE CONDEMN STATE SURVEILLANCE OF THE MUSLIM, ARAB, AND SOUTH ASIAN COMMUNITIES

3. WE CHALLENGE THROUGH OUR WORDS AND ACTIONS INSTITUTIONALIZED RACISM AND STATE-SANCTIONED ANTI-BLACK VIOLENCE

4. WE PROTEST THE USE OF ISLAMOPHOBIA AND ANTI-ARAB RACISM TO JUSTIFY ISRAEL'S REPRESSIVE POLICIES AGAINST PALESTINIANS

5. WE FIGHT ANTI-MUSLIM PROFILING AND RACIAL PROFILING IN ALL ITS FORMS

6. WE CALL FOR AN END TO RACIST POLICING #SAYHERNAME #BLACKLIVESMATTER

7. WE STAND AGAINST U.S. POLICIES DRIVEN BY THE "WAR ON TERROR" THAT DEMONIZE ISLAM AND DEVALUE, TARGET, AND KILL MUSLIMS

8. WE WELCOME SYRIAN REFUGEES AND STAND STRONG FOR IMMIGRANTS' AND REFUGEE RIGHTS

In addition to these actions, NAI developed a modular

curriculum, freely available on JVP's website, designed for both community building as well as sharpening political analysis of those engaging in this work locally.[27] The modules included an introductory session on challenging Islamophobia and racism; practical sessions on planning an action, coalition building, and bystander intervention; and deeper dives into more analytical topics, such as the ways that race, racism, and racialization are constructed in relation to US Muslims from Middle Eastern and South Asian immigrant communities, Arab Americans, and Black American Muslims; the ways that liberal Islamophobia is present in the US today; and how it affects people's perceptions of Muslims and connects to cultural and structural racism and government policies. There are also sessions that dig into the networks and resources undergirding the Islamophobia industry and its relationship to Israel, including looking at the legacy Jewish organizations that have a history of funding anti-Muslim hate groups. The hope was that these sessions would facilitate JVP members and chapters becoming more effective, principled, creative, thoughtful partners to Muslims.

Once Trump was elected in 2016, the urgency of NAI's work skyrocketed. Because of JVP's long-standing work on Islamophobia and deep relationships with Muslim social justice community leaders, JVP chapters mobilized communities around the country against the Muslim ban. Because we had already articulated our politics and this was an area of work we were already experienced in, our members were ready in January 2017, when thousands of us joined broad coalitions that flooded airports across the country, protesting Trump's Muslim ban executive order. JVP chapters sprang into action to canvass in their communities to get businesses, houses of worship, and homes to display in their windows our poster with the simple message "Refugees are welcome here." In dozens of cities, JVPers went door-to-door to store owners with a simple script: "We are concerned about the growing Islamophobic sentiment in this country. We are hoping you share this concern, and that in this season you are open to displaying a message of welcome and support for the Muslim community. We have posters we would love for you to hang in your window. Is it OK to hang them?" Soon, JVP was getting messages and reports of our posters everywhere in the US.

The work of NAI was multifaceted, bridging internal political education, public actions, and cultural commemoration. No matter your style of activism, there was a way for you to plug in to fighting Islamophobia while bringing more people along with you. This work also reflected JVP's understanding that the fight against Islamophobia and Israeli apartheid were manifestations of our Jewish lives and part of building a world of safety for us all, through solidarity. The internal education strengthened our members' confidence and inspiration to take up the fight, and the public actions generated media attention that let Muslims know there are others out there who despise anti-Muslim hatred. Our partners were buoyed by this support, and our demonstrated commitment created bonds of trust and love that allowed us to keep building and showing up for each other. Through this work, JVP's long-term partners got to see the depth of our commitment, not just to saying the right thing but also doing the work to ensure our members are able to notice Islamophobia where they might have missed it, and that the way we organize prioritizes the right relationship with Muslims in our communities. The primary reward of this work was the maturation of our Muslim partners' trust and reliance on JVP, and vice versa.

Reflecting on this and other successes at growing JVP, we are aware that the success was not just about our capabilities but also about our Jewish identity. We didn't have to contend with Islamophobia. There was an inherent anti-Arab racism in the way in which critical Jewish voices, white voices in particular, were taken more seriously than those of Palestinians who were experiencing dispossession firsthand. And, of course, we were catnip for coverage in the press because our existence upended expectations of Jewish positions on Israel. There was always a question of when centering ourselves and our Jewish positioning in any given media debate or campaign would be strategic, and when it would be a manifestation of the anti-Palestinian racism that animates our culture, where Palestinians are not taken as credible narrators of their own experiences. There were some issues—such as taking on the fight against the weaponization of antisemitism—where our Palestinian partners clearly asked us to lead. We relished such moments, when we were able to take the guesswork out of our own motivations.

Unlike for anti-Zionist Jews, there is no opting out of being Palestinian, with all the challenges that entails. For us Jews, we could (heaven forbid), conceivably, publicly declare our embrace of Zionism to once again find a warm welcome in Jewish communities that currently reject us as anti-Zionists. There is a conditionality to our outcast-ness, which can give our organizing a moral power while also creating a sense of precarity. It makes sense that this can amount to a fundamental trust question between comrades in solidarity movements and takes enormous amounts of work and communication to overcome. This is not unique to Jews and Palestinians; it is, in fact, inherent to all solidarity politics and presents a challenge and hurdle for those of us with privilege to confront and transcend as an ongoing practice and principle in our organizing.

We Will Outlive Them

The litany of pressure, intimidation, attacks, harm, and attempted harm to those speaking out can be overwhelming—and is unfortunately not uncommon. While the named tactics are specific to this movement, they most likely feel familiar to just about anyone in any movement working to disrupt power and the unjust status quo, from reproductive justice to Indigenous struggles to climate crisis to trans rights to the fight against white supremacy and emergent fascism.

The costs to doing this work, any movement work, are real and serious, and they fall unevenly on those who do it, in the same deeply grooved patterns of racism and white supremacy that create uneven impacts in every aspect of our lives. Our intention in naming these patterns is not to deter people from pursuing justice work but the opposite. Understanding the logic of these tactics is a powerful tool to fight back against them and understand your own power.

Within the movement for Palestinian freedom, the pressure is even more intense on anyone not Jewish, and that goes more than double for Palestinians and other people of color, Black people in particular. But naming and understanding these tactics as a strategy of the opposition offers energy and power to the fight against them. In fact, the Palestinian rights movement has strengthened itself and built entire organizations, such as Palestine Legal, which focuses on legal defense, specifically to be prepared to fight back. As a result, the movement has made enormous strides. Sharing these tactics among movements can help break all of us out of our isolation and offer tools and resiliency to continue to fight.

At the most fundamental level, JVP's primary response to the mounting impact of these tactics is to consciously live out an alternative vision of how we want the world to be. After the devastating massacre at the Tree of Life synagogue in Pittsburgh in 2018, Rabbi Miriam Grossman gave voice to this vision at a rally in Brooklyn, saying,

> Our liberations are all bound up with each other. Which means the only real way to safety is together. We will not

silence our grief, our rage, or our joys. As the Yiddish saying goes, *"Mir velen zei iberleben.* We will outlive them,"
loudly, in full solidarity with all people whose humanity
is threatened by systems of domination and abuse. Jewish
friends, family, community—we are not alone. And our
ancestors, I am so sure, are with us today and always.

In fact, we were offered a glimpse of what this vision could look
and feel like from our comrades in Gaza after the murders at
Tree of Life. Is there anything more galvanizing than being fully
seen by those with whom you are working together, from opposite sides of the globe? Ahmed Abu Artema, one of the leaders
of the Great March of Return, sent Rebecca this moving letter
at the time:[28]

> On behalf of the organizers of the Palestinian Great
> March of Return in Gaza I would like to express to you
> and to all Jews in America our profound sympathy and
> solidarity in the face of the recent tragic massacre at the
> Tree of Life Synagogue in Pittsburgh.
>
> Palestinians in Gaza share with American Jews the
> fear and pain that comes from racist action.
>
> In America, Jews were targeted because they are Jews.
>
> In Palestine, we are cooped up in the tiny space of
> Gaza, and not allowed to return, because we are NOT
> Jews.
>
> We thank you for your many years of courageous
> support of the human rights of Palestinians. We wish
> to share with you that we stand in support of equality
> and the human rights of Jews in America and around the
> world.

For us, resilience is communal. When we are part of a collective of care, support, understanding, and healing, we are better

able to continue to struggle. This is not to downplay the cumulative impact of being individually targeted—sometimes it simply becomes too much. What we know for sure is that having a political home, a community that is linked to other communities that offer solidarity and a sense of safety, is the best antidote to the threats of those who seek to destroy movements for justice and all people who are committed to them.

Organizing Strategy Reflection Questions

Weathering Repression

1. Which items on the list of strategies of repression do you see operating in your own movement? How are you preparing for or mitigating against the harm from these strategies to your staff, members, and partners?

2. If you are in a position of relative power, how can you flank your allies? Who are the bridge builders in your community whom you can call on to build solidarity, beyond the usual suspects?

3. Are you effectively recognizing opportunities to move from a reactive to proactive stance, thereby interrupting the status quo? What are creative ways you can expand the lens of crucial conversations, and who can participate in them? For example, how can you use the virulent opposition of the right to your advantage to draw attention and media coverage?

4. How are you approaching the real need for security without impeding your organizing? How do you evaluate the balance between ignoring fringe attacks and recognizing when they start to impact public opinion?

5. How can you keep a vision for liberation at the center of your day-to-day work as a way to weather the repressive strategies of your adversaries?

6. What spiritual, emotional, and physical protections are you

offering yourself and your people from relentless attacks? What are strategies you have in place to resist the chilling effect these repression strategies can have on organizing?

Conclusion

Solidarity Is the
Political Version of Love

I n the fall of 2019, Representative Rashida Tlaib was informed
that the Israeli government would not allow her to enter the
country. They later reversed themselves and agreed to let her
come in, but only if she would agree to curtail her planned
speech, specifically in support of BDS, during the trip. She was
not willing to accept those conditions and therefore returned to
her hometown of Detroit, her hopes of being able to enter her
homeland and visit her grandmother cruelly dashed.

This happened on the same day that JVPAction was launched,
a 501(c)(4) sister organization to JVP that would legally allow for
lobbying Congress and endorsing candidates. It also was a symbolic
moment: JVP had amassed enough grassroots power that we were
ready to engage on an electoral level; the election of the Squad the
year before had ushered in an unprecedented era in Congress, in
which the Palestinian solidarity movement had a group of actual
allies in Congress. It was a moment to acknowledge the organizing, effort, and energy that had gotten JVP to the point of being
ready to engage more directly with Congress and elections, to step
into a new phase of contesting for actual political power and policy

change in just the way our theory of change had anticipated. But what had happened to Representative Tlaib that day, and the US government's lack of an adequate reaction, also showed just how far there still was to go. Bruised and disappointed, Representative Tlaib arrived back home, only to go directly to a Friday evening Shabbat in a local park at the invitation of JVPAction in Detroit, which covers her district, surrounded by signs that said "Jews Love Rashida" and "Dignity from Detroit to Palestine."[1] Rashida said movingly at the event, "I cannot tell you how much love I feel here . . . thank you for hearing me, thank you for seeing me, thank you for loving me. And thank you for allowing me to be not just your congresswoman but also a granddaughter of a grandmother living under occupation."[2]

Solidarity, at that moment, was truly the political version of love. And that moment, for all its pain, also illustrated the deep partnership and serious commitment to building a new world that solidarity organizing embodies in its best moments.

Power Building Is Solidarity

That moment was one of both solidarity in practice and an elucidation of why power building is crucial to a genuine dedication to solidarity. Solidarity is not just about having the "right" position but also the often grinding labor of creating a political force that can help drive action. As organizers, our job is to constantly be thinking about power: how to build it, how to exert it, how to fight it, how to bait it into response. This is true no matter what momentous shift your organizing is working to bring to fruition.

The power building we do as organizers exists inside complicated power relationships, mediated by gradations of race, class and ethnicity, positionality, public influence, and relationships to allies. This was particularly true for JVP, since the power we were building was as Jews in solidarity with Palestinians organizing for their freedom. Even now, JVP and JVPAction are far outside the mainstream of Jewish communal standards. But, unlike the early years, by the end of our tenure, JVP had commanded a measure of grudging respect, a recognition of our strong membership base, the significant shifts in the narrative in our direction, and the consistent numbers of people, in particular young people, JVP was attracting. During those years, JVP built a warm and welcoming political home for tens of thousands of people. We notched quite a number of campaign victories and had strong working relationships with congresspeople, public intellectuals, and celebrities. In other words, JVP started to develop some degree of power—power that could be further developed and wielded as part of the greater solidarity movement for Palestinian freedom.

Solidarity is full of contradictions. During our time at JVP, those contradictions included being rejected from Jewish communities we grew up in, but also through force of will making it possible to build new communities that match our values and vision for a Judaism beyond Zionism. It meant finding a community as Jewish anti-Zionists because of the brutality Palestinians face. It is about organizing toward an end of forced exile for Palestinians even as we embrace diaspora for ourselves. Through our organizing, we have found meaning and satisfaction in this work but also tapped into painful levels of despair.

Solidarity requires that we know who we are, what we believe, where we come from, and where we want to see ourselves go, all while not being so rigid that we can't be influenced and even transformed by those we struggle alongside. Building enough power to force change starts from this commitment.

Solidarity Is a Practice

Our time at JVP taught us that the daily work of solidarity is a practice. You're learning as you go, you make mistakes, fall short, get distracted, reflect, learn, repair, reassess, make strides, level up. The practice involves being attentive to the visions and demands of the people with whom you are in solidarity, while carving out roles that allow you to bring your strengths to growing and sustaining the movement broadly and not neglecting impacts on your own community. It includes flanking those being targeted, organizing those you have unique access to, designing strategic campaigns, and integrating your own sense of stake in the issue you are organizing around into your programs.

Solidarity isn't about being neutral, unfeeling, or deferring to others without hesitation. It instead requires we bring our full selves to the work of movement building and freedom fighting. Solidarity means knowing there will be personal costs and risks involved. Solidarity means feeling the pain of the struggle. But also the joy.

We are inspired by the proud lineage of unlikely freedom fighters who confronted their own community as their values demanded. The White Rose, white German Christians who rose up against the Nazis at the cost of their lives. The white members of SNCC who took part in the Freedom Rides in the US South in the 1950s and other white Southerners, like Mab Segrest and Anne Braden, who rejected their families' pride in the legacy of slavery and anti-Black racism. In fact, beloved JVP elder Dorothy Zellner, who had been a key member of SNCC and focused on Palestinian freedom in later decades, provided a crucial living link between our movements. While we have not made that level of sacrifice, these histories are the ones we want to resurrect, to remind ourselves that in response to every authoritarian government and in the face of devastating violence and oppression, voices of resistance emerge not just from those being oppressed but also from the children, cousins, classmates, nieces, friends, coworkers, and neighbors of the oppressors.

It's a comfort to know that we are not the first, the only, or the last to reject those that use dominance, violence, and hatred in our name or ostensibly in our interest. We do so not just out of solidarity or magnanimity but out of a deep-rooted, self-interested understanding that a world where oppression thrives is not a world of freedom or safety for anyone. So, we find the moral and political courage to confront our own community. The root of this courage to confront is knowing that a world where Palestinians—or anyone—live under apartheid and constant violence is not a world we want to live in. At the same time, we are also motivated by a sense of guardianship of the sacred legacy of Judaism. We want to nurture the evolution of Judaism beyond Zionism, as we have experienced it in our own communities.

In confronting our community for its support of Israeli apartheid, we hold in one hand our fury at the ongoing violence and degradation of Palestinian life under apartheid, and in the other we hold our vision of a Jewish future that cherishes the values of dignity, justice, and freedom for all people. We are always seeking to balance our accountability to Palestinians, leading the movement for their liberation and the self-interest we have as Jews to liberate Judaism from Zionism.

For those who are confronting their communities in other struggles, whether complicity in environmental racism, religious nationalism, exploitation of workers, or the myriad other issues plaguing our world, we hope the manifestation of solidarity we practiced and tried to portray for you here will aid your efforts. Whatever your version of solidarity, may you practice it as an expression of love. A love that manifests as raging at the world as it is, and at the same time developing smart, intentional plans to realize the world as it should be. Transforming your community into one you can be proud of passing on to the next generation, as you align your actions with the visions and demands of those you are in solidarity with. Love, like solidarity, lives in the both/and.

For my sake the world was created.
I am but dust and ashes.

One of the fruits of organizing from within a cultural tradition is being able to reach back to ancestors or predecessors for wisdom when you feel confused or defeated or uncertain. For example, a story is passed down in Jewish tradition that Reb Simcha Bunem, a late eighteenth-century Hasidic rabbi, carried two slips of paper, one in each pocket. One was inscribed with the saying he plucked from roughly the fifth century of the common era: *Bishvili nivra ha-olam*, "For my sake the world was created."[3] On the other, he wrote a phrase that reached even further back, to the biblical patriarch Abraham: *"V'anokhi afar v'efer,"* "I am but dust and ashes."[4] As the story goes, Reb Bunem would take out and read whichever slip of paper he needed at that moment. Unwittingly and almost instinctively, that is what we as leaders of JVP sought to do moment to moment—balancing our power with humility and accountability.

Reflecting on our time at JVP now, we can see that the way we found to confront our community is beautifully reflected in Reb Bunem's practice of reminding himself: the world is made for me; I am nothing but ashes. We moved between pressing forward and retreating, from demanding space for our voices and evaluating where we might have gone too far. Instead of seeking to resolve contradictions that are inherent and irresolvable, we must learn how to work with them toward justice. In honor of the ethical legacy of Jewish tradition and the radical political lineages we draw from, thousands of us built a home for people who believe and are willing to act on the simple yet radical idea that Palestinians must be free.

Afterword

What Will It Take?

As JVP's current executive director I have many reflections about the organizing lessons detailed in these pages and in the four years since. But I am writing to you from an entirely different time zone: we are 230 days into Israel's ongoing genocide of Palestinians in Gaza. Our focus at JVP is wholly on showing up to this moment. So that's where I write to you from.

May 23, 2024: Day 230

I pick up my five-year-old from school knowing that the Israeli military has already killed over 14,000 children. In the time between when I dropped my son off on Monday morning and when I picked him up on Friday afternoon, Israel murdered more than 400 Palestinian children—nearly the same number of students that fill his entire school.

An untold number of other children are still trapped under rubble—each a universe annihilated. Gone are their wild imaginations and favorite after-school snacks, the silly games they made up with their cousins, and the pet names from their grandfathers.

Adults in Gaza—exhausted, traumatized, and likely starving—struggle to find rations and water, to seek shelter when nowhere is safe, to distract their surviving children from the unrelenting grief and terror. Over 1.4 million Palestinians who have been forced to flee and flee again are now in Rafah, where the Israeli military is continuing to bomb and invade while blocking all food and other essential humanitarian aid from entering.

The ways Israel's assault on Palestinians in Gaza exceed the horror of nearly all wars in recent memory are too many to list: more children killed, more journalists killed, more bombs dropped, more homes destroyed, more internally displaced people, more targeting of hospitals, schools, mosques, churches, and refugee camps. That's because it's simply not a war—it's a genocide.

As Israeli officials follow through on their public pledges to commit genocide against Palestinians in Gaza, the Biden administration has been a full partner in the crimes. Six months into this horror, the US government sent the Israeli military more than $14 billion in funds for weapons and destruction, on top of its annual $3.8 billion. They have continued shipping billions in weapons. While Biden leads cynical public relations stunts—such as dropping food aid from the sky or building an ineffective floating pier for aid distribution—he continues sending bombs to Netanyahu and smearing international bodies that attempt to hold the Israeli government accountable, such as the United Nations, the International Court of Justice, and the International Criminal Court.

For nearly eight months, the massive, intersectional, global movement for Palestinian liberation has been pushing for a ceasefire and end to Israeli impunity with constant action. The stories in this book share some of the groundwork laid to build relationships across movements, relationships that are now multiplying in truly unprecedented ways to meet this moment. From the center of complicity here in the United States, a united front is growing with Palestinian leadership at the core, including many leaders and organizations from climate to labor, immigrant rights to housing, from racial justice to electoral groups in battleground states.

Millions of people have mobilized, shutting down highways and federal buildings, clogging congressional phone lines, hunger striking and blocking boats holding weapons shipments, bird-dogging President Biden and setting up encampments on college campuses to demand universities divest from the US-Israel war machine.

B'tselem Elohim

At JVP, we have never been so grateful to be embedded and woven into this movement, answering the call of Palestinians fighting for their own lives. On October 18th, two dozen rabbis led five hundred people in a sit-in at the Capitol rotunda, while five thousand others rallied outside—the largest such Jewish action in history—and a week later in New York, thousands took over Grand Central Station, catapulting #CeasefireNOW to number one on Twitter. Since then we have stayed constant in our disruption, aiming with each and every day to escalate our pressure on decision-makers and the material impact of our actions on the levers of power upholding the US-Israel alliance.

Through action, we endeavor to embody the value of *B'tselem elohim*: we are, each of us, made in the image of the divine. We know intrinsically that there is no contradiction between grieving Palestinian loved ones and Israeli loved ones, or between mourning those killed by Hamas on October 7 and fighting for Palestinian liberation. In fact, for us, there is no other way.

Most Jewish Americans were raised to understand the danger of authoritarian rulers, fascism, and the dehumanization of "the other." At JVP, we know that the lesson of the Holocaust and all other genocides is that all human life is sacred and that we must struggle against any systems of power that say otherwise. For all of us who understand that "Never again" must mean *for anyone*, there has been no question about what is demanded of us in this time: unrelenting action, mobilization, and disruption. Everything we can to stop this. We have held nothing back in working to bring an end to this horror.

Not in spite of our Jewishness, *but because of it*. As Israeli forces plant giant menorahs on the decimated remnants of bombed-out refugee camps in Gaza, we resist this brutal co-optation through action and reclamation. Many JVP actions include anti-Zionist song, prayer, and poetry, extending the millennia of Jewish cultural life preceding the state of Israel. On the eighth night of Hanukkah, eight JVP chapters shut down eight bridges across the country to say: No business as usual while the US government is funding and arming genocide. During Passover, we held Seders in the Streets to call for the United States to stop arming Israel—hosted in dozens of cities and campuses—harkening back to the Freedom Seder tradition, organized in 1969 by Arthur Waskow to connect the Jewish liberation story with the struggles against anti-Black racism in the United States and against the war in Vietnam. At the New York City seder, over three thousand Jews gathered and then blocked traffic outside the home of Chuck Schumer hours after he voted to send over $14 billion in military funding to Israel.

Divesting from Zionism while holding close to our Jewishness and Judaism is critical to our resistance in this time. While Zionism enlists our community into complicity with Israeli apartheid, solidarity calls forward the best of our traditions and heritage. At the Passover action in New York City, Naomi Klein told the crowd: "We don't need or want the false idol of Zionism. We want freedom from the project that commits genocide in our name."[1]

The supposed center of the Jewish communal world has dropped away, as liberal Zionist organizations that claim to care about Palestinians and peace have been reluctant—at best—to join antiwar calls for an end to arming and funding this violence. Our anti-Zionist resistance and refusal must be loud enough to form a counterweight to the war drums.

Over the last eight months, our specific mandate within the broader Palestinian liberation movement has become even more clear. And tens of thousands of Jews have joined the organization to expand the reach of our message and say, with more power than we've ever mustered: "Not in our names."

Our dues-paying membership has doubled or more, by nearly every measure. Our chapters and pods, in over ninety cities and campuses across the country, are working to welcome and mobilize new members constantly. Our largest chapters include thousands of active and engaged participants. Every day, more Jews are breaking away from Zionism and the violence of the Israeli state and joining the movement for Palestinian liberation and a future in which all people—without exception—can live in freedom.

Escalation

As the Israeli government's brutal violence and destruction of Gaza worsens with each passing day, and the US government continues to arm and fund this genocide at full speed, the movement for Palestinian liberation has risen to meet the moment. JVP chapters have been part of that escalation from coast to coast. Durham, North Carolina, leaders shut down the interstate, calling in to representative Valerie Foushee's virtual town hall as they sat on the freeway surrounded by police. A few weeks later, she finally called for a ceasefire. In Los Angeles, three thousand people shut down Hollywood Boulevard in the rain. The very next day, the *LA Times* editorial board called for a ceasefire. Biden's fundraisers have been plagued by constant disruption, and divestment campaigns are picking up steam in local and state coalitions around the country. And as Biden continues sending billions to arm this genocide, the movement keeps pressing forward in its demands for an arms embargo and an end to US funding of the Israeli military with even more persistent protest.

The Uncommitted National Movement brought the demands for a ceasefire and to stop arming Israel to the ballot box. Kicked off in Michigan's Democratic presidential primary, more than one hundred thousand voters cast ballots marked "uncommitted," a message to President Biden that voters demanded a drastic shift to end his complicity in genocide. Since then, other states, such as Minnesota, Washington, and Wisconsin, picked up the idea, organizing rapidly to turn out hundreds of thousands in battleground states, warning Biden they held his margin for victory.

Perhaps unsurprisingly, the burgeoning power of the Palestinian freedom movement has also found a renewed expression on college campuses. At Columbia University, where the administration banned campus chapters of Students for Justice in Palestine and JVP, students erected an encampment, calling for an immediate ceasefire and demanding the school divest from Israel. In a matter of days, Gaza solidarity encampments sprung up on over a hundred and thirty university campuses across the United States. The student movement draws inspiration from similar encampments during the struggle to end apartheid in South Africa, from the civil rights movement and the antiwar protests that swept US universities in the 1960s, as well as from the Black-led uprising of 2020.

As encampments emerged across the country, students took steadfast, principled, and peaceful action demanding university divestment from Israel's oppression of Palestinians. In response, many school administrations dispatched militarized police onto campuses to violently crack down on their own students.

The iteration of tactics and strategy throughout the global movement illuminates the relationships within the struggle for Palestinian liberation, how many groups have been building collective power, strategy, and organization for years. Those connections and structures have been critical for guiding the masses of newly outraged people into effective action.

Together, we are illustrating the isolation of the warmongers from the will of people all over the world. The US and Israeli governments are committing this genocide against a backdrop of nearly unanimous outcry from people of conscience, including the majority of world governments and substantial numbers of voters in the United States. We have made clear the political popularity and moral indisputability that we must end this genocide and win a future rooted in freedom, equality, and justice for Palestinians.

Never Again Is Now

At the same time, our movement has not built enough power to change the fact that the US and Israel are continuing these historic atrocities with utter impunity. After 230 days, the Biden administration has watched without action as Netanyahu has crossed each of Biden's supposed "red lines."

In order to silence the massive and growing movement calling for an end to genocide, the Biden administration and Congress are unleashing new levels of state repression. Right-wing slander against the movement is gaining momentum and is seamlessly translated into antidemocratic legal and legislative attacks. Our opposition, with the weight and might of the US-Israel alliance and megadonor groups like AIPAC behind it, is building new tools to crush our growing power.

Yet this movement persists. As we take to the streets again and again, the carnage and destruction the Israeli government has wrought is hard to fathom. From the outset of this latest assault, Palestinians have been saying that Israel is aiming for nothing less than full expulsion of Palestinians from the Gaza Strip. This is the continuation of the unchanged goal from the very founding of the state, beginning with the 1948 Nakba.

The escalation of this logic since October 7th is consistent through the entirety of historic Palestine. In East Jerusalem and the West Bank, Palestinian villages and towns are undergoing a catastrophe that is virtually blacked out by Western media. Israeli police are arresting large numbers of residents. Settlers who have been carrying out pogroms in Palestinian villages for years are now directly armed by the government with semiautomatic weapons and are violently driving out Palestinians at a rate we haven't seen since the creation of the state.

Israel's campaign of forced starvation is also catastrophic. On May 6th, the UN World Food Program said northern Gaza has entered full-blown famine, and these disastrous levels of malnutrition and dehydration are increasing throughout the entire besieged Gaza Strip. Disabled people, children, infants, and pregnant and breastfeeding parents are suffering and dying first. So many of us grew up with the images of emaciated men, women, and children, intentionally starved in ghettos and concentration camps. Today's photos from Gaza are a rattling echo. I know how painful it is for Jews to grasp that a Jewish state could possibly commit a genocide. But speaking with moral clarity about what is happening to Palestinians at this moment is the only thing "Never Again" means, if it is to mean anything at all.

This is the contradiction we must face each day: the Palestinian freedom movement has more grassroots power than it has ever had; we're mobilizing with more force and sophistication and in wider alliance and deeper relationships than ever. Yet we are horrifyingly aware that, with everything we are doing, the United States is still fully complicit in this genocide. That said, in the words of Nelson Mandela, "It always seems impossible until it's done." Now is the moment for us to organize with every single bit of power we have until we end the US-Israeli genocidal war machine.

Endurance

There is a cruel calculus of the war criminals in Tel Aviv and Washington, DC. They believe we will become overwhelmed, slow down, give up, give in. Palestinian poet, novelist, and clinical psychologist Hala Alyan writes, "We owe Gaza endurance. . . . All relentless entities depend enormously on a few things: Your fatigue. Your hopelessness. Your turning away." But, she goes on, "we belong to long, gorgeous lineages of endurance. we are all here because someone, somewhere, endured."[2]

On the night of Biden's White House Hanukkah party, December 11, 2023, eighteen elder Jewish women chained themselves to the White House gates to demand he immediately stop arming Israel's genocide of Palestinians. Most of these women were key leaders of the stories in this book, within the founding and growing of JVP. And they bring decades of organizing not only within JVP but also across most justice movements in living memory. They are veterans of ACT UP and the civil rights movement, the struggle against South African apartheid and the Vietnam War. They are longtime labor leaders and helped grow queer liberation movements.

As they prepared for the action, the activists talked about how their endurance through decades of liberation struggle had led them all to a shared conclusion: this moment is the most urgent call to action of our lives.

As I draw on the endurance of our elders, the question I keep asking myself about JVP is not *What can we do?* It is *What will it take?*

What will it take to reach a ceasefire, the release of all imprisoned people, an end to Israeli siege, occupation, and apartheid? What will it take to end US support for Israeli oppression and colonization of Palestinians? What will it take to see our Jewish communities join the freedom side of history, divesting from Zionism and investing in movements for collective liberation?

What will it take to build a world where this nightmare is unthinkable, where every single life is precious, where all children run safely into their parent's arms at the end of the school day?

It is unbearable to not have the answers. But I do know this: the only thing greater than our horror, more profound than our heartbreak, bigger than our overwhelm at the task at hand must be our determination to answer the questions through action.

—Stefanie Fox
JVP Executive Director
May 23, 2024

Appendices

JVP Documents and Statements

Appendix A

JVP's 2015 Strategic Filters

A. Primary Considerations
(all things must align) "Must"

- Align with guiding principles and mission
- Add value without privileging Jews over others
- We have the capacity and can manage the risk
- Decouples being Jewish and support for Israeli policies that oppress Palestinians
- Is responsive and accountable to others in the broad movement

B. Secondary Considerations
(depending upon circumstances) "It's best if it does"

- Connects us with larger movements
- Multiple constituencies can be engaged at multiple levels
- Opens space for people to join (relationships)
- Helps build leadership/capacity
- Leverages our Jewish privilege to elevate the voices of our Palestinian allies
- Is winnable and/or strategically worth it
- Mobilizes and creates pathways for engagement
- Our involvement provides a unique contribution
- Builds a narrative that explains our values in human terms
- Helps us build/broaden resources/reach

C. General Discernment Questions
(big picture questions to keep in mind)

- Does it open new tactics for the movement?
- Is this the leadership we want to develop?
- Does it avoid normalization?
- Does it force people to take sides as a way to build grassroots?
- Does this perpetuate a dynamic we're looking to dismantle?
- Are we communicating in a way we can be heard?

Appendix B

JVP's "Guiding Principles
for How We Work Together"

Grassroots Organizing, Leadership Development and Relationships: We believe in building a movement rooted in relationships in order to create change from the grassroots. Within our relationships we translate our political values into action through how we treat one another. These types of relationships take work and intention.

Capacity for People to Change: We are all here because of chances we've been given or had to take in order to grow and evolve. Our work is about making space for others to question their political assumptions, get uncomfortable, and move to new understandings. If we ask it of others, we're also obligated to make sure each of us is committed to getting and doing better all the time.

Solidarity and Accountability: We see accountability as a process of deep listening, continual relationship-building and genuine re-assessment. It is a set of discrete actions we take: it's how we check-in, set strategy, share resources, and take action together. This is not abstract—we do this both through organizational commitments within the movement, and also through living those values out interpersonally within JVP.

Respect for the Humanity of All People: It's simple, but it's everything. We treat one another with respect. And we reach for dignity and a belief in everybody's fundamental humanity even in the face of vicious attacks from our opposition.

Jewish Community Centered on Justice: Radically inclusive Jewishness. We are a Jewish organization committed to the liberation of Palestine and we are building the alternative, vibrant Jewish community we want to call home, which includes and welcomes non-Jewish members, staff, board. We believe strongly that there is no such thing as a hierarchy of Jewishness based on observance, Jewish background, or parentage. As we build a political home together, we intentionally create space for lots of ways to be Jewish. Recognizing the multiplicity of Jewishness and exploring how Ashkenazi and white privilege plays out in Jewish communities in the U.S. and in Israel/Palestine allows JVP to better understand the different levels of privilege of Jews and how to deploy that privilege in the most strategic and effective ways.

Flexibility and Tenacity for the Long Haul: We want to be in this, together, until justice, equality and dignity for all people of Israel/Palestine is a reality. That means we are going to need to shift and grow with each other many times over. Let's start by assuming best intentions, being patient with each other, and understanding that we're all working toward that same vision of justice even in moments of disagreement.

Collective Liberation is About All of Us: Our work for Palestinian rights is bound up in a vision of collective liberation aimed at ending global white supremacy in the U.S. and its practice under Israeli apartheid. We are not in this work out of a desire to "save" or "rescue" Palestinians, but rather as a fight we all require to be fully free. We do our work from our own shared stake and a deep sense of solidarity, with Palestinians as equals. We are committed to doing the work to articulate and understand our own stake in this work.

Building Cultures of Consent: In order to build together for the long haul, we must be building cultures of consent and respecting people's boundaries. Our job as organizers is to ask and invite people's participation and give them the opportunity to be part of an incredible movement. We know that we are doing our job well when we are asking enough people that we hear no. To build a consent based culture we must respect people's boundaries—with their times, capacity and bodies.

272 Solidarity Is the Political Version of Love

Appendix C

Zionism Statement

"Solidarity is the political version of love."
—Melanie Kaye/Kantrowitz z"l, Jewish American
feminist, author and activist (1945–2018)

Jewish Voice for Peace is guided by a vision of justice, equality and freedom for all people. We unequivocally oppose Zionism because it is counter to those ideals. We know that opposing Zionism, or even discussing it, can be painful, can strike at the deepest trauma and greatest fears of many of us. Zionism is a nineteenth-century political ideology that emerged in a moment where Jews were defined as irrevocably outside of a Christian Europe. European antisemitism threatened and ended millions of Jewish lives—in pogroms, in exile, and in the Holocaust.

Through study and action, through deep relationship with Palestinians fighting for their own liberation, and through our own understanding of Jewish safety and self determination, we have come to see that Zionism was a false and failed answer to the desperately real question many of our ancestors faced of how to protect Jewish lives from murderous antisemitism in Europe.

While it had many strains historically, the Zionism that took hold and stands today is a settler-colonial movement, establishing an apartheid state where Jews have more rights than others. Our own history teaches us how dangerous this can be.

Palestinian dispossession and Occupation are by design. Zionism has meant profound trauma for generations, systematically separating Palestinians from their homes, land, and each other. Zionism, in practice, has resulted in massacres of Palestinian people, ancient villages and olive groves destroyed, families who live just a mile away from each other separated by checkpoints and walls, and children holding onto the keys of the homes from which their grandparents were forcibly exiled.

Because the founding of the state of Israel was based on the idea of a "land without people," Palestinian existence itself is resistance. We are all the more humbled by the vibrance, resilience, and steadfastness of Palestinian life, culture, and organizing, as it is a deep refusal of a political ideology founded on erasure. In sharing our stories with one another, we see the ways Zionism has also harmed Jewish people. Many of us have learned from Zionism to treat our neighbors with suspicion, to forget the ways Jews built home and community wherever we found ourselves to be. Jewish people have had long and integrated histories in the Arab world and North Africa, living among and sharing community, language and custom with Muslims and Christians for thousands of years.

By creating a racist hierarchy with European Jews at the top, Zionism erased those histories and destroyed those communities and relationships. In Israel, Jewish people of color—from the Arab world, North Africa, and East Africa—have long been subjected to systemic discrimination and violence by the Israeli government. That hierarchy also creates Jewish spaces where Jews of color are marginalized, our identities and commitments questioned & interrogated, and our experiences invalidated. It prevents us from seeing each other—fellow Jews and other fellow human beings—in our full humanity.

Zionist interpretations of history taught us that Jewish people are alone, that to remedy the harms of antisemitism we must think of ourselves as always under attack and that we cannot trust others. It teaches us fear, and that the best response to fear is a bigger gun, a taller wall, a more humiliating checkpoint.

Rather than accept the inevitability of Occupation and dispossession, we choose a different path. We learn from the anti-Zionist Jews who came before us, and know that as long as Zionism has existed, so has Jewish dissent to it. Especially as we face the violent antisemitism fueled by white nationalism in the United States today, we choose solidarity. We choose collective liberation. We choose a future where everyone, including Palestinians and Jewish Israelis, can live their lives freely in vibrant, safe, equitable communities, with basic human needs fulfilled. Join us.

Appendix D

JVP Endorses BDS

FEBRUARY 20, 2015

THE ONLY RECOGNIZABLE FEATURE OF HOPE IS ACTION.
—Grace Paley, Jewish American author and activist

Jewish Voice for Peace endorses the call from Palestinian civil society for Boycott, Divestment, and Sanctions (BDS) as part of our work for freedom, justice and equality for all people. We believe that the time-honored, non-violent tools proposed by the BDS call provide powerful opportunities to make that vision real.

We join with communities of conscience around the world in supporting Palestinians, who call for BDS until the Israeli government: ends its Occupation and colonization of all Arab lands occupied in June 1967 and dismantles the Wall; recognizes the fundamental rights of the Arab-Palestinian citizens of Israel to full equality; and respects, protects and promotes the rights of Palestinian refugees to return to their homes and properties as stipulated in UN Resolution 194.

In the long and varied history of Jewish experience, we are inspired by those who have resisted injustice and fought for freedom. We strive to live up to those values and extend that history. By endorsing the call, we make our hope real and our love visible and we claim our own liberation as bound with the liberation of all.

JVP is committed to supporting and organizing all kinds of powerful and strategic campaigns to secure a common future where Palestinians, Israeli Jews, and all the people of Israel/Palestine may live with dignity, security, and peace.

Appendix E

JVP Response to M4BL

Policy Platform

AUGUST 4, 2016

The Jews of Color Caucus, organized in partnership with Jewish Voice for Peace, has released a full statement in solidarity and co-resistance with the Movement for Black Lives. Read the statement here.

Jewish Voice for Peace is following the leadership of Jews of Color in partnership with JVP as to how we can best contribute to realizing the demands and vision for Black lives laid out in the inspiring, bold Movement for Black Lives platform. Because the leadership team of JVP is currently all white Ashkenazi Jews, we are slowing down to ensure our members who are Jews of Color can lead the way, particularly in matters of racial justice. This is part of our ongoing project to dismantle white supremacy inside of JVP.

We are deeply disappointed by the response from a number of Jewish organizations to the platform, particularly the "Invest-Divest" section that endorses the Boycott Divestment and Sanctions (BDS) movement and makes a clear call for Black/Palestinian solidarity. These Jewish organizations are rejecting a thorough and inspiring transformational set of policy ideas developed by a broad coalition of Black leaders simply because these Black leaders have explicitly linked the experiences and struggles of Palestinians with their own.

JVP endorses the Movement for Black Lives platform in its entirety, without reservation.

Appendix F

YJP Declaration

A vision of collective identity, purpose and values written by and for young Jews committed to justice in Israel and Palestine. It is an invitation and call to action for both our peers and our elders, launched as a counter-protest at the 2010 Jewish Federation General Assembly in New Orleans.

I. we exist.

We exist. We are everywhere. We speak and love and dream in every language. We pray three times a day or only during the high holidays or when we feel like we really need to or not at all. We are punks and students and parents and janitors and Rabbis and freedom fighters. We are your children, your nieces and nephews, your grandchildren. We embrace diaspora, even when it causes us a great deal of pain. We are the rubble of tangled fear, the deliverance of values. We are human. We are born perfect. We assimilate, or we do not. We are not apathetic. We know and name persecution when we see it. Occupation has constricted our throats and fattened our tongues. We are feeding each other new words. We have family, we build family, we are family. We renegotiate. We atone. We redraw the map every single day. We travel between worlds. This is not our birthright, it is our necessity.

II. we remember.

We remember slavery in Egypt, and we remember hiding our celebrations and ritual. We remember brave, desperate resistance. We honor a legacy of radical intellectuals and refugees. We remember the labor movement. We remember the camps. We remember when we aged too quickly. We remember that we are still young, and powerful. We remember being branded as counterrevolutionaries in one state and hunted during the red scare of another. We remember our ancestors' suffering and our own. Our stories are older than any brutal war. We remember those who cannot afford to take time to heal. We remember how to build our homes, and our holiness, out of time and thin air, and so do not need other people's land to do so. We remember solidarity as a means of survival and an act of affirmation, and we are proud.

III. we refuse.

We refuse to have our histories distorted or erased, or appropriated by a corporate war machine. We will not call this liberation. We refuse to knowingly oppress others, and we refuse to oppress each other. We refuse to be whitewashed. We will not carry the legacy of terror. We refuse to allow our identities to be cut, cleaned, packaged nicely, and sold back to us. We won't be won over by free vacations and scholarship money. We won't buy the logic that slaughter means safety. We will not quietly witness the violation of human rights in Palestine. We refuse to become the mother who did not scream when wise King Solomon resolved to split her baby in two. We are better than this. We have ancestors to honor. We have allies to honor. We have ourselves to honor.

IV. we commit.

We commit ourselves to peace. We will stand up with honest bodies, to offer honest bread. We will stand up with our words, our pens, our songs, our paintbrushes, our open hands. We commit to re-envisioning "homeland," to make room for justice. We will stand in the way of colonization and displacement. We will take this to the courts and to the streets. We will learn. We will teach this in the schools and in our homes. We will stand with you, if you choose to stand with our allies. We will grieve the lies we've swallowed. We commit to equality, solidarity, and integrity. We will soothe the deepest tangles of our roots and stretch our strong arms to the sky. We demand daylight for our stories, for all stories. We seek breathing room and dignity for all people. We are committed to the struggle. We are the struggle. We will become mentors, elders, and radical listeners for the next generation. It is our sacred obligation. We will not stop. We exist. We are young Jews, and we get to decide what that means.

Appendix G

GLOSSARY

Jewish Cultural Lineages

Jews have always been a multiethnic and multiracial exilic people, who have made their homes across the globe by choice and by force. Jews often identify themselves according to their geographical heritage, which comes along with a set of languages, customs, foods, and rituals, and also according to experiences of trauma, inclusion, precarity, and safety. The four most common cultural lineages within Jewishness include Ashkenazi, Sephardi, Mizrahi, and Ethiopian.

"Ashkenazi" (plural: Ashkenazim) refers to Jews who descend from communities in Central, Western, and Eastern Europe that primarily spoke various dialects of Yiddish. Ashkenazim were the primary Jewish victims of the Nazi Holocaust. Ashkenazi Jews currently make up the supermajority of Jews in the United States (66 percent according to the Pew Research Center) and dominate the political elite in Israel.

"Sephardi" (plural: Sephardim) refers to Jews who descend from communities in the Iberian Peninsula that spoke Spanish and Ladino. Ashkenazi and Sephardi are used to distinguish between the dominant liturgical traditions and melodies, holiday customs that evolved over the centuries influenced by their surrounding cultural milieus. Sephardi Jews were some of the first to immigrate to United States, beginning in the seventeenth century, and they participated in colonial settlement and the slave trade here. But Sephardi synagogues in the US are few in number and are primarily Orthodox. It is important to note that not all Ashkenazi Jews are white and not all Sephardi Jews are people of color. These ethnic categories do not neatly map onto racial categories as we use them today and have evolved into references for cultural legacies that people of many races and ethnicities are a part of.

"Mizrahi" (plural: Mizrahim) is an umbrella term for Jews who descend from the Middle East and North Africa, including but not limited to Morocco, Tunisia, Iran, Iraq, Afghanistan, Yemen, Uzbekistan, Lebanon, Turkey, India, and Pakistan. "Mizrahi" is the Hebrew word for East or "Oriental" and thus has been a controversial term that many are choosing to reclaim. In Israel, a majority of the Jewish Israeli population have Mizrahi or Sephardi heritage. The most recent polls of US Jews by the Pew Research Center in 2020 found 1 percent of US Jews identify as Mizrahi, 3 percent as Sephardi, and another 7 percent as some combination of Ashkenazi, Sephardi, and Mizrahi.

Ethiopian Jews, known as "Beta Israel," make up a community of Jews that today lives in Israel but up until the late twentieth century lived in the Amhara and Tigray regions of Ethiopia. Beta Israel practice of Judaism rooted in the laws and customs found in Torah, not Talmud.

In addition to these ethnic categories, over the past decade an umbrella term "Jews of Color" (JoC) has been used to describe Jewish people of Color. Jews of Color Initiative commissioned "Beyond the Count: Perspectives and Lived Experiences of Jews of Color," which reported,

> Those who self-identified as JoC in this study used the term in a multiplicity of ways: as a racial grouping (e.g.

Black, Asian, and multiracial Jews); to indicate national heritage (e.g. Egyptian, Iranian, and Ethiopian Jews); to describe regional and geographic connections (e.g. Latina/o/x, Mizrahi, Sephardic Jews); and to specify sub-categories (e.g. transracially adopted Jews and Jewish Women of Color).

Of the over one thousand survey respondents they engaged for their study, 42 percent identified as Ashkenazi, and 66 percent identified as "biracial, mixed, multiracial." Relevant to the struggles inside JVP over our ability to be an inclusive space for Jews of Color, over 80 percent of their survey respondents reported experiencing discrimination in Jewish settings.[1]

Throughout our discussion of Jews of Color at JVP we use the acronym JOCSM, which stands for Jews of Color, Sephardi, Mizrahi. This was a term developed by JVPers to capture their understanding that those identities are uniquely yet commonly marginalized by white supremacy and Zionism.

Jewish Communal Organizations

Please note: this is not at all a comprehensive list, but is meant as a guide to the range of organizations that are mentioned in the text. An asterisk indicates "legacy Jewish institution."

American Israel Public Affairs Committee (AIPAC): The leading pro-Israel lobby group in Washington, DC. Founded in 1953, AIPAC began its rise to power in the 1970s during the presidencies of Gerald Ford and Jimmy Carter. One of AIPAC's most successful strategies has been bundling campaign contributions for candidates for office in order to ensure pro-Israel support upon their election. AIPAC officially supports a two-state solution but opposes criticisms of Israeli policy in the West Bank and Gaza. For several years now, one of AIPAC's top policy agendas has been to impose heavy sanctions on Iran and sink any possible negotiated settlement on the nuclear issue.

American Jewish Committee (AJC)*: This global Jewish advocacy organization based in the United States describes its work by saying it "stands up for Israel's right to exist in peace and security; confronts antisemitism, no matter the source; and upholds the democratic values that unite Jews and our allies around the world." The AJC commissioned the definition of antisemitism that became the International Holocaust Remembrance Alliance (IHRA) definition. The lead author, Kenneth Stern, was AJC's director on antisemitism, hate studies, and extremism from 1989 to 2014. Stern has since come out vigorously against the misuse of the definition by governments and institutions.[2]

Anti-Defamation League (ADL)*: A Jewish nongovernmental organization based in the United States, the stated mission of which is "to stop the defamation of the Jewish people and to secure justice and fair treatment to all." In recent years, the ADL has sought to define all activity in support of Palestinian human rights as antisemitic and has come under scrutiny for its past activities surveilling US Muslim communities and allowing its focus on Israel advocacy to overshadow its civil rights work.

Bend the Arc: A national organization that brings together progressive Jews to fight for justice and equality for all.

Center for Jewish Nonviolence (CJNV): Brings Jewish activists from around the world to Israel/Palestine to join in Palestinian-led, nonviolent, civil resistance to occupation, apartheid, and displacement.

Hillel International: "The foundation of Jewish campus life," Hillel holds offices on thousands of college campuses for Jewish students. Hillel's Israel guidelines forbid Hillel member groups from partnering with supporters of BDS and opponents of Israel. They are targeted by the Open Hillel campaign.

IfNotNow: A movement of American Jews organizing the Jewish community to end US support for Israel's apartheid system and demand equality, justice, and a thriving future for all Palestinians and Israelis.

International Jewish Anti-Zionist Network (IJAN): An international network of Jews committed to struggles for human survival and emancipation, of which the liberation of the Palestinian people and land is an indispensable part.

Jewish Community Relations Councils (JCRC):* A group of 125 Jewish organizations nationwide that work on promoting community relations between the Jewish community and the community at large.

Jewish Council for Public Affairs (JCPA)*: An umbrella organization that deals specifically with the issue of how the Jewish community relates with the community at large. It provides advice and support to the 125 Jewish Community Relations Councils that operate in their own locales. The JCPA regularly issues policy positions in the areas of "Equal Opportunity and Social Justice," "Jewish Security and the Bill of Rights," and "Israel, World Jewry and International Human Rights."

Jewish Federations of North America (JFNA)*: The umbrella organization for the 146 local Jewish Federations in North America. The JFNA and the local federations engage in charity work in the United States and abroad, support local Jewish communities and heavily promote Israel advocacy. Their annual General Assembly is one of the most important national gatherings of Jewish professionals and community leaders.

Jews for Racial & Economic Justice (JFREJ): The home for Jewish New Yorkers organizing with our neighbors and allies to transform New York from a playground for the wealthy few into a real democracy for all of us, free from all forms of racist violence.

J Street: Formed in 2008, J Street is a US lobbying organization promoting a two-state solution. They've established themselves as the "pro-Israel, pro-peace" liberal alternative to AIPAC. They also advocate against BDS.

Judaism On Our Own Terms (JOOOT): A national movement of independent campus Jewish organizations committed to promoting student self-governance and radical inclusivity, both on individual campuses and in the wider Jewish community. JOOOT was born out of student tussles with Hillel. During our tenure it was called Open Hillel.

New Israel Fund (NIF): Provides grant-making and capacity-building support to progressive organizations in Israel.

Simon Wiesenthal Center: Researches and educates about the Holocaust and antisemitism through the lens of Israel advocacy. They operate several "Museums of Tolerance," one of which is built atop a demolished Muslim cemetery in Jerusalem. Their director of government affairs, Mark Weitzman, is a member of the official US delegation to the IHRA, where he chaired the Committee on Antisemitism and Holocaust Denial, spearheading its adoption of the IHRA "Working Definition of Antisemitism."

Stand With Us: An international, right-wing Israel advocacy organization with a focus on supporting students and faculty on college campuses to oppose BDS and forward the idea that critique of Israel is antisemitic.

T'ruah: Brings together rabbis to advance "democracy and human rights for all people in the United States, Canada, Israel, and the occupied Palestinian territories."

Palestine Solidarity Organizations

Adalah Justice Project (AJP): "A Palestinian-led advocacy organization based in the U.S. that builds cross-movement coalitions to achieve collective liberation. [Their] work is rooted in the conviction that drawing the linkages between US policy abroad and repressive state practices at home is crucial to shifting the balance of power." www.adalahjusticeproject.org

Al-Shabaka: The Palestinian Policy Network: An independent, nonpartisan, and nonprofit organization, the mission of which is to educate and foster public debate on Palestinian human rights and self-determination within the framework of international law. "Al-Shabaka," which means the network, is a think tank without borders or walls. www.al-shabaka.org

American Friends Service Committee (AFSC): A Quaker institution that advocates and organizes around a range of social justice and human rights issues. Their work with Palestine predates the founding of the state of Israel. www.afsc.org

American Muslims for Palestine: "Works to educate, organize, and mobilize the Muslim-American community, as well as allies in other communities, to advance Palestinian rights." www.ampalestine.org

Arab Resource & Organizing Center (AROC): "Serves poor and working class Arabs and Muslims across the San Francisco Bay Area, while organizing to overturn racism, forced migration, and militarism." https://aroc.herokuapp.com/

CODEPINK: "A feminist grassroots organization working to end U.S. warfare and imperialism, support peace and human rights initiatives, and redirect resources into healthcare, education, green jobs, and other *life-affirming* programs." www.codepink.org

Friends of Sabeel–North America (FOSNA): "An interdenominational Christian organization seeking justice and peace in the Holy Land through education, advocacy, and nonviolent action. https://www.fosna.org

Israel/Palestine Mission Network of the Presbyterian Church (USA): The IPMN was established by action of the Presbyterian Church (USA)'s 2004 General Assembly with the mandate to advocate for Palestinian rights. www.theipmn.org

The Institute for Middle East Understanding (IMEU): "An independent non-profit organization that provides journalists with quick access to information about Palestine and the Palestinians, as well as expert sources, both in the United States and in the Middle East." www.imeu.org

National Students for Justice in Palestine: "Seeks to empower, unify, and support student organizers as they push forward demands for Palestinian liberation & self-determination on their campuses." www.nationalsjp.org

Palestine Legal: "Founded in 2012, Palestine Legal is an independent organization dedicated to protecting the civil and constitutional rights of people in the US who speak out for Palestinian freedom. Palestine Legal is the only legal organization in the United States exclusively dedicated to supporting the movement for Palestinian rights." www.palestinelegal.org

US Campaign for Palestinian Rights (USCPR): "Provide[s] resources and strategic support to the U.S.-based Palestine solidarity movement, channeling grassroots power into positive change in U.S. policy and public opinion." www.uscpr.org

US Palestinian Community Network (USPCN): "A Palestinian and Arab community-based organization, founded in 2006 to revitalize grass-roots organizing in Palestinian and Arab communities in the U.S., as part of the broader Palestinian nation in exile and the homeland." www.uspcn.org

Acknowledgments

As we found out as we were writing this book, memory is a tricky thing! We are so grateful to the JVP member leaders, staff, former staff, former board members, and movement partners who spent time with us to share their recollections. Together, we were able to reconstruct how things went down. We held roundtables and individual conversations and also asked some folks to read and review specific parts of the text. Even before we began to write, we had conversations that helped us shape the scope of the book. Everyone's willingness to share their perspectives was moving and absolutely invaluable to our own understanding and recounting. Of course, any mistakes or differences are entirely our own.

Thank you to Alana Krivo Kaufman, Amira, Andrew Kadi, Ari Belathar, Arielle Angel, Ari Wohlfeiler, Audrey Bruner, Beth Bruch, Beth Miller, Cecilie Surasky, Cindy Shamban, Dana Bergen, Danny Bryk, Donna Nevel, Elena Stein, Ellen Brotsky, Elsa Auerbach, Estee Chandler, Esther Farmer, Ezra Nepon, Grace Lile, Henri Picciotto, Lana Dee Povitz, James Schamus, Jennifer Bing, Jethro Eisenstein, Lara Friedman, Laura Tichler, Leila, Lesley Williams, Marc Scheiner, Margaret DeReus, Michael Deheeger, Mike Merryman Lotze, Nadia Hijab, Nadia Saah, Nava EtShalom, Noura Erakat, Noushin Framke, Penny Rosenwasser, Peter Beinart, Rabbi Brian Walt, Rabbi Jessica Rosenberg, Rabbi Laurie Zimmerman, Rabbi

Lynn Gottlieb, Rabbi May Ye, Rachel Kipnes, Rebecca Subar, Riham Barghouti, Sa'ed Atshan, Sandra Tamari, Shirly Bahar, Stefanie Fox, Stephanie Roth, Sydney Levy, Tallie Ben Daniel, Wendy Somerson.

Additionally, we are very thankful to Liz Ingenthron, who fielded our multiple requests for access to the JVP online archives and other admin needs with her usual grace and kindness.

We feel incredibly lucky to have a set of friends and comrades who so generously agreed to spend the time to read and offer feedback on an entire draft of the book. Getting honest feedback from such a smart and committed group of readers was a crucial step in the book's development. Thank you to Lesley Williams, Lilah Saber, Jeremy Siegman, Rabbi Ellen Lippman, and Nadia Saah for your thoughtful contributions and suggestions.

A few people read the book, or sections of the book, with a fine-toothed comb, offering incredibly detailed and honest feedback that immeasurably improved the final version. Enormous thanks for your time and generosity to Dania Rajendra, Shanée Garner, Shari Silberstein, Stefanie Fox, Ari Wohlfeiler, Omar Barghouti, Ari Belathar, and Sydney Levy. We were deeply thrilled that our friend and comrade Wendy Elisheva Somerson designed the gorgeous cover for the book.

When we began the process of thinking about writing a book, the only publisher we ever imagined having was Haymarket Books. Haymarket's commitment to making books a vibrant part of social movements and the development of a critical and engaged internationalist left made it a perfect home for us. We are so grateful to Julie Fain for ushering us through the proposal process, and we are deeply honored to be among the Haymarket authors.

Throughout the long process of writing and rewriting, our editors, John McDonald and Charlotte Heltai, read and responded to endless drafts, offered emotional support, and gently guided us through the totally new-to-us process of writing and publishing. They always offered an enormous commitment to the book and our voice being what we wanted and needed it to be, while also offering innumerable valuable suggestions both large and small. Thank you so much, Charlotte and John! We were incredibly impressed by the care and thoroughness with which Carrie Luft copy edited the final document.

Huge thanks to Noor Shefani and Erin Solokas for your crucial support, which allowed us to have the time we needed to write.

We both found our political homes and a place to do our life's work at JVP. It is hard to describe how important JVP has been, and continues to be, in both our lives. Thank you to everyone at JVP, who have put in grueling and joyful hours to make JVP a force to be reckoned with! We especially want to thank our beloved Stefanie Fox for leading JVP with such brilliance, care, and power in the years since we left.

The two of us also grew to know and love one another during our years at JVP. Throughout the time we were writing the book, we often commented to each other that the reason the writing was not just smooth but a delight was because we knew so well how to communicate and work with one another. We truly appreciate the book being a container that gave us space to reflect upon the frenetic and essential JVP years. We offer our love and appreciation to each other as writing partners, comrades, and for the profound friendship that carried us through.

We are who we are thanks to our beloved families, who have offered their ongoing love and support throughout our lives, even when, at times, we have disagreed in our politics! Our love and thanks always to David Vilkomerson, Barbara Vilkomerson, and Sara Vilkomerson; and to Joyce Kamen and Ron Wise. And extra thanks to Barbara and David, who several times over the course of our writing opened their home (Rebecca's childhood home!) for our writing retreats.

Our children—Tali, Amalia, Sammy, Lev, and Samara—have grown up as the JVP second gen. On a daily basis, we draw on their love, cuddles, silliness, and, as they grew older, serious questions, and support of our work as inspiration and reminder of why this work matters so much to us. We love you.

Our partners—Yoni and Stefan—have put up with a lot. We've been at times distracted, rant-y, exhausted, and far from home. Through it all, you never wavered in your belief in and support of the work we do. We love you and are lucky to have you.

Notes

Foreword

1. Quoted in Fayez A. Sayegh, *Zionist Colonialism in Palestine* (Beirut, Lebanon: Palestine Liberation Organization's Research Center, 1965).
2. Palestinian BDS National Committee, "BDS@10: Boycott Movement Leaders Address Press Conference," BDS Movement.net, July 9, 2015, https://bdsmovement.net/news/bds10-boycott-movement-leaders-address-press-conference.
3. I use "accumulate" to echo Keeanga-Yamahtta Taylor's notion that history is "cumulative, not cyclical." Keeanga-Yamahtta Taylor (@KeeangaYamahtta), "This is so true. History is cumulative; it is not cyclical. Today's protests are much more intense and more generalized today than 2014 because of the political failures in substantively addressing the grievances then. Ferguson gave way to protests but nothing on this scale." X post with link, May 31, 2020, https://twitter.com/KeeangaYamahtta/status/12671511 99041736704?s=20&t=umMsZryIghs92XHPJWbjZQ.
4. "Our Approach to Zionism," Jewish Voice for Peace, https://www.jewishvoiceforpeace.org/resource/zionism/.
5. The quoted phrase appears in chapter 5 of this book.
6. "Jewish Voice for Peace Unequivocally Opposes the IHRA Working Definition of Antisemitism," Jewish Voice for Peace, statement, February 8, 2021, https://www.jewishvoiceforpeace.org/2021/02/08/ihra/.
7. I.F. Stone, "Holy War," *New York Review*, August 3, 1967, https://www.nybooks.com/articles/1967/08/03/holy-war/.

Introduction

1. "Data on Demolition and Displacement in the West Bank,"
   United Nations Office for the Coordination of Humanitarian
   Affairs, https://www.ochaopt.org/data/demolition.
2. "The Discriminatory Laws Database," Adalah, September 25,
   2017, https://www.adalah.org/en/content/view/7771.
3. Laurie Goodstein, "Presbyterians Vote to Divest Holdings to
   Pressure Israel," *New York Times*, June 20, 2014, https://www.
   nytimes.com/2014/06/21/us/presbyterians-debating-israeli-occu-
   pation-vote-to-divest-holdings.html.
4. Human Rights Watch, "A Threshold Crossed: Israeli Authorities
   and the Crimes of Apartheid and Persecution," HRW.org,
   April 27, 2017, https://www.hrw.org/report/2021/04/27/thresh-
   old-crossed/israeli-authorities-and-crimes-apartheid-and-per-
   secution; Amnesty International, "Israel's Apartheid against
   Palestinians: Cruel System of Domination and Crime against
   Humanity," Amnesty.org, February 1, 2022, https://www.
   amnesty.org/en/documents/mde15/5141/2022/en/; "A Regime of
   Jewish Supremacy from the Jordan River to the Mediterranean
   Sea: This Is Apartheid," *B'Tselem*, 2021, https://www.btselem.
   org/publications/fulltext/202101_this_is_apartheid.
5. Robert Mackey, "Advice for Ferguson's Protesters from the
   Middle East," *New York Times*, August 14, 2014, https://www.
   nytimes.com/2014/08/15/world/middleeast/advice-for-fergusons-
   protesters-from-the-middle-east.html.
6. See appendix for list of Palestinian organizations we worked with
   most closely during our tenure at JVP.
7. See appendix for definitions of different Jewish populations.
8. Karen Brodkin, *How Jews Became White Folks and What That Says
   about Race in America* (New Brunswick, NJ: Rutgers University
   Press, 1998).
9. See appendix for more on these organizations. While
   Palestinians and many others define Zionism as inherently racist
   and therefore not liberal in any form, we use these terms because
   they are widely recognized.
10. Peter Beinart, "The Failure of the American Jewish Establishment,"
   New York Review of Books, June 10, 2010, https://www.nybooks.
   com/articles/2010/06/10/failure-american-jewish-establishment/.

11. Pew Research Center, "Jewish Americans in 2020,"
    PewResearch.org, May 11, 2021, https://www.pewresearch.org/
    religion/2021/05/11/jewish-americans-in-2020/; Lydia Saad,
    "Democrats' Sympathies in Middle East Shift to Palestinians,"
    Gallup, March 16, 2023, https://news.gallup.com/poll/472070/
    democrats-sympathies-middle-east-shift-palestinians.aspx.
12. See appendices for more detailed definitions of different Jewish
    populations.
13. Shout-out to Cindy Greenberg, who created and facilitated the
    process.
14. Rabbi David Basior, "Jewish Voice for Peace: An Analysis"
    (unpublished manuscript, 2013).
15. See appendix for the list of people interviewed.
16. We spell *antisemitism* without the hyphen following advice of
    scholars in Jewish studies who made a compelling case for this
    spelling. For a fuller explanation, see Jewish Voice for Peace,
    On Antisemitism: Solidarity and the Struggle for Justice (Chicago:
    Haymarket Books, 2017), xv.
17. See appendix for names of specific organizations.
18. Z"l is an acronym for *zichrona livracha*, may her memory be a
    blessing. See appendix for the full statement and chapter six for a
    fuller accounting of that process.

Chapter 1: Building a Political Home

1. Elliott batTzedek and Rabbi Alissa Wise coauthored the ritual text.
2. The Jewish Labor Bund was a secular Jewish socialist party initially
   formed in the Russian Empire and active between 1897 and 1920.
3. Founded in the US in the early twentieth century,
   Reconstructionism is one of the five major movements of Judaism,
   next to Orthodox, Conservative, Reform, and Humanist.
4. Pew Research Center, "The Size of the U.S. Jewish Population,"
   PewResearch.org, May 11, 2021, https://www.pewresearch.org/
   religion/2021/05/11/the-size-of-the-u-s-jewish-population/.
5. See appendix for definitions.
6. See appendix.
7. Evan Serpick, "Embracing Israel Boycott, Jewish Voice
   For Peace Insists on Its Jewish Identity," *The Forward*,
   March 28, 2015, https://forward.com/israel/217528/

embracing-israel-boycott-jewish-voice-for-peace-in/.

8. Many legacy Jewish communal organizations are hyper focused on the rates of Jews marrying non-Jews in the United States and what that will mean for the continuation of Jewish life.

9. *Havurah* is Jewish spiritual community that is layperson led.

10. See appendix for list of our most frequent partners.

11. Israel's "Law of Return" gives the right to any Jewish person with one Jewish grandparent or married to a Jewish person to relocate to Israel and immediately be granted citizenship.

12. Shout-out to Sarah Sills and Micah Bazant of the JVP Artist Council for their leadership in this work.

13. Jewish prayer recited in honor of the deceased.

Chapter 2: Building a Movement Inside a Nonprofit

1. INCITE!, *The Revolution Will Not Be Funded: Beyond the Non-Profit Industrial Complex* (Durham, NC: Duke University Press, 2017).

2. Jo Freeman, "The Tyranny of Structurelessness," https://www.jofreeman.com/joreen/tyranny.htm.

3. For more info see https://www.momentumcommunity.org/.

4. Saul Alinsky, *Rules for Radicals: A Pragmatic Primer for Realistic Radicals* (New York: Vintage, 1989).

5. Shout-out to Sam Brotman, who took the reins of our membership program so ably, developing the systems and practices to tend to our members.

6. Maurice Mitchell, "Building Resilient Organizations: Toward Joy and Durable Power in a Time of Crisis," *Convergence Magazine*, November 29, 2022, https://convergencemag.com/articles/building-resilient-organizations-toward-joy-and-durable-power-in-a-time-of-crisis/.

7. See appendices for filters and guiding principles.

8. Tema Okun, "Sense of Urgency," WhiteSupremacyCulture.info, accessed August 11, 2023, https://www.whitesupremacyculture.info/urgency.html.

9. Highlander Center (@HighlanderCtr), "This Black History Month we are shining a light on some of the brilliant Black folks who have shared Highlander's history and work. Ella Baker, born December 13, 1903 in Norfolk, Virginia, was a largely behind the scenes organizer whose career lasted over 5 decades." Twitter

post, February 15, 2022, https://twitter.com/HighlanderCtr/
status/1493625258338836482?s=20.
10. "Facing the Nakba," Jewish Voice for Peace, https://www.jewish-
voiceforpeace.org/facing-the-nakba/.
11. Shout-out to Naomi Dann and Granate Kim, who successively
took on the communications role after Cecilie with great success.
12. This predates Rebecca and Alissa on staff. Rebecca was a member
leader at the time in the Bay Area chapter.
13. Shout-out to Audrey Bruner, Maya Berkowitz, and Mike
Heinrich, who did so much to build fundraising practices.

Chapter 3: Confronting Our Own Community

1. Adam Horowitz, "Video of Activists Disrupting Netanyahu at
Jewish Federations General Assembly," *Mondoweiss,* November
9, 2010, https://mondoweiss.net/2010/11/video-of-activists-dis-
rupting-netanyahu-at-jewish-federations-general-assembly/.
2. Cecilie Surasky, "Shouting to Be Heard," *The Forward,*
November 24, 2010, https://forward.com/opinion/133406/
shouting-to-be-heard/.
3. Shoutout to Mirit Mizrahi, who predrafted and finalized the
declaration.
4. Full text of the declaration can be found in the appendix.
5. Jewish Voice for Peace, "Jewish Voice for Peace: Young Jewish
Proud Declaration," video, September 25, 2011, https://www.
youtube.com/watch?v=BAV-3-AqP9M.
6. Olúfẹ́mi O. Táíwò, *Elite Capture: How the Powerful Took Over
Identity Politics (And Everything Else)* (Chicago: Haymarket
Books, 2022), 22.
7. See appendix.
8. Jewish Social Justice Roundtable, "About Us," https://www.
jewishsocialjustice.org/mission, accessed September 5, 2023.

Chapter 4: Fighting Antisemitism and Its Weaponization

1. Jewish Voice for Peace, *On Antisemitism: Solidarity and the
Struggle for Justice* (Chicago: Haymarket Books, 2017), 213–16.
2. Jewish Voice for Peace, *On Antisemitism: Solidarity and the*

Struggle for Justice (Chicago: Haymarket Books, 2017).

3. Keeanga-Yamahtta Taylor (@KeeangaYamahtta), "This is so true. History is cumulative; it is not cyclical. Today's protests are much more intense and more generalized today than 2014 because of the political failures in substantively addressing the grievances then. Ferguson gave way to protests but nothing on this scale." Twitter, May 31, 2020, https://twitter.com/KeeangaYamahtta/status/1267151199041736704.

4. "White Nationalist Richard Spencer Backs Israel's Contentious Nation-state Law," *Haaretz*, July 22, 2018, https://www.haaretz.com/israel-news/2018-07-22/ty-article/israeli-nation-state-law-backed-by-white-nationalist-richard-spencer/0000017f-dbb1-d3ff-a7ff-fbb1567d0000.

5. John Brown, "John Brown's Flow Chart on Why Many on the Israeli Right Don't Condemn neo-Nazis," *Haaretz*, August 17, 2017, https://www.haaretz.com/israel-news/2017-08-17/ty-article/why-many-on-the-israeli-right-dont-condemn-neo-nazis/0000017f-e2cb-d9aa-afff-fbdb94a50000.

6. Meirav Zonsein, "After the Pittsburgh Shooting, Israeli Politicians Sound Even More Like Trump," *Washington Post*, October 30, 2018, https://www.washingtonpost.com/outlook/2018/10/30/after-pittsburgh-shooting-israeli-politicians-sound-even-more-like-trump/

7. Aaron Blake, "Trump's Long History of Trafficking in Antisemitic Tropes," *Washington Post*, October 17, 2022, https://www.washingtonpost.com/politics/2022/10/17/trump-history-antisemitic-tropes/

8. Antony Lerman, *Whatever Happened to Antisemitism?: Redefinition and the Myth of the "Collective Jew"* (London: Pluto Press, 2022).

9. See glossary for more on the AJC; Kenneth Stern, "I Drafted the Definition of Antisemitism. Rightwing Jews Are Weaponizing It," *The Guardian*, December 13, 2019, https://www.theguardian.com/commentisfree/2019/dec/13/antisemitism-executive-order-trump-chilling-effect.

10. "What Is Antisemitism?" International Holocaust Remembrance Alliance, https://www.holocaustremembrance.com/resources/working-definitions-charters/working-definition-antisemitism.

11. See "Distorted Definition: Redefining Antisemitism to Silence Advocacy for Palestinian Rights," Palestine Legal, https://palestinelegal.org/distorted-definition#timeline.

12. Christians United for Israel, "CUFI Reaches 10 Million

Members," press release, December 22, 2020, https://cufi.org/press-releases/cufi-reaches-10-million-members/; Lynn Gottlieb, "The Anti-Semitic Theology behind the Christian Zionist Lobby," July 8, 2019, https://religionnews.com/2019/07/08/the-anti-semitic-theology-behind-the-christian-zionist-lobby/. As of 2020 Pew Research Center counted 5.8 million Jews in the US. See Pew Research Center, "The Size of the U.S. Jewish Population," PewResearch.org, May 11, 2021, https://www.pewresearch.org/religion/2021/05/11/the-size-of-the-u-s-jewish-population/.

13. Jews for Racial and Economic Justice, "Understanding Antisemitism: An Offering to Our Movement," JFREJ.org, November 2017, https://www.jfrej.org/assets/uploads/JFREJ-Understanding-Antisemitism-November-2017-v1-3-2.pdf.

14. Editorial Board, "The New School's Fake Panel 'to Combat Anti-Semitism,'" *New York Post*, November 19, 2017, https://nypost.com/2017/11/19/the-new-schools-fake-panel-to-combat-anti-semitism/.

15. Editorial Board, "Bigotry's Leader: Linda Sarsour to Speak at Antisemitism Discussion," *Jerusalem Post*, November 19, 2017, https://www.jpost.com/opinion/bigotrys-leader-514563.

16. Jonathan Greenblatt (@JGreenblattADL), "Having Linda Sarsour & head of JVP leading a panel on #antisemitism is like Oscar Meyer leading a panel on vegetarianism. These panelists know the issue, but unfortunately, from perspective of fomenting it rather than fighting it." Twitter, November 13, 2017, https://twitter.com/JGreenblattADL/status/930197451797020672.

17. Brett Stephens, "Steve Bannon Is Bad for the Jews," *New York Times*, November 16, 2017, https://www.nytimes.com/2017/11/16/opinion/steve-bannon-israel-anti-semitism.html.

18. Seth Frantzman, "Non-Jews, Anti-Israel Activists Dominate 'Antisemitism' Panel," *Jerusalem Post*, November 22, 2020, https://www.jpost.com/diaspora/antisemitism/why-does-a-dismantling-antisemitism-panel-have-anti-israel-commentators-649873.

19. @BariWeiss, "'Antisemitism is used to manufacture division and fear.' Aha, I see. So 'dismantling antisemitism' is actually about dismantling *accusations* of antisemitism. Watch with me in real time as 'antisemitism' is transformed into 'right-wing disinformation.'" Twitter, November 20, 2020, https://twitter.com/bariweiss/status/1329904611117830144.

20. See appendix for full list of all six principles.
21. Shout-out to Sharon Goldtzvik of Uprise Consulting, who first framed antisemitism this way.

Chapter 5: Nurturing Movement Partnerships

1. See appendix for full statements.
2. See filters in appendix and more in-depth discussion of them later in this chapter.
3. An original version of this section, as well as the section on the BDS decision in chapter 5, was included in the anthology edited by Carolyn Karcher, *Reclaiming Judaism from Zionism* (Northampton, MA: Olive Branch Press, 2019). Thank you to Carolyn Karcher for permission to adapt it.
4. See appendix.
5. *Klezmer* is a Yiddish word that refers to the musical tradition of Ashkenazi Jews from Eastern and Central Europe that began in the late sixteenth century and evolves to this day.
6. These moments of discord with some of our Palestinian partners are noteworthy because they have been few and far between. Through intentional work, we have enjoyed synergistic collaborations overwhelmingly, and we raise these moments of disconnection because they are openings for explorations toward more complicated and mature solidarity stances.
7. More full explanations of this principles can be found in the appendix.
8. The US Campaign for Palestinian Rights also cut ties around the same time.
9. In 2012, the divestment resolution failed in favor of an "invest not divest" measure, before divestment passed in 2014.
10. AFSC is a Quaker institution that advocates and organizes around a range of social justice and human rights issues. Their work with Palestine pre-dates the founding of the State of Israel.
11. We won this campaign in part in 2012 when TIAA-CREF divested from Caterpillar stock in their socially responsible investment fund. Naomi Zeveloff, "Israel Was Key Issue in Caterpillar Dump," *The Forward*, June 26, 2012, https://forward.com/news/158433/israel-was-key-issue-in-caterpillar-dump.

Chapter 6: Growing While Sharpening Our Politics

1. "Hillel Israel Guidelines," Hillel International, https://www. hillel.org/israel-guidelines/. The organization Open Hillel was founded by students at several campuses in 2012 to fight the guidelines. Some supported BDS, but others simply believed all Jewish students should be welcome at Hillel.

2. Palestinian Civil Society, "Palestinian Civil Society Calls for BDS," bdsmovement.net, July 9, 2005, https://bdsmovement.net/ call, accessed September 5, 2023.

3. JVP-NYC was also embarking on a parallel chapter-based process at the time, which resulted in a theater piece and eventually a book titled *A Land with a People: Palestinians and Jews Confront Zionism*, edited by Esther Farmer, Rosalind Petchesky, and Sarah Sills (New York: Monthly Review Press, 2021).

4. Shout-out to Tallie Ben Daniel, who did the lion's share of drafting and editing on the final statement, which is included in the appendix.

5. Jeremy Ben-Ami, "J Street's Commitment to Israel's Future," Jstreet.org, January 23, 2019, https://jstreet.org/j-streets-commitment-to-israels-future/; Rabbi Jill Jacobs, Manijeh Nasrabadi, Rabbi Michael Davis, Shaul Magid, and Sherene Seikaly, "Roundtable: The Jewish Voice for Peace Statement on Zionism," *Jewish Currents*, March 25, 2019, https://jewishcurrents.org/ roundtable-the-jewish-voice-for-peace-anti-zionism-statement-2; Michael Schaeffer Omer-Man, "JVP Just Declared Itself anti-Zionist and It's Already Shifting the Conversation," *+972 Magazine*, January 30, 2019, https://www.972mag.com/ jvp-anti-zionist-rebecca-vilkomerson-2/.

6. Daisy Pitkin, *On the Line: Two Women's Epic Fight to Build a Union* (Chapel Hill, NC: Algonquin Books, 2023).

7. Shoutout to Karen Ackerman, Rabbi Yoseph Berman, Estee Chandler, Naomi Dann, Stefanie Fox, Alana Krivo-Kaufman, Beth Miller, Seth Morrison, and Ari Wohlfeiler, who were early advocates for and architects of our congressional work.

8. Jeremy Ben-Ami, "J Street Letter to Congress on Netanyahu Address," Jstreet.org, February 10, 2015, https://jstreet. org/j-street-letter-to-congress-on-netanyahu-address_1/.

9. Jewish Voice for Peace, "#SkiptheSpeech Campaign Update," June,

2015 https://www.jewishvoiceforpeace.org/wp-content/uploads /2015/06/SkipTheSpeech-JVP-Campaign-Update.pdf. Partners on this action included AMP, Code Pink, Sabeel, and USCPR.

10. Rebecca Vilkomerson, "Netanyahu Does Not Speak for All American Jews," *Washington Post*, February 20, 2015, https:// www.washingtonpost.com/national/religion/netanyahu-does-not-speak-for-all-american-jews-commentary/2015/02/20/9c456ecc-b943-11e4-bc30-a4e75503948a_story.html.

11. Shoutout to Elana Baurer, who did the behind-the-scenes operational and legal work of preparing to launch JVPAction successfully.

Chapter 7: Transforming JVP's Approach to Racial Justice

1. Shirly Bahar, Danny Bryck, and Sydney Levy, "Letters / On 'What Comes Next for Jews of Color Activism?'" *Jewish Currents*, March 23, 2023, https://jewishcurrents.org/letters/ on-what-comes-next-for-jews-of-color-activism.

2. Staff, "Detention Centers Are 'Worthy of Your Disgust' in Their Own Right, Says Jewish Latina Activist," *The World*, July 11, 2019, https://theworld.org/stories/2019-07-11/detention-centers-are -worthy-your-disgust-their-own-right-says-jewish-latina; Michal David and Shahar Zaken, "Mizrahi Jews Speak in Support of the California Ethnic Studies Curriculum," *Unruly: A Blog of the Jews of Color Caucus*, April 22, 2020, http://jocsm.org/mizrahi-jews -speak-in-support-of-the-ca-ethnic-studies-curriculum; Jewish Voice for Peace, "A Black Lens on Palestinian Liberation," video, June 18, 2021, webinar, 2:26:37, https://www.youtube.com/watch ?v=SrY0EPpIYHI; "Mimouna," 3 Dollar Bill, https://www .3dollarbillbk.com/rsvp/2023/4/13/mimouna, accessed September 8, 2023; "Reuven Abergel in NYC: Mizrahi Struggles, Solidarity with Palestinians, the World We Build," *Jewish Currents*, April 6, 2022, https://jewishcurrents.org/event/reuven-abergil-in-nyc-mizrahi -struggles-solidarity-with-palestinians-the-world-we-build; "From the Personal to the Political: Mizrahi and JSWANA Families' Migration Stories & Global Struggles for Justice," workshop series, February–March 2023, https://docs.google.com/forms /d/e/1FAIpQLSdTXGnZcRTcu1KxvHeMnO5_ 8PKszrbX0XEArtMye9gCqHRHHw/viewform.

3. This quote is Shirly Bahar, Danny Bryck, and Sydney Levy,

"Letters / On 'What Comes Next for Jews of Color Activism?'" *Jewish Currents*, March 23, 2023, https://jewishcurrents.org/letters/on-what-comes-next-for-jews-of-color-activism. The JOCSM Caucus statement defending the M4BL is in *Unruly: A Blog of the Jews of Color Caucus*, http://jocsm.org/jews-of-color-caucus-statement-in-solidarity-with-the-movement-for-black-lives-matter/, retrieved September 9th, 2023.

4. Jewish Voice for Peace, "Fact Sheet: Jews from the Middle East," JVP.org, https://www.jewishvoiceforpeace.org/wp-content/uploads/2015/07/JVP-Jews-of-the-middle-east-fact-sheet.pdf, accessed June 19, 2023.

5. Quoted from the Discovery Report prepared by Amadee Braxton and Sarah Jaffe of Dragonfly Partners, https://www.dragonfly-partners.com/

Chapter 8: Weathering Repression

1. A reference to Jewish victims of the Holocaust who were forced to do work for the Nazis, it is the worst insult that a Jewish person can make toward another Jew.

2. San Francisco Jewish Voice for Peace, "StandWithUs Member Attacks Jewish Voice for Peace Activists," *Electronic Intifada*, November 16, 2010, https://electronicintifada.net/content/standwithus-member-attacks-jewish-voice-peace-activists/9764.

3. @marcowenjones, "A few people are reporting a sudden influx of suspicious followers today, including @abierkhatib . I crunched the numbers and yes, it's very anomalous, and very weird. Read on for some weird stats and possible explanations." Twitter, April 29, 2022, https://twitter.com/marcowenjones/status/1519978209126850560.

4. Isabel Kershner, "Israeli Airport Detention of Prominent U.S. Jewish Journalist Prompts Uproar," *New York Times*, August 14, 2018, https://www.nytimes.com/2018/08/14/world/israeli-airport-detention-of-prominent-us-jew-prompts-uproar.html.

5. Isaac Chotiner, "Is Anti-Zionism Anti-Semitism?" *New Yorker*, May 11, 2022, https://www.newyorker.com/news/q-and-a/is-anti-zionism-anti-semitism.

6. #DropTheADL, "Open Letter: The ADL Is Not an Ally," August 2020, https://droptheadl.org/.

7.   For example, The Israel on Campus Coalition, The Conference of Presidents of Major American Jewish Organizations, and the Jewish Council on Public Affairs are three of the major organizations that serve in the US as umbrella organizations for Jewish communal organizations through which strategic coordination takes place around messaging, communications, advocacy, and beyond.

8.   Staff, "Israel to Bankroll NIS 1m StandWithUs Venture," *Times of Israel*, January 15, 2015, https://www.timesofisrael.com/israel-to-bankroll-nis-1m-standwithus-venture/.

9.   For example, in the spring of 2022, Stand with Us was found to have advised a donor to the University of Washington who successfully negotiated with the university to return a donation of $5 million for an endowed chair that had been filled by a non-Zionist professor; Mari Cohen, "The Fight for the Future of Israel Studies," *Jewish Currents*, September 28, 2022, https://jewishcurrents.org/the-fight-for-the-future-of-israel-studies.

10. Center for American Progress, "Fear, Inc.: The Roots of the Islamophobia Network in America," August 26, 2011, https://www.americanprogress.org/article/fear-inc/.

11. Tahere Herzallah and Ben Lorber, "In the US, We Need a Muslim-Jewish Alliance" *Al Jazeera*, January 23, 2017, https://www.aljazeera.com/opinions/2017/1/23/in-the-us-we-need-a-muslim-jewish-alliance/.

12. Louise Cainkar, "The Muslim Ban and Trump's War on Immigration," *Middle East Research and Information Project* 294 (Spring 2020), https://merip.org/2020/06/the-muslim-ban-and-trumps-war-on-immigration-2/.

13. 7amleh documented almost 500 cases of censorship in May 2021 alone, ranging from removed posts to adding sensitivity labels to account suspensions and closures. See 7amleh, "The Attacks on Palestinian Digital Rights," May 6–19, 2021, https://7amleh.org/2021/05/21/7amleh-issues-report-documenting-the-attacks-on-palestinian-digital-rights.

14. Glenn Greenwald, "Facebook Says It Is Deleting Accounts at the Direction of the U.S. and Israeli Governments," *The Intercept*, December 30, 2017, https://theintercept.com/2017/12/30/facebook-says-it-is-deleting-accounts-at-the-direction-of-the-u-s-and-israeli-governments/.

15. See Palestine Legal's legislative map for updated statistics on bills

that have been introduced, passed, and overturned: https://legislation.palestinelegal.org/.

16. Nathan Thrall, "How the Battle Over Israel and Anti-Semitism Is Fracturing U.S. Politics," *New York Times*, https://www.nytimes.com/2019/03/28/magazine/battle-over-bds-israel-palestinians-antisemitism.html, retrieved September 9, 2023.

17. #DropTheADL, "Open Letter: The ADL Is Not an Ally," August 2020, https://droptheadl.org/.

18. Charity and Security Network, "USA v Holy Land Foundation for Relief and Development," CharityandSecurity.org, August 24, 2020, https://charityandsecurity.org/litigation/holy-land-foundation/.

19. On October 19, 2021, Israel's Defense Minister Benny Gantz designated six leading Palestinian human rights and civil society groups as "terrorist organizations" under Israel's domestic Counter-Terrorism (Anti-Terror) Law (2016). The six groups are Addameer, Al-Haq, Bisan Center for Research and Development, Defence for Children International – Palestine (D.C.I-P), the Union of Agricultural Work Committees (UAWC), and the Union of Palestinian Women's Committees (UPWC). The Israeli military commander also outlawed all six groups under the 1945 Emergency (Defense) Regulations, declaring them "unlawful associations."

20. Richard Engel, Aggelos Petropoulos, and Kennett Werner, "Black Cube: Inside the Shadowy Israeli Firm Accused of Trying to Undermine the Iran Deal," NBC News, May 25, 2018, https://www.nbcnews.com/news/world/black-cube-inside-shadowy-israeli-firm-accused-trying-undermine-iran-n877511.

21. Amir Oren, "Israel Setting Up 'Dirty Tricks' Unit to Find, Spread Dirt on BDS Groups," *Haaretz*, June 20, 2016, https://www.haaretz.com/israel-news/2016-06-20/ty-article/.premium/israel-setting-up-dirty-tricks-unit-to-spread-dirt-on-bds-groups/0000017f-db20-df62-a9ff-dff7d6e20000.

22. Ali Abunimah, "Israel Using 'Black Ops' against BDS, Says Veteran Analyst," *Electronic Intifada*, September 5, 2016, https://electronicintifada.net/blogs/ali-abunimah/israel-using-black-ops-against-bds-says-veteran-analyst.

23. See "The Palestine Exception to Free Speech" report by the Center for Constitutional Rights and Palestine Legal for a more in-depth discussion of anti-BDS laws as a tactic, https://ccrjustice.org/the-palestine-exception.

24. Elly Bulkin and Donna Nevel, *Islamophobia and Israel* (Mishawaka, IN: Better World Books, 2014).

25. Jewish Voice for Peace, "Rekindling Our Commitment to Justice on Chanukah," JVP.org, December 6, 2015, https://www.jewishvoiceforpeace.org/2015/12/rekindling-our-commitment-to-justice-on-chanukah/.

26. Micah Bazant, "Micah Bazant," https://www.micahbazant.com/welcome-here, accessed August 11, 2023.

27. Jewish Voice for Peace, "Workshop Curriculum Challenging Islamophobia and Racism," JVP.org, 2017, https://www.jewishvoiceforpeace.org/2017/01/free-workshop-curriculum-challenging-islamophobia-and-racism/.

28. Regular demonstrations held on the Gaza-Israel border beginning in March 2018 demanding Palestinian refugees be able to return to the lands their families were violently displaced from as part of Israel's founding in 1948.

Conclusion: Solidarity Is the Political Version of Love

1. Shout-out to JVPAction organizer Reuben Telushkin, who organized the event with the Detroit chapter.

2. Marcy Oster, "Rashida Tlaib Attended JVP Shabbat Service after Cancellation of Israel Trip," *The Forward*, August 18, 2019, https://forward.com/fast-forward/429759/rashida-tlaib-israel-trip-jewish-voice-for-peace-shabbat/.

3. Babylonian Talmud, Sanhedrin 37b.

4. Genesis 18:27.

Afterword

1. Naomi Klein, "We Need an Exodus from Zionism," *Guardian*, April 24, 2024, https://www.theguardian.com/commentisfree/2024/apr/24/zionism-seder-protest-new-york-gaza-israel.

2. Hala Alyan (hala.n.alyan), "We owe Gaza endurance . . ." Instagram post, December 4, 2023, https://www.instagram.com/p/C0bxvCdOA3l.

Appendices

1. Tobin Belzer, et al., *Beyond the Count: Perspectives and Lived Experiences of Jews of Color* (New York: Jews of Color Initiative, 2021), ii, https://jewsofcolorinitiative.org/wp-content/uploads/2021/08/BEYONDTHECOUNT.FINAL_.8.12.21.pdf.
2. Kenneth Stern, "I Drafted the Definition of Antisemitism. Rightwing Jews Are Weaponizing It." *Guardian*, December 13, 2019, https://www.theguardian.com/commentisfree/2019/dec/13/antisemitism-executive-order-trump-chilling-effect.

Index

Reform Judaism, 14–15
Reframing Anti-Semitism: Alternative Jewish Perspectives (JVP), 121
"Refugees Are Welcome Here" poster, 239–240
repression
and building a political home, 236
disproportionate impact on Palestinians of, 5, 126–127, 231–232, 245, 251–252
disproportionate impact on people of color of, 5, 231, 236, 245
experienced by JVP, 233–234
impacts of, 5, 222, 235–237
solidarity as resistance to, 239, 245–247
repression tactics
harassment as, 224–225
Islamophobia as, 226–227, 230–231
lawfare as, 228–229
online censorship as, 227–228, 306n13
overview of, 221–222
social pressure as, 223–224
surveillance as, 229–230
terrorism designations as, 230–231, 307n19
used by Israeli government, 221–222, 224–225, 226, 228, 230
used by legacy Jewish institutions, 225–226, 304n9
weaponization of antisemitism as, 223–227

See also "new antisemitism"; "war on terror"
The Revolution Will Not Be Funded: Beyond the Non-Profit Industrial Complex (INCITE! Women of Color Against Violence), 60
right to return, 8, 251–252
Rosen, Brant, 102–103

Sarsour, Linda, 129
Second Intifada, 1, 16, 158
secret girlfriend phenomenon, 110–112
separationist theory, 119
See also antisemitism; Zionism
Sephardi Jews, 11–12, 280
See also Jews of Color and Sephardi/Mizrahi (JOCSM) Caucus
settler colonialism, ix, xi–xii, xiv–xv, xvii, xix, 7–8, 15–16, 50, 107, 119, 123, 168, 272
sharpening politics, 165–166, 180, 190–191
SJP. *See* Students for Justice in Palestine (SJP)
#SkipTheSpeech campaign, 187–189
solidarity
accountability as central to, 107, 138, 141, 145–147
contradictions within, 253
power building as, 252–253
as a practice, 253–254
as resistance to repression, 239, 245–247
Spencer, Richard, 123
Stand With Us, 221, 285